ASEAN Beyond the Regional Crisis

ASEAN Beyond the Regional Crisis

Challenges and Initiatives

Edited by **Mya Than**

Institute of Southeast Asian Studies
Singapore

First published in Singapore in 2001 by
Institute of Southeast Asian Studies
30 Heng Mui Keng Terrace
Pasir Panjang
Singapore 119614

Internet e-mail: publish@iseas.edu.sg
World Wide Web: http://www.iseas.edu.sg/pub.html

ISEAS Library Cataloguing-in-Publication Data

ASEAN beyond the regional crisis : challenges and initiatives / edited by Mya Than.
   Papers originally presented at the ASEAN Roundtable, Singapore, 5–6 November 1999.
   1.   ASEAN—Congresses.
   2.   ASEAN countries—Economic integration—Congresses.
   3.   ASEAN countries—Economic conditions—Congresses.
   I.   Mya Than.
   II.   ASEAN Roundtable (1999 : Singapore)
HC441 A843 1999   2001   sls2000057539

ISBN 981-230-099-6

Typeset by International Typesetters Pte. Ltd.
Printed in Singapore by Seng Lee Press Pte Ltd.

CONTENTS

LIST OF TABLES

LIST OF FIGURES

GLOSSARY

AAECP	ASEAN-Australia Economic Co-operation Programme
ADB	Asian Development Bank
AERR	ASEAN Emergency Rice Reserves
AFSR	ASEAN Food Security Reserve
AFSRB	ASEAN Food Security Reserve Board
AFTA	ASEAN Free Trade Area
AIA	ASEAN Investment Area
AIC	ASEAN Industrial Complementation (scheme)
AICO	ASEAN Industrial Co-operation (scheme)
AIJV	ASEAN Industrial Joint Ventures
AIP	ASEAN Industrial Projects
AMAF	ASEAN Ministers of Agriculture and Forestry
ANZCERTA	Australia-New Zealand Closer Economic Relations and Trade Agreement
APEC	Asia-Pacific Economic Co-operation
ARF	ASEAN Regional Forum
ARIC	Asian Recovery Information Centre
ASC	ASEAN Standing Committee
ASEM	Asia-Europe Meeting
ASP	ASEAN Surveillance Process
ASQ	ASEAN Surveillance Quality (Unit)
BBC	Brand to Brand Complementation (scheme)
BIS	Bank for International Settlements
BPA	Bilateral Payments Arrangements
CEPT	Common Effective Preferential Scheme
CLMV	Cambodia, Laos, Myanmar, and Vietnam
COFAF	Committee on Food, Agriculture and Forestry
CSCAP	Council on Security Co-operation in the Asia-Pacific
ECB	escape-clause-based
ECOTECH	economic and technical co-operation
EFTA	European Free Trade Area
EIP	Environment Improvement Project
EMEAP	Executives' Meeting of East Asia-Pacific (Central Banks)
EU	European Union

EVSL	Early Voluntary Sectoral Liberalization
EPG	Eminent Persons Group
FAO	Food and Agriculture Organization
FDI	foreign direct investment
FTA	Free Trade Area
FTAA	Free Trade Area of the Americas
G-7	group of seven industrialized countries
GATS	General Agreement on Trade in Services
GATT	General Agreement on Tariffs and Trade
GDP	gross domestic product
GNP	gross national product
GSP	Generalized System of Preferences
HSBC	Hongkong Shanghai Banking Corporation
HYVs	high yielding varieties
IAP	Individual Action Plan
IILP	Inter-Institutional Linkages Program
IL	Inclusion List
ILLR	international lender of last resort
IMF	International Monetary Fund
ITTO	International Tropical Timber Organization
LIBOR	London Interbank Offer Rate
LLR	lender of last resort
MAPA	Manila Action Plan for APEC
MEM	Meeting of Economic Ministers
MERCOSUR	Mercado Comun del Cono Sur (including Argentina, Brazil, Paraguay, and Uruguay)
MFN	most-favoured-nation
MOP	margin of preference
NAFTA	North American Free Trade Agreement
NEACD	Northeast Asian Co-operation Dialogue
NGOs	non-governmental organizations
NTBs	non-tariff barriers
NTMs	non-tariff measures
OECD	Organization for Economic Co-operation and Development
PITO	Private Investment and Trade Opportunities (Project)
PIWP	Policy Implementation and Work Programme
PTA	Preferential Trading Arrangement
REMU	Regional Economic Monitoring Unit
RETA	regional technical assistance

RLLR	regional lender of last resort
RTA	Regional Trading Arrangement
SAARC	South Asia Association for Regional Co-operation
TAC	Treaty of Amity and Co-operation
TEL	Temporary Exclusion List
TEMSEA	transitional economies of mainland Southeast Asia
TIPP	Trade and Investment Promotion Program
TRIMs	Trade-related Investment Measures
TRIPs	Trade-related Aspects of Intellectual Property Rights
UNDP	United Nations Development Programme
UNEP	United Nations Environment Programme
WTO	World Trade Organization

CONTRIBUTORS

Dr Florian A. Alburo is Professor of Economics in the School of Economics, University of the Philippines.

Dr Nick J. Freeman is a Senior Fellow at the Institute of Southeast Asian Studies, Singapore.

Dr H. S. Kartadjoemena is Vice-Chairman and Executive Director of the Center for Economic and Business Negotiations and Dispute Settlement, Jakarta. He was formerly Ambassador of Indonesia to the GATT during the Uruguay Round negotiations (1986-94).

Professor Rolf J. Langhammer is Head of Department at the Kiel Institute of World Economics, Germany.

Dr Cornelis P. F. Luhulima is Research Professor and Senior Research Associate at the Centre for Strategic and International Studies, Jakarta.

Professor Mahani Zainal Abidin is with the Department of Applied Economics at the Faculty of Economics and Administration, University of Malaya.

Dr Mya Than is a Senior Fellow at the Institute of Southeast Asian Studies, Singapore.

Dr Nattapong Thongpakde is Research Director of the International Economic Relations Program at the Thailand Development Research Institute.

Dr Ramkishen S. Rajan is a Lecturer in the School of Economics at the University of Adelaide, and Divisional Associate at the Research School of Pacific and Asian Studies (Economics), Australian National University.

Mr Simon Tay is Chairman of the Singapore Institute of International Affairs.

Professor Wing Thye Woo is with the Department of Economics at the University of California, Davis.

1

ASEAN Beyond the Crisis: A Bird's-eye View

MYA THAN

Leaving behind the worst part of the "Asian flu", ASEAN is entering the new post-crisis era. With the entry into the new era, ASEAN will have to contend with new challenges and unresolved issues as well as opportunities in terms of political, strategic, institutional, economic, and social and cultural dimensions.

As the regional financial and economic crisis seems to have bottomed out, and ASEAN economies are on the recovery path, it would be opportune to carry out a post-mortem on the crisis to evaluate the sustainability of the recovery and the long-term direction of the ASEAN economies. In addition, as challenges and competitiveness have become significant issues for the ASEAN economies in the post-recovery process, it is important to address these issues. Similarly, after achieving the ASEAN Free Trade Area's (AFTA's) objectives by 2002, as pledged by all members at the Hanoi Summit in 1998, the progress of AFTA should be analysed, and challenges explored in order to deepen ASEAN co-operation. Many academics and policy-makers have questioned whether ASEAN should perhaps go beyond the free trade area to an economic union, following the example of the European Union (EU).

The thirty years experience of ASEAN indicate that the member countries still have much room to improve in economic and financial co-operation. The fact that ASEAN cannot solve the regional crisis on its own shows that it is important to take measures towards avoiding a recurrence of another crisis. Although ASEAN has already agreed to introduce a surveillance mechanism, to establish an ASEAN Investment Area (AIA), the ASEAN Vision 2020, and an "ASEAN roadshow" to promote trade and investment, there is a need to reassess ASEAN economic and financial co-operation.

To address the economic issues alone is not enough; there are also issues encompassing human and social dimensions, such as food security, poverty, and cross-border pollution to be dealt with.

Furthermore, in the wake of the regional crisis, ASEAN has been criticized as being ineffective. Many suggest that ASEAN needs to change to meet its future needs of peace, stability, and prosperity in the region with confidence as it moves into the information age. In other words, there is a need to evaluate ASEAN on whether it is still relevant in its present form and contents, and if not, what changes should be introduced.

In short, the regional crisis has led to a re-examination of the regional grouping and its relevance, challenges, and opportunities as it enters the new millennium. With these objectives, the Institute of Southeast Asian Studies, Singapore, organized the ASEAN Roundtable 1999, the traditional annual meeting of ASEAN experts including academics, policy-makers, businessmen, and journalists, in Singapore on 5–6 November 1999.

The ASEAN Roundtable 1999

The ASEAN Roundtable 1999 focused on the issues outlined above: that is, to perform an evaluation on ASEAN in crisis and its future challenges in the light of global and regional economic, political, strategic, security, and social developments. Accordingly, the following topics relating to ASEAN were discussed:

1. ASEAN Economies: Crisis and Recovery
2. ASEAN Economies: Challenges and Competitiveness
3. ASEAN Free Trade Area: Progress and Challenges
4. ASEAN Investment Area: Progress and Challenges
5. Financial and Macroeconomic Co-operation in ASEAN: Issues and Policy Initiatives

6. Food Security in ASEAN
7. Environment and ASEAN Co-operation
8. ASEAN Co-operation and the World Trade Organization
9. ASEAN and Inter-regional Linkages
10. Is ASEAN Still Relevant?

The last topic was the subject of a panel discussion. Four panelists presented their views, followed by open discussion. The presentations of two panellists are attached as Appendices I and II.

Summary of the Contributions

ASEAN Economies: Crisis and Recovery

This volume begins with Woo Wing Thye's presentation on the ASEAN Economies' Crisis and Recovery. In it, he carried out a post-mortem on the regional crisis, its impact on the ASEAN economies, and the ongoing process of recovery in these economies. The author concluded, based on his analysis of the regional financial crisis, that there is a clear need for important reforms in many areas, including domestic markets, domestic institutions, international organizations, and international financial architecture.

Woo proposed policy actions on seven fronts. They are, among others, strengthening of prudential regulation and supervision of financial markets; increased and improved external supervision; democratization and transparency of the International Monetary Fund (IMF); establishment of regional bodies by the new monetary system and an international bankruptcy court; redesigning of international rescue packages; stricter and internationally co-ordinated regulation and monitoring of international capital markets; decisive and quick resolution of the bad debts of the financial and corporate sectors; and improvement in the long-term competitiveness of Asia, which rests as much on "getting the institutions right" as on "getting the prices right".

Competitiveness and Sustainable Growth in ASEAN

The chapter by Florian A. Alburo focuses on two key issues facing the ASEAN economies in the post-crisis recovery process. After tracing the broad economic effects of the crisis, it attempts to determine whether the ASEAN economies have seen the crisis bottoming out and whether recovery is really on the way. It also addresses the issues related to the sustainability of the recovery and growth and the prospects for the region's competitiveness.

The author finds that the ASEAN economies hit by the crisis have indeed "bottomed out" and are on the way to recovery and return to growth. The speed of the recovery, somewhat surprisingly, indicates its critical importance. The chapter also argues that the uneven speed of adjustment processes suggests offhand that there is no assurance of sustainability.

As far as competitiveness of the ASEAN economies is concerned, the chapter discusses three points. First, the events up to the crisis and the crisis itself may have altered the pattern of productivity growth for all the ASEAN countries, and thus their competitiveness. Secondly, the importance of foreign direct investment (FDI) to productivity is emphasized. The crisis may have encouraged significant inflows but the task is in capitalizing on those flows to improve technological capacities, marketing networks, and product techniques. Thirdly, the threat of the economic and social effects of the crisis on long-term sustainability of growth can be seen not only in real productivity per worker but also on the wave of future global trade concentrating on high technology products and R&D-intensive goods.

ASEAN Free Trade Area: Progress and Challenges

The chapter on "ASEAN Free Trade Area: Progress and Challenges" first gives an overview of ASEAN economic co-operation before and after the establishment of the ASEAN Free Trade Area. It then analyses the achievements and shortcomings of AFTA since its establishment in 1993 in the light of its objective to liberalize trade, create a more integrated regional market, and attract more foreign investment. The achievements of AFTA are mainly the deepening of co-operation in areas such as the reduction of tariffs, trade in services, ASEAN investment area, customs harmonization, and growth areas (for example, Indonesia-Malaysia-Singapore Growth Triangle). Other achievements include the integration of all the Southeast Asian countries, tariff reduction, increasing intra-ASEAN trade, setting clear objectives and directions for economic co-operation, enhancing trade negotiation capability, and fostering unilateral liberalization.

The author, Nattapong Thongpakde, also mentions the shortcomings of AFTA as modest intra-regional trade (compared to the European Union [EU] and the North American Free Trade Agreement [NAFTA]), difference in the stage of economic development of the members, and weakened prospects of economic growth. The author also addresses the challenges of AFTA as a result of ASEAN enlargement, the Asian crisis, and acceleration of the AFTA process. These are, among others, recovery from the crisis with sustained growth and stability, avoiding protection pressure from the members, speeding up liberalization, and further strengthening of trade negotiation capability.

ASEAN Investment Area: Progress and Challenges

Nick J. Freeman's chapter on "ASEAN Investment Area: Progress and Challenges" gives a brief background of the AIA and analyses its recent development although it is too early to assess it. He not only explores the recent trends in ASEAN's FDI inflows and the impact of the regional crisis on FDI, but also the portfolio investment and capital flows within AIA. The main challenge is seen as the practical and policy dilemmas of going forward. "Therefore, as a forward-looking instrument, the AIA needs to be 'ahead of the curve', delivering the sort of strategy that will stimulate the next generation of foreign investment activity within ASEAN".

In his conclusion, the author suggests, among other things, that the AIA's success will not only be dependent in large part on the commitment of the ten-member countries, but the AIA arrangement will also not be a substitute for the ASEAN countries' own unilateral FDI-friendly policy measures. Hence, although the sorts of policies contained within the AIA framework agreement are necessary to attract FDI interest in the region, member countries will need to improve various other elements of their own host-country business regimes if they are to successfully attract foreign investment inflows.

Financial and Macroeconomic Co-operation in ASEAN

This chapter by Ramkishen S. Rajan, firstly, outlines the analytical basis for enhanced regional co-operation in the spheres of financial and monetary co-operation. The emphasis is on detailing the various transmission channels leading to regional contagion or negative spillovers from a speculative attack, and the resulting devaluation-induced recession in one economy possibly infecting neighbouring economies. Secondly, the author gives concrete policy proposals for future co-operation. Among the proposals, an important one is the expansion of the role of the Executives' Meeting of East Asia-Pacific Central Banks (EMEAP), so as to act as the central co-ordinating body for regional financial and macroeconomic co-operation. This is because the EMEAP might be the appropriate body within which a regional monetary facility could be established.

In the conclusion, the author suggests that, given the absence of substantive steps towards the reform of the monetary and financial architecture at an international level, alternative policies and initiatives for regional financial and macroeconomic co-operation need to be put forward as a "self-help" mechanism for the small open economies in East Asia in this era of the globalization of capital flows.

Food Security in ASEAN

Mya Than, the author of the chapter on "Food Security in ASEAN", tries to assess the recent experiences, policies, and issues on food security in the ASEAN nations. He finds that agricultural and food production during the last decade was quite impressive in almost all the ASEAN member countries. Although the setback witnessed during the crisis was due to financial turmoil and the *El Nino* effect, it seems that the agriculture sector recovered together with the economy in 1999 and 2000. The short-term prospects are favourable; however, for the longer-term, the situation may depend on macroeconomic and technological factors, and climatic conditions.

Food availability (in terms of calorie supply) and accessibility (in terms of poverty indicators) are also important in assessing food security in the region. The study finds that overall food availability has become more stable except during the regional crisis period. Poverty indicators are also more positive in the region and there is an improvement in nutrition status in most of the ASEAN countries. All these indicators suggest that the food security situation in Southeast Asia is satisfactory, at least in the short-term perspective. However, for the longer term, the region needs to improve agriculture and food technology, introduce correct development strategies, appropriate macroeconomic policies (such as domestic market reforms) and agricultural and rural development policy, as well as credible measures for poverty alleviation and population control.

Environment and ASEAN Co-operation

Since the cross-border environmental issues in ASEAN — specifically the haze problem spreading from Indonesia to the neighbouring countries — have forced the member countries to co-operate, the focal point of Simon Tay's chapter on "ASEAN Co-operation and the Environment" is environment control in ASEAN. Among other issues related to the field of environmental co-operation, the chapter argues that although ASEAN's attitude towards this problem is changing, the pace of change in response to the crisis of fires and haze have not been radical enough since the changes have not been sufficiently effective in addressing the immediate problems. This is because of the mode of ASEAN co-operation, known as the "ASEAN way", which does not serve well in dealing with environmental challenges. The emphasis is on co-operative measures, or giving carrots instead of sticks. The environmental institutions foster compliance with assistance and the reporting mechanism, rather than penalities and sanctions. In short, ASEAN has so far failed to tackle the environmental problems.

As such, the chapter suggests that perhaps the best hope is that the "ASEAN way" be changed without being either ossified or abandoned. "Such evolution and change has implications not only for the environment, but also for the future shape of ASEAN".

ASEAN and the International Trading System: Regional Trade Arrangement versus the WTO

As ASEAN's trading system is now moving forward on two tracks — regional and multilateral — the chapter by H. S. Kartadjoemena addresses the multilateral trading system of ASEAN, that is, ASEAN co-operation with the World Trade Organization (WTO). The author focuses on the issues that the government of an ASEAN country should keep in mind when considering the position to take in relation to regional integration and the multilateral system. He also looks at the European experience briefly to compare notes.

The chapter assumes that it is the intention of the ASEAN countries to continue economic co-operation undertaken since its creation but they should also obtain the benefits of World Trade Organization membership.

The chapter concludes that, intellectually, an effective and open global system, operating on a non-discriminatory basis, is clearly in the best interest of the ASEAN countries, individually and as a group. However, it suggests that intra-regional integration in ASEAN, if pursued with realism, can help the member countries to cope more quickly and more effectively with the global system, irrespective of the immediate impact of regional integration on trade expansion. In this context, the author suggests taking an approach of "constructive ambiguity", or "soft" integration in ASEAN.

After all, ASEAN needs to ensure that the global system remains open and to develop the capability to compete globally.

ASEAN and Inter-Regional Economic Links

Since the importance of regional trade co-operation among countries in ASEAN is not just intra-regional, but also inter-regional, the chapter by Mahani Zainal Abidin explores and analyses the trends in ASEAN's relations with individual countries (Dialogue Partners) and other regional groupings, such as ANZCER, APEC, NAFTA, EU, MERCOSUR and SAARC. ASEAN's relations with these groupings are restricted to trade and investment liberalization because wider co-operation needs a longer time to establish.

It also examines bilateral economic co-operation with "Dialogue Partners" and a "sectoral partner" (Pakistan). In these relationships, developmental co-operation and the promotion of trade and investment are the hallmarks. Thus, the Dialogue Partners have widened the scope of co-operation to cover more specific areas, particularly in science and technology, human resources, cultural and social development, and the environment. The regional crisis has opened a new challenging dimension: the formulation of joint support measures to revive the ASEAN economies, including financial support and programmes to mitigate the social impact of the crisis.

The chapter also discusses issues which may determine the future direction of ASEAN's external relationships. Other issues addressed are the pace of progress within each grouping, the enlargement of ASEAN, the progress of liberalization efforts under the auspices of the WTO, identification and prioritization of new areas of co-operation, the need for a review of the role of its Dialogue Partners in the context of inter-regional relations, and the possibility of the emergence of mega-regional groupings, such as those between the European Union (EU) and the United States, and the Free Trade Area of the Americas. The author concludes that ASEAN is too small to remain inward-looking, and only by expanding its external relations can ASEAN be a key player in the international arena. Strong external partnerships will give ASEAN the opportunity to garner political support and form a collective stand on common concerns at the international level. Furthermore, the chapter states that the most significant achievement of ASEAN's external relationship is the role it has played in propelling the ASEAN economies into the international arena. It further suggests that economic links will be more effective if there is active participation from the private sector.

Is ASEAN Still Relevant?

In the last few years, especially during the regional economic crisis, many critics of ASEAN have questioned more vociferously whether ASEAN is still relevant. This is because the severe financial and economic crisis which had profound effects on the security outlooks and designs of the ASEAN countries seem to have shattered ASEAN's dreams and simultaneously exposed the fragility of ASEAN as a regional institution. Dr Suthad Setboonsarng, Deputy Secretary-General at the ASEAN Secretariat, Professor Rolf J. Langhammer, Head of Department of the Kiel Institute of World Economics, Professor Cornelis Luhulima, Research Professor at the Centre for Strategic and International Studies, Indonesia, and Dr Kao Kim Hourn, Executive Director of the Cambodian Institute for Co-operation and Peace, Phnom Penh, contributed their enlightening views during the discussion on the topic.

All four contributors unanimously concluded on an optimistic forward-looking note with some reservations, as the entire ASEAN rehabilitation programme, in general, is inseparably linked to the political stabilization and economic recovery in Indonesia. ASEAN still has a very important role to play in safeguarding the region from internal and external threats to its development, and to its modernization programmes and processes as a consequence of unfettered globalization and fierce competition. In other words, ASEAN is still very relevant in the field of politics and security, especially to moderate political and security disagreements among members; however, it seems to be less effective in the field of economics. The contributions by Luhulima and Langhammer are presented in Appendices I and II.

To conclude, the ASEAN Roundtable 1999 was held to explore, analyse and make suggestions for solutions to current issues and to address challenges and initiatives facing ASEAN in the wake of the regional crisis.

The editor would like to express his sincere appreciation to all the contributors to this volume for their patience and close co-operation. Thanks are also due to the Konrad Adenauer Stiftung (KAS), Germany, for its generous financial support for the ASEAN Roundtable 1999 on "ASEAN Beyond the Regional Crisis: Challenges and Initiatives", from which this book has emanated.

2

East Asia:
Crisis and Recovery

The period 1997–98 was a very difficult time for Pacific Asia. Indonesia, Malaysia, South Korea, and Thailand experienced their worst economic performance in the last three decades, with their output in 1998 declining from 6 to 14 per cent. The resulting economic hardship sparked off political changes and social turmoil in these countries. The governments in Indonesia, South Korea, and Thailand were replaced, and a bitter power struggle broke out in once politically quiescent Malaysia. These were the very countries that the World Bank identified to be the "miracle economies" — the models of economic development for the rest of the developing world to emulate.[1] This turn in events has caused many observers to revisit their development paradigms, and to ask whether the Pacific Asian economies were not "mirage economies" like those of the Soviet bloc. Is crony capitalism fatally flawed like central planning?

The claim that the Pacific Asian economies had imperfect economic institutions (for example, inadequate banking supervision and collusive relations between big businesses and government officials) is surely correct, but to go on to claim that these flawed economic institutions ("soft rot") had reached breaking points

11

simultaneously and thereby ignited the region-wide economic crisis is also surely incorrect. The second claim would be like focusing exclusively on deforestation in Central America when discussing the damage wrought by Hurricane Mitch, while ignoring the damage from the hurricane itself. Yes, policy failures matter, but they are only part of the story in Asia's financial storm. As much attention should be paid to the financial "hurricane" itself, specifically, the tendency for international financial markets to over-react both to positive and negative news. It was financial panic among international investors that brought Pacific Asia to its knees in 1998. Fortunately, the underlying fundamental strengths of the region are bringing about an economic recovery faster than has been widely predicted.

In general terms, we can say that there was little particularly "Asian" about the Asian financial crisis. Even though official Washington, led by the International Monetary Fund (IMF), proclaimed the crisis to be one of Asian capitalism, the more generic character of the crisis became all too clear during 1998, as the crisis spread to Russia, South Africa, and Latin America. Rather than an Asian crisis, the world was experiencing a type of global crisis that reflected the rapid arrival of global capitalism, in a world economy not yet used to the integration of the advanced and developing countries. The 1994–95 foreign exchange crises in Mexico and Argentina and, less severely, in the rest of Latin America via the "Tequila effect" of 1995, were the high-profile precursors to the financial market crisis that hit Pacific Asia in mid-1997. The Asian financial crisis is really another example of financial panic involving international creditors, though of course the onset of financial panic reflected some of the conditions specific to Asia in 1997.

The extent of economic devastation in each Asian country differed according to specific national structural conditions and policy reactions; for example, the amount of international debt, the proportion of international debt that was short-term, the adequacy of financial sector regulation, the amount of foreign reserves available to the monetary authorities, the tenacity with which the country defended its exchange rate, the degree to which IMF-style high interest rates and bank closing were implemented (with adherence to IMF programmes often doing more, rather than less, short-term damage), and the ability of the political system to preserve social stability while coping with economic shocks. The solutions to the crisis require responses both at the international level — to address shortcomings in the nascent global capitalist system — and at the regional and national levels, so that Asia can maintain and improve its competitiveness in a globalized economy.

Naturally, there remains a deep division of professional opinion about the sources of the crisis (national versus international), the reasons for Asia's extreme vulnerability (poor policies versus private-sector instabilities), the appropriate policy responses (financial orthodoxy *á la* the IMF versus financial heterodoxy of various forms), and the best ways to guard against a recurrence of crisis in the future (national level reforms versus a new global architecture). In our view, the crisis was built on national weaknesses that were greatly magnified by a flawed international financial system; the initial policy recommendations from Washington, especially to raise interest rates sharply and to close a large number of financial institutions, were deeply flawed, and made matters worse, not better; and long-term crisis prevention requires actions both at the national and international levels, including a basic change of strategy in exchange rate management and recognition of the inherent destabilizing risks of short-term capital flows.

The many competing explanations of the Asian financial crisis bring to mind the analogy of autopsies performed on the victims after a hurricane has blown through. Some of the deaths were due to pneumonia caught by the physically weak who had not taken care of their health (the "soft rot" explanation). A second group died because they were crushed by fallen trees (the financial contagion explanation). Finally, a third group died in the ambulance on the way to the hospital because nitrogen, rather than oxygen, was administered to them (macroeconomic malpractice by the IMF). In our assessment, only the initial July devaluation of the baht could be credibly attributed to the "soft rot" explanation.[2] The collapse of Thailand that began in August 1997 after the signing of the first IMF programme was the result of macroeconomic malpractice, which inflamed a financial panic. The subsequent devaluations in the other East Asian countries were largely the result of financial contagion, and in some cases the output declines were also due to inappropriately austere macroeconomic policies. The fact that IMF programmes in Thailand, Indonesia, and South Korea after mid-1998 reversed the macroeconomic policies of the first IMF programmes imposed on these countries is admission by the IMF of macroeconomic malpractice.

The most general and important point is that global capitalism has to be understood better by global policy-makers, national political leaders, and business people in all parts of the world. All of these participants in the new global economy have to recognize the types of shocks that have been magnified and rendered more common by the processes of deep economic integration and of institutional harmonization that are key forces of global capitalism. Only with a better comprehension of the new realities will the world community be able to take true precautionary measures to head off a future crisis, and will Asia be able to make a swift recovery from the deep crisis which engulfed the region. In short, we need to rise to the challenge of developing a new policy framework and new business strategies that are appropriate for global capitalism.

The main conclusions of our analysis are as follows. The financial crisis resulted from the interaction of, firstly, problematic macroeconomic policies (especially exchange rate policies) in the emerging markets; secondly, shortcomings in the financial sectors of the borrowing countries; and thirdly, intrinsic instabilities in the global financial markets. These problems interacted with some deeper weaknesses in Asian competitiveness to trigger the recent financial crisis. The sharp rebound (V-shaped recovery) of the Asian crisis economies in 1999 is at odds with the IMF's view that "soft rot" was the primary cause of their output collapse, and that recovery could come only after extensive economic restructuring. So, while we agree with the IMF's recommendation that substantial internal policy reforms are needed, we think that there should also be substantial reform of the international financial architecture, including macroeconomic policy design in developing countries; the regulation of international capital flows; the revision of the roles of the IMF, the United Nations agencies, and other institutions; and the redesign of international financial assistance itself, including accelerated debt reduction.

Understanding Financial Crises

Before we delve into the specifics of the Asian crisis, we need a general theoretical understanding of how international capital markets work — or fail to work — in the new global capitalist system. Thus, we start with some general theoretical ideas, and only afterwards focus on the Asian experience.[3]

Emerging market financial crises, such as occurred in Asia in 1997–98, are characterized by an abrupt and significant shift from net capital inflow to net capital outflow from one year to the next. These crises typically reflect a three-stage process that hits a developed country engaged in large-scale international borrowing. In the first stage, the exchange rate becomes overvalued as a result of internal or external macroeconomic events. In the second stage, the exchange rate is defended, but at the cost of a substantial drain of foreign exchange reserves held by the Central Bank. In the third stage, the depletion of reserves, usually in combination with a devaluation, triggers a panicked outflow by foreign creditors holding short-term claims. The trigger in most cases is the devaluation itself, resulting from the exhaustion of reserves. The panicked outflow of short-term capital leads to macroeconomic collapse, characterized by a sharp economic downturn, soaring interest rates, depressed equity prices, and a plummeting currency.

Some observers have attributed such crises to currency devaluation, since the panic has almost always followed a movement in the currency. This was certainly the case in Asia, since the Asian crisis followed soon on the heels of the unexpected devaluation of the Thai baht, on 2 July 1997. Similarly, Korea's extreme crisis came in December 1997, following the devaluation of the Korean won. As a result of these instances, and the earlier case of Mexico's devaluation in December 1994, these observers concluded that currencies should be fixed in value and never allowed to weaken. We disagree with these observers. In our view, it is not the devaluation, but rather the defence of the exchange rate preceding the crisis that opens the door to financial panic. A gradual weakening of the currency by itself is not harmful — as exemplified by the successes of many countries with flexible exchange rate arrangements, including Chile, Canada, Australia, and New Zealand.

The real harm comes from the depletion of foreign exchange reserves while trying to defend an overvalued currency. A devaluation which follows the depletion of reserves can indeed trigger a panic, but the lesson is to allow the currency to weaken *before* the reserves are depleted. When foreign reserves are depleted, short-term interbank credits in particular become subject to an abrupt, self-fulfilling loss of confidence. In summary, the devaluation signals the depletion of reserves; the depletion of reserves signals the inability of the Central Bank to act as a lender of last resort *vis-à-vis* foreign creditors; the short-term foreign creditors flee in panic; and the macroeconomy collapses as a result of the creditor flight.

The ubiquitous feature of recent emerging market crises is that the exchange rate defence, typically ending in a devaluation, has often been followed by a rapid and ferocious withdrawal of credits by foreign investors. It is the panic, not the devaluation itself, which leads to the acute damage to the emerging market and to the creditors.

Typically, some key segments (for example, banks, non-financial enterprises, and government) of the fast-growing Asian economies are heavily in debt to foreign investors, including international banks, hedge funds, and other investment funds. Much of this debt is short-term, that is, with maturity of less than one year. Additionally, much of the debt has trigger clauses, such that repayment is immediately accelerated in the event of a contractual default by the debtor to other creditors. The borrowing, in general, has been converted into long-term, relatively illiquid investments. As a result, total short-term debt is often significantly greater than the available short-term assets that might be mobilized to repay creditors in the event of a withdrawal of new lending.

The level of central bank forex reserves is crucial because the central bank is widely, and rightly, understood to be the lender of last resort not only to the banks, but to the government and corporate sector as well, in the event of an external creditor panic. Suppose that foreign banks begin to withdraw credit lines from domestic banks, demanding repayment of outstanding loans. This immediately leads to financial distress in the banking system, since the banks have transformed the foreign loans into long-term investments. The bank may, to some extent, use liquid domestic assets to purchase dollars in the foreign exchange market, but even so, the bank is unlikely to have sufficient liquid assets on hand to meet a large-scale withdrawal of funds. Thus, the central bank will almost surely have to extend credit, either directly as foreign exchange loans, or as domestic credit which is then sold in the forex market. In the latter case, of course, the exchange rate will depreciate in the absence of official intervention.

Once forex reserves have been depleted, the central bank's lender-of-last-resort functions are deeply compromised, and international creditors understand this fact very well. In these circumstances (depletion of forex reserves, and a high level of short-term debt), the economy becomes vulnerable to a self-fulfilling run. Even if economic fundamentals are adequate to ensure long-term debt servicing without default, they are not adequate to guarantee short-run debt servicing in the event of a panic. Thus, a panic can unfold simply by the self-fulfilling belief of creditors that it will indeed occur. This explains the finding by Radelet and Sachs that when the ratio of short-term debt to forex reserves is greater than 1, the country is prone to a creditor panic.[4]

In the past four years, financial panic has been triggered mainly by three types of events:

1. the sudden discovery that reserves are less than previously believed;
2. unexpected devaluation (often in part for its role in signalling the depletion of reserves); and
3. contagion from neighbouring countries, in a situation of perceived vulnerability (low reserves, high short-term debt, overvalued currency).

It is interesting and important to stress that currency devaluation, following a long defence of the exchange rate, has typically been the most important trigger of panic. This seems to be the result of several factors. First, many investors have been caught off-guard by the devaluation even when it has been widely discussed. These investors seem, incredibly enough, to have taken at face value, the solemn commitments of governments not to devalue. Secondly, the devaluations are often the signal that forex reserves are lower than publicly announced up to that point. In Mexico, the late-December 1994 devaluation "revealed" the steep loss of reserves in early December 1994. In Thailand, the 2 July 1997 devaluation was followed by public announcements that the Thai Central Bank had a large book of forward dollar sales. These dollar sales were not previously announced, and came as a large jolt to the market. In Korea, the December 1997 devaluation was the occasion for revealing that much of the Central Bank's announced forex reserves were actually illiquid claims on Korean banks, the result of unannounced deposits of the reserves in offshore Korean banks experiencing a run on inter-bank loans (in effect, the Central Bank had been making unannounced extensions of credit to offshore

Korean banks). Speaking in the most general terms, the collapse of pegged exchange rate regimes appeared to have been regarded as "serious breaches of faith" by foreign investors, causing them to recall their loans even though the devaluation had already occurred.

When the panic gains full force, the effects are devastating. The rational behaviour of each short-term creditor is to demand repayment as rapidly as contractually possible, and to suspend routine inter-bank lines which support letters of credit and other standard trade-financing operations. Long-term fundamentals cease to play any role in investor thinking, since the logic of *sauve qui peut* dominates in a creditor scramble in which creditors are serviced on a first-come, first-served basis. The macroeconomic results are a huge overshooting: (1) debt is drawn down even when domestic investments (such as in working capital, letters of credit, etc.) have a rate of return vastly greater than the world cost of capital; (2) the real exchange rate depreciates sharply, far overshooting any real correction that needs to be made; (3) the current account swings wildly from deficit to outright surplus; (4) the banking system suffers illiquidity, and perhaps an ancillary panic by domestic savers; (5) market real interest rates soar to astronomical levels, as each borrower scrambles to mobilize funds to avoid default; and (6) partial default on forex obligations becomes almost assured. The key effects on macroeconomic contraction are, firstly, the collapse of bank lending, leading to a collapse of trade and production; and secondly, the conversion of illiquidity into insolvency in the course of a few months, as loans become non-performing under the weight of reduced production and sales, and the crushingly high interest rates on working capital.

Economic Policies During a Financial Panic

In order to minimize the output collapse, it is imperative that the central bank takes the following two steps to keep the payments mechanism of the economy intact. The first step is to prevent the generalized panic, sparked off by the failure of the bad banks, from rendering the good banks illiquid and causing them to fail too. This means that the central bank must extend sufficient reserves to the good banks to meet the withdrawal of deposits but not sufficient for them to extend new loans to finance speculation against the currency.

The second step to protect the payments mechanism is for the central bank to ensure that the good customers (especially if they are exporters) of the failed banks continue to receive working credit to keep production going. This means that the central bank must keep the operations of failed banks going while restructuring their balance sheets for eventual sale. Again, the emphasis is on maintaining the volume of working credit to existing clients. The crucial point to keep in mind is that the creation of new reserves is to accommodate the private sector's shift out of bank deposits into currency, and not to fuel the run from domestic assets to foreign assets.

During a financial panic, the central bank has to choose maintenance of the domestic payments system and output level over maintenance of the existing exchange rate. The central bank should float the currency and allow currency depreciation to discourage capital outflow. Some banks may fail because of the exchange-rate-induced increase in the value of their foreign liabilities, and the central bank must keep the operations of these banks going in order to keep production credit going to the good firms. With the amount of working credit in the economy unchanged by the financial panic, domestic firms can increase exports to take advantage of the currency depreciation.

The resulting growth in exports, coupled with the stability of output, will help to restore confidence in the economy, prompting domestic agents to repatriate their capital from abroad and foreign creditors to resume lending, and the final outcome will be an appreciation of the currency from its over-depreciated value (although it may not be up to its pre-crisis value). The important implication is that banks that had been rendered bankrupt by the exchange-rate-induced increase in the value of their foreign liabilities are now likely to be solvent again.

In light of the analysis above, we see the error of the first IMF packages that were implemented in Thailand, South Korea, and Indonesia. The tightening of monetary policy in order to raise interest rates to prevent further currency depreciation, the abrupt closure of bad financial institutions, and the raising of prudential ratios, all created a tremendous credit crunch that dramatically deepened the output decline, and that inflamed the panic. The closure of the bad financial institutions, particularly in Indonesia where there was no depositor insurance, spread the financial panic to the good banks.

The fact that fiscal policy was also tightened ensured the crashing of these economies.

Our objection to the first IMF packages that were implemented in the crisis countries should not be interpreted as a general objection to the closing of bad banks or the adoption of higher BIS-style prudential ratios. We are only objecting to the implementation of these two actions in the middle of a financial crisis. It is the timing of the implementation of these two policies that was wrong.

Applying the Framework to Asia

Our interpretation of financial crises is a general one, not specific to Asia, but the analysis fits the Asian experience very well. All the countries that got into trouble in Asia (especially Indonesia, Korea, Malaysia, and Thailand) shared three main characteristics. First, they were very successful economies, so that they were able to attract significant inflows of capital during the 1990s. Secondly, all the countries maintained exchange rates that were practically fixed to, or depreciating at a predetermined rate against, the U.S. dollar during the 1990s. Thirdly, the combination of capital inflows and fixed exchange rates pushed the economy into a position of vulnerability, characterized by an *overvalued currency, falling foreign exchange reserves*, and *a high level of foreign debt*, especially short-term debt. As discussed earlier, once the overvaluation of the currency became apparent to investors (by the end of 1996 in the case of Thailand, and by mid-1997 in the case of the other economies), currency speculation led to the worst of all evils. To honour their exchange rate commitments, these countries simply depleted their foreign exchange reserves in defending their overvalued currencies. When reserves fell to low levels, the foreign creditors panicked and demanded immediate repayments of loans, rather than rolling the loans over — which would have been mutually beneficial for the creditors and the debtors alike.

In fact, in the case of Asia, we can definitely view the crisis as a "crisis of success" rather than a crisis of failure. Only successful economies would have been able to attract so much capital inflow as did the Asian economies. Ironically, these economies did not really need so much foreign capital. During their high growth phase of the 1980s, the Asian countries tended to save around 25–30 per cent of gross domestic product (GDP) and to invest a similar amount, so that they relied little on foreign borrowing. In the early 1990s, these countries liberalized their financial markets, with the effect that domestic banks and corporations could suddenly borrow from abroad, thereby raising the investment rates even higher than the already high levels of domestic savings. There was certainly no shortage of willing foreign lenders. As a result, the ratio of investment to GDP rose to about 35 per cent or more, with 5 per cent of GDP or more being financed by foreign loans.

There is ample evidence that neither the foreign nor domestic financial markets were able to allocate the increased investments very efficiently. Both microeconomic and macroeconomic data support the view that the incremental investments in the 1990s were only moderately profitable. Too much money was poured into speculative real estate projects, for example, in downtown Bangkok. There was also a fairly clear over-investment in sectors such as memory chips, especially among the copy-cat Korean *chaebols*. Still other investments were thoroughly wasted in crony projects, such as the abortive "national car" programme linked to former President Soeharto's family. Yet, even though the incremental investments added little to economic growth, they were hardly a disaster on average, and certainly not a sufficient explanation for an abrupt economic collapse.

The collapse came mainly because of the macroeconomic problems outlined earlier, not the microeconomic inefficiencies of the investment boom, although such inefficiencies certainly added to the troubles. More important was the fact that the investments were financed by short-term loans, under conditions of pegged exchange rates (or, in the case of Indonesia, a crawling peg). As the capital inflows proceeded in the 1990s, domestic prices and wages were bid higher. As a result, the wage level expressed in dollars began to creep up to unsustainable levels. The steady devaluation of the Chinese yuan in 1991–94 (through the swap market mechanism) further decreased the competitiveness of these countries. Then, when the U.S. dollar appreciated sharply relative to the Japanese yen and the European currencies in 1995 and 1996, these currencies appreciated alongside the dollar, further eroding the international competitiveness of these countries. Export growth faltered severely in 1996 as a result. By the end of 1996, market participants began to suspect the need for a currency depreciation in several Asian countries, most notably Thailand.

The rest, as they say, is history. Thailand depleted its foreign reserves in an ill-fated attempt to stabilize its currency. After using most of its reserves, it announced defeat on 2 July 1997, allowing the baht to depreciate. The IMF announced several Draconian measures for the Thai economy, most notably a sharp increase of interest rates, a significant cut in budget outlays, and a dramatic closure of 58 finance companies. The combination of depleted foreign reserves, high levels of foreign short-term debt, and market anxieties surrounding the tough IMF measures, all conspired to produce a full-fledged financial panic. The panic spread to the rest of Pacific Asia, engulfing Indonesia and Malaysia in the Fall of 1997, and Korea in December 1997. This reversal of capital flow is captured in Table 2.1 below, which shows the composition of net capital flows to Indonesia, Malaysia, Philippines, South Korea, and Thailand in the 1994–99 period.

It is instructive to note that the panic was greatest among the commercial banks. Their lending to the five Asian countries jumped from US$24 billion in 1994 to US$63 billion in 1996, and then became *negative* US$21 billion in 1997, *negative* US$36 billion in 1998, and (expected) *negative* US$16 billion in 1999. The much-maligned hedge funds were presumably captured in the sum of "portfolio equity" and "non-bank creditors", and their operations became dwarfed by those of the commercial banks, being US$35 billion in 1996, US$16 billion in 1997, *negative* US$1 billion in 1998, and (expected) US$4 billion in 1999. Foreign direct investment into these five Asian countries (direct equity) actually increased after 1996, rising steadily from US$5 billion in 1996 to (expected) US$13 billion in 1999.

When the crisis hit, many observers began to point out some of the weaknesses of the Asian economies: poor banking supervision; excessive lending in the 1990s; cronyism in the allocation of loans; and so forth. These weaknesses were, and are, real but they hardly explain Asia's collapse. The Asian economies were not "miracle" economies to be sure, but they were also not impending disasters; they were victims of global panic. These economies were, overall, ranked mid-way among the world's major economies in terms of institutional quality, good enough to achieve rapid growth given that they were starting at fairly low levels of income (and therefore with plenty of room to import technologies to catch up with the leaders). For example, the World Economic

TABLE 2.1
External Financing of Indonesia, Malaysia, South Korea,
Thailand, and Philippines[5]
(In billions of US dollars)

	1994	1995	1996	1997	Estimates 1998	Forecasts 1999
Current Account balance	−24.6	−40.6	−54.8	−26.1	69.2	44.6
External Financing, net	47.4	83.0	99.0	28.3	−4.2	7.8
1.0 Private flows, net						
Direct equity	4.7	4.2	4.7	5.9	9.5	12.5
Portfolio equity	7.6	11.0	13.9	−1.5	4.3	6.0
Commercial banks	24.0	53.2	62.7	−21.2	−36.1	−16.0
Non-bank private creditors	4.2	12	21.0	17.1	−5.3	−2.3
2.0 Official flows, net	7.0	2.6	-3.3	28.1	23.4	7.6
Other Financing (include monetary gold & errors and omissions)	−17.5	−28.3	−27.3	−33.7	−22.9	−21.0
Reserves excluding gold (− = increase)	−5.4	−14.1	−16.9	31.5	−42.1	−31.4

SOURCE: Institute of International Finance, *Capital Flows to Emerging Market Economies*, 29 January 1998; and 25 April 1999.

Forum's Global Competitiveness Reports consistently ranked the Asian economies just a little above average in overall competitiveness. For example, of the 53 countries evaluated for competitiveness in 1997, Indonesia ranked fifteenth, Thailand ranked eighteenth, and South Korea ranked twenty-first. Investors knew about the weaknesses, at least in broad terms, but they also knew about Asia's great strengths: high rates of domestic savings; export promotion policies; a skilled and disciplined labour force; and private-market orientation. What nobody counted on was a sudden withdrawal of foreign credits that would bring these economies to their knees.

Prognosis for Selected Pacific Asian Countries

Before assessing the economic prospects of selected Pacific Asian countries, it is important to note that there have been at least four instances of financial panic in the first half of the 1990s: Argentina and Mexico in 1995, Turkey in 1994, and Venezuela in 1994. Part A of Table 2.2 shows the GDP growth rates of these economies for the period of two years before the panic and two years after the crisis (except for Venezuela which shows the figure for three years after the crisis). In three of the four cases — Argentina, Mexico, and Turkey — the financial panic caused a sharp drop in output for one year, followed by a sharp rebound. The result was a V-shaped movement in gross national product (GNP).

Part B of Table 2.2 shows a similarly sharp output decline for Indonesia, Malaysia, and South Korea in 1998 following a slowdown in growth in 1997. If the previous experiences of Argentina, Mexico, and Turkey apply to Malaysia, South Korea, and Thailand (three countries that are not embroiled in the severe political crisis like Indonesia), the financial panic explanation would predict their output collapses to be short-lived. The IMF, on the other hand, predicted in December 1998 that recovery in 1999 would be weak because it attributed the financial crisis to be a structural collapse

TABLE 2.2
Financial Panic and Real GDP Change
(In per cent)

Part A: The Precedents

	T-2	T-1	T	T+1	T+2	T+3
	(T=year of panic given next to country)					
Argentina, 1995	5.7	8.0	−4.0	4.8	8.6	
Mexico, 1995	2.0	4.5	−6.2	5.2	7.0	
Turkey, 1994	6.4	8.4	−5.0	6.7	7.3	
Venezuela, 1994	7.3	0.3	−2.9	3.4	−1.6	5.1

Part B: The Pacific Asia Cases

	1995	1996	1997	1998[6]
Indonesia	8.2	8.0	4.6	−13.6
Malaysia	9.5	8.6	7.7	−7.5
South Korea	8.7	7.3	5.5	−5.8
Thailand	8.8	5.5	−0.4	−8.0

SOURCE: Except as noted, data are from IMF, *International Financial Statistics*, December 1999.

TABLE 2.3
Predictions of Economic Growth

Agency:	IMF	IMF[7]		HSBC[8]		HSBC[9]	
Date:	Dec. 1998	October 1999		October 1999		March 2000	
Year:	1999	1999	2000	1999	2000	1999	2000
Indonesia	−3.4	−0.8	2.6	−0.5	4.0	0.2	4.0
Malaysia	−2.0	2.4	6.5	4.5	5.5	5.4	5.5
S. Korea	−1.0	6.5	5.5	7.5	6.0	9.4	6.3
Thailand	1.0	4.0	4.0	3.9	3.4	3.9	5.3

that was waiting to happen, just like the centrally-planned economies of Eastern Europe and Russia on the eve of 1990.

The IMF predictions of December 1998 have turned out to be badly wrong for the crisis countries (see Table 2.3). By mid-1999, it was clear that regional recovery was on the way, and the IMF revised its predictions upwards in October 1999. Because of the IMF's "soft-rot" perspective, its upward adjustments were not enough to anticipate the true extent of the recovery. For example, it was more pessimistic than the HSBC (Hongkong and Shanghai Banking Corporation) growth projections for Korea and Malaysia that were released at about the same time. The latest indications in March 2000 suggest that output in South Korea in 1999 is likely to rise by about 9.4 per cent instead of declining 1 per cent as predicted by the IMF in December 1998, while that of Malaysia is likely to grow by 5.4 per cent in 1999, and that of Thailand by 3.9 per cent instead of 1 per cent and *negative* 2 per cent respectively. The strong recovery in 1999 in all these countries certainly negate the "soft rot" explanation of the Asian financial crisis. The V-shaped recovery pattern in these countries is more compatible with the financial contagion explanation.

The financial contagion explanation not only predicted a V-shaped recovery, but also that the robust recovery would be sustained in 2000. Most of the prominent investment banks like HSBC have also given the same predictions. The view in March 2000 was that growth in Indonesia and Thailand would be higher in 2000 than in 1999, and that Malaysia's growth in 2000 would likely be the same as in 1999. To its credit, even the IMF has come round to recognizing the V-shaped recovery, and the strong underlying economic strength of the crisis countries in Asia — as evidenced by its October 1999 predictions of growth in 2000.

The Seven Pillars of Reform

Our analysis of the Asian financial crisis indicates the clear need for important reforms in many areas, including domestic markets, domestic institutions, international organizations, and international financial architecture. Based on the analysis here, we propose policy actions on seven fronts.

First and foremost, the financial markets in developing countries require root-and-branch reform in many cases. In order to enhance the resilience of the financial system to creditor panic, prudential regulation and supervision must be strengthened, accounting practices brought up to international standards, balance sheets of financial institutions reported more fully, more frequently, and more timely, and the entry of foreign banks relaxed.

Secondly, the performance of the IMF has left much to be desired. The IMF actually contributed to the financial panic that helped to bring down the Asian economies. External supervision of the IMF must be increased and improved, and this requires the decision-making process within the IMF to be more transparent, and more democratic to include a larger number of developing countries.

Thirdly, the IMF cannot, and should not, be either the international lender of last resort or the international deposit insurance agency. In such circumstances, generalized floating of exchange rates should be the norm for the international monetary system. The new monetary system should establish regional monetary bodies, and an international bankruptcy court to speed up international debt restructuring.

Fourthly, the failure of the first IMF programmes for Thailand, Indonesia, and South Korea, as well as subsequent programmes for Russia and Brazil, makes it clear that international rescue packages must be redesigned. Among other things, there should be ways to "bail in", rather than bail out, the foreign creditors. Debt relief, standstills for existing debt, priority payment for new loans, and other standard features of domestic bankruptcy procedures should be part of international rescue packages. IMF funds should certainly not be used to defend overvalued exchange rates, as was done (unsuccessfully) in Russia and Brazil.

Fifthly, the regulation and monitoring of international capital markets should be stricter and internationally co-ordinated. The chief regulatory reforms are prudential restrictions on short-term capital inflows, and the further liberalization of long-term foreign direct investments. The United Nations should take the lead in convening a meeting of international organizations on this important question, a meeting that can help to bridge the differences and misunderstandings between the developed and developing countries.

Sixthly, the bad debts of the financial and corporate sectors in Pacific Asia must be decisively and quickly resolved because they are paralysing the credit system and inhibiting investment. The key steps to recapitalizing the banking sector are the infusion of public money, and the takeover of some large domestic banks by foreign banks. Moreover, the key steps to reviving the corporate sector are debt write-downs and debt-equity swaps.

Seventhly, there is a serious mismatch in Pacific Asia, particularly in most of Southeast Asia, between investment in physical hardware — factories and machinery — and investment in social software — scientific research centres, administrative and judiciary systems, and the growth of civil society. While it is now increasingly recognized that the enrichment of the domestic scientific base is crucial for sustaining high economic growth, it is less recognized that Asia's flawed social infrastructure and inadequate political institutions — which have allowed for too much corruption and mismanagement — are a cause for serious concern. In a world of growing international competitiveness, when foreign direct investors are courted not just by Asia but also Central Europe and Latin America, the concerns over governance are bound to grow, and to weigh increasingly heavily on the unreformed countries of Asia. In short, the long-term competitiveness of Asia rests as much on "getting the institutions right" as on "getting the prices right".

NOTES

*   I am most grateful to Florian Alburo, Chia Siow Yue, William James, Kao Kim Hourn, Wisarn Pupphavesa, Hadi Soesastro, Nattapong Thongpakde, Mya Than and the other participants of the Roundtable for excellent criticisms that have helped to improve this paper. The paper draws in part upon research undertaken jointly with Jeffrey Sachs.

1 World Bank, *The East Asian Miracle: Economic Growth and Public Policy* (New York, N.Y.: Oxford University Press, 1993).
2 Wing Thye Woo, in "Managing the Instability from the Globalisation of Financial Markets", *ASEAN Economic Bulletin* 17, no.2 (August 2000), makes this argument by using the movements in the risk premia of the Eurodollar bonds issued by enterprises from each Asian country.
3 The financial contagion phenomenon is theoretically compatible with rational expectations; see Wing Thye Woo, "Some Evidence of Speculative Bubbles in the Foreign Exchange Markets", *Journal of Money, Credit and Banking* (November 1987).
4 Steven Radelet and Jeffrey Sachs, "The East Asian Financial Crisis: Diagnosis, Remedies, Prospects," *Brookings Papers on Economic Activity* 1 (1998): 1–90.
5 Data from Institue of International Finance, *Capital Flows to Emerging Market Economies*, 29 January 1998; and 25 February 1999.
6 The estimates are from HSBC, *Asia Economics Weekly*, 11 October 1999.
7 IMF, *World Economic Outlook*, October 1999.
8 HSBC, *Asia Economics Weekly*, 11 October 1998.
9 HSBC, *Asia Economics Weekly*, 6 March 2000.

REFERENCES

HSBC. *Asia Economics Weekly*, 11 October 1998; and 6 March 2000.
Institute of International Finance. *Capital Flows to Emerging Market Economies*, 29 January 1998; and 25 February 1999.
International Monetary Fund. *World Economic Outlook*, October 1999.
Radelet, Steven and Jeffrey D. Sachs. "The East Asian Financial Crisis: Diagnosis, Remedies, Prospects." *Brookings Papers on Economic Activity* 1 (1998): 1–90.
Woo, Wing Thye. "Some Evidence of Speculative Bubbles in the Foreign Exchange Markets." *Journal of Money, Credit and Banking* (November 1987).
Woo, Wing Thye. "Coping with Capital Flows Accelerated by the Globalisation of Financial Markets." *ASEAN Economic Bulletin* 17, no. 2 (August 2000).
World Bank. *The East Asian Miracle: Economic Growth and Public Policy*. New York: Oxford University Press, 1993.

3

Competitiveness and Sustainable Growth in ASEAN

FLORIAN A. ALBURO

Overview

More than a year after the outbreak of the Asian financial crisis, there still does not seem to be a consensus on the proximate causes and hence what measures ought to be taken to avert its recurrence. Despite the numerous papers (scholarly as well as popular), conferences, publications, and official meetings that have proliferated since the start of the crisis, there is no convergence on its explanation — its unpredicted occurrence, its severity, and its wide spread across Asia and the rest of the world. At one extreme is a school of thought that the crisis was caused by fundamental weaknesses in the economies of the affected countries, manifested by macroeconomic imbalances, excessive borrowings, overvalued currencies, and poor investments, among other things (Moreno, et al. 1998; Glick 1998). At the other extreme is an argument that the crisis was triggered by speculators and their panic behaviour by withdrawing from the emerging markets in fear of losses (Moreno et al. 1998; Montes 1998). Between these two extremes are various shades of explanation. There is the notion of a lack of governance in both public and private transactions, especially in terms of close relationships between financial institutions and regulators.[1] There is the notion that corruption weakened the system of investment decision-making in the emerging markets. There is the notion that "Asian values" had dictated the manner of financial exchanges. There is the notion that the crisis was essentially a bubble crisis (Nomura 1999). While the truth may lie somewhere between these two extremes, they have different policy implications. If the crisis was caused by fundamental weaknesses in the economy, the crisis-hit countries should carry out reforms to improve the foundation for sustainable development. On the other hand, if the crisis was caused by the sudden loss of confidence among short-term investors and speculators not directly related to country fundamentals, then the essential task is not really reforms, nor would they be necessary. Restoring confidence where the basic fundamentals are "correct" may require other measures that would bring back investors.[2] Without a clear explanation for the crisis in the affected countries, it would be difficult to prescribe policy options.

There have been many attempts to assess the impact of certain factors in the evolution of the Asian crisis but events remain fluid and although there is a definite "bottoming out" and a return to the growth experiences of the past, their sustainability remains to be seen. What seems evident, however, is the finding that weaknesses in the financial systems in Asia were stronger explanations for the crisis than basic fundamental flaws in the economy (McKinnon and Pill 1998). The unusually large flows of short-term capital in these countries exposed them to inevitable reversals when investors panicked, eventually draining reserves and squeezing liquidity. Moreover, one particular reason for the spread of the crisis from Thailand in July 1997 to the other Southeast and East Asian countries was the high degree of financial and trade integration among them (Glick and Rose 1998). The vulnerability of the financial sector to external shocks was not a product of economic fundamentals but of micro aspects of the sector, such as less-than-arms-length transactions and poor risk management, which led to unusual credit booms. Indeed, there is an argument that none of these explanations suffice since the Asian crisis was a bubble crisis, which had its beginnings well before the explosion in Thailand, and ran across most of Southeast and East Asia (Ichimura et al. 1997).

In the more formal theoretical models of foreign exchange crisis, second-generation and third-generation models emphasize the importance of the governments' conflicting objectives and interaction between the banking sector and the balance of payments. In this sense, the second-generation models show that domestic policy failures do not necessarily precede a crisis to enable governments to make decisions to alter its exchange rate policy. A domestic banking crisis, however, often precedes a payments crisis among the third-generation models. The Asian crisis itself has spawned some theoretical explanations for the tendency of agents and institutions to over-borrow and to rely on government guarantees under fixed exchange rates (Krugman 1998; and Montes 1998).

Despite the lack of consensus on the root causes of the Asian financial crisis, there is growing evidence that it has largely subsided and bottomed out. What is not so clear is whether the recovery in the affected countries is sustainable and when growth will get back on track. The ASEAN economies have been badly hit by the crisis although the extent of the damage has not been uniform across the region. At one extreme are the economies of Indonesia and Thailand (which some have identified as the source of the conflagration) which seem to have suffered the most. At the other extreme are the new members of the region, which appear to have been insulated from the direct impact of the crisis. In between are the other members, which have been partially affected. Judging by the growth rates of aggregate output, the economies that have been in the direct path of the crisis are the five ASEAN economies of Indonesia, Malaysia, Philippines, Singapore, and Thailand. Indeed, in 1998, the first full year after the start of the crisis, these ASEAN economies experienced sharp falls in their gross domestic product (GDP) growth rates, in magnitudes that were way out of their usual pace in the recent past. If we look into their quarterly growth rates, all of them were technically in recession. However, recovery now seems to be taking place among these affected ASEAN economies, and the prospects of an earlier full recovery are now greater than previously anticipated. The more important question in the region is the strength of this recovery and how the ASEAN economies will fare in the long haul. While there is the rest of the world's economies to contend with, it may be possible to examine ASEAN's own prospects.

This chapter will focus on two main aspects. After tracing the broad economic effects of the crisis, we attempt to determine whether the crisis has bottomed out and recovery is really on the way. We also consider issues related to the sustainability of the recovery and the growth and prospects for the region's competitiveness. Finally, some conclusions are drawn.

Figure 3.1 shows the annual growth rate of GDP for five of the ASEAN economies hit by the crisis between 1995 and 1998. These annual growth rates highlight the severity of the decline in growth in the year after the crisis broke out. Except for Singapore, all the rest suffered negative growth rates in 1998. Indeed, these annual figures show how the ASEAN economies (with the exception of the Philippines) had been used to growth rates of 7–9 per cent annually in contrast to the rate in 1998. The figure also shows that perhaps the source of the crisis was Thailand, given the drop in its GDP growth rate from 1996 and even a negative growth rate as early as 1997. On the other hand, the severity of the decline in Indonesia was a combination of the contagion effect and the ensuing political turmoil that transmitted itself into the economic front, which cumulatively contributed to the severe decline in the growth rate. The two countries which were least affected, Singapore and the Philippines, had the smallest decline in GDP growth rates, as shown

FIGURE 3.1
GDP Growth Rates

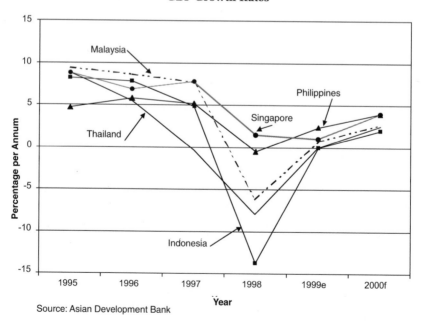

Source: Asian Development Bank

in the figure. Of course, these aggregate figures do not just reflect the impact of the crisis. They are also the outcomes of many interactive policies, and are not only driven by financial difficulties.

Since the ASEAN economies are open and trade vigorously in the international market, their trade sectors contribute significantly to overall growth. Similarly, sharp declines in trade performance also contribute to growth declines. Figure 3.2 gives this telling picture. Indeed, in these economies the declines in export (of merchandise) growth rates have also been prominent. While the Philippines managed to keep a double-digit growth rate throughout the period, its absolute export size is the smallest among the group (Figure 3.2).

What is missing from this discussion is the oft-repeated assertion that the Asian crisis was a financial one. Invariably, the identified causes ranged from a narrow peg of the exchange rates to lack of transparency and prudential regulations among banks. Moreover, the crisis was the occasion for calling attention to the weaknesses of the financial systems of the affected countries, wherein there existed close relationships between the government and institutional credit. Indeed, the crisis was partly triggered by cronyism and corruption, and there was lack of effective governance among the institutions concerned. In the tradition of sequencing issues, the crisis highlighted the "disorder" by which the capital account was liberalized without the concomitant checks in place, namely, banking reforms, standards, and transparency. However, the more formal of these explanations of financial behaviour identified some of the causes, ranging from a narrow peg of the exchange rates to lack of transparency and prudential regulations among banks. These posit that, with respect to foreign fund borrowings, the private sector behaves as if there is an implied government guarantee against exchange losses, and thus there is a tendency to overborrow when the exchange rate is fixed. The magnitudes involved in the transaction of foreign funds and the implied behaviour are thus obvious. The surge of capital flows into the Asian region in the nineties associated with capital account liberalization was mainly in the form of portfolio investments and debt capital (through banks and non-bank financial institutions) rather than foreign direct investments (FDI). Thus, much of the growth in the region during this time may have been driven by (private) debt capital. For example, the Institute for International Finance (IIF) reported that

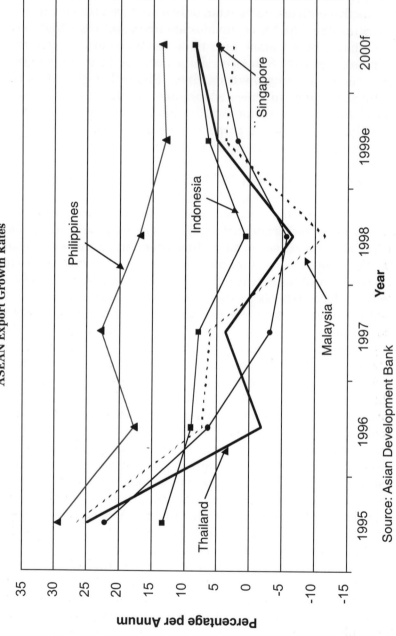

FIGURE 3.2
ASEAN Export Growth Rates

Source: Asian Development Bank

of the US$44.8 billion net private flows into the five affected economies in the Asian region (Indonesia, South Korea, Malaysia, Philippines, Thailand) in 1993, only US$4.5 billion were in net direct equity investment and the rest were in portfolio equity investments, net lending by commercial banks, and other private creditors (IIF 1998). By 1996, the total net private flows into these countries amounted to US$97 billion, of which only US$6.2 billion were in net direct equity investments. By the end of 1997, net private flows indicated an outflow of US$11.9 billion, with FDI increasing slightly. The private capital from abroad therefore augmented domestic private sector resources, creating capital stock essential to growth and development. However, the question whether financial forces drove the crisis in the ASEAN economies is not germane to our interest here. The question is whether economic recovery and growth sustainability are assured in the countries concerned. It is here perhaps that the underlying forces of the crisis become relevant. We turn to this as we attempt to search for recovery signs in the region.

Recovery Signs

We have argued elsewhere that while the crisis left economic devastation in the region, the very foundation of these economies was not lost. This needs to be emphasized as we identify signs of a "bottoming out" and an early recovery of growth. It is important to point out in the aftermath of the crisis that while the affected countries and the entire region experienced recession, the growth potential remains and the region's productive capacities have not evaporated because of it. It is of course true that one sees the "waste" (for example, empty condominiums, unoccupied houses, buildings, malls, golf courses, etc.) around, the social as well as political costs, and the widespread poverty created by the collapse of the region's economies — and the toll continues. Yet, in a real sense, the crisis highlighted the behaviour of these economies that led to the region's solid economic growth which created a productive capacity that can help the economies to turn around. Indeed, this should matter in the policy adjustment of the region.

Firstly, macroeconomic parameters of the regional economies in the nineties show that both inflation and government budgetary deficits were well managed. The convergence of inflation rates and the movement of overall surplus (deficit) of the central government during the period 1990–95 verifies this. There may have been some divergence in the early nineties for the ASEAN countries but the numbers narrowed by 1995. Some data may not be comparable, yet the trend reflects fiscal stability not profligacy; monetary discipline and conservatism, not irresponsibility. This is in relation to government policy behaviour rather than that of the private sector.

Secondly, the ASEAN economies have sustained an industrial development drive and have therefore seen a rising share of industry in the overall economy. In terms of real value-added in manufacturing, with the exception of the Philippines, their growth rates had narrowed by 1995. In both Indonesia and the Philippines, the share of industry was below 30 per cent of GDP, while for the other three countries, industry occupied 30 per cent or more of their GDP. This pattern has not just been for the first five years of this decade but has in fact been true for the last two decades for some of the other three ASEAN economies. The record of the period 1990–95 shows that these countries have developed a strong industrial sector.

Thirdly, both the real growth rates in manufacturing and the significant share of industry in GDP are reflected in the greater diversity of markets and in the share of manufactures in total exports. A comparison is made for these countries between 1980 and 1995 in terms of export destination to East Asia (that is, for trade among themselves and with the rest of the region) and the share of manufactured goods to total exports. Except for Thailand (which had only a marginal increase in exports to East Asia between 1980 and 1995), all the other countries expanded their exports into the region by at least 50 per cent (See Alburo [1998] for the data to support these). Looking back into their economic history, there was a dramatic surge of manufactured exports between 1980 and 1995. In addition, it is also well documented that with the exception of the Philippines there has been significant diversification of manufactured exports by the ASEAN economies, especially during the decade or so before the onset of the crisis in the region, suggesting both maturity and deepening.

Finally, sustained growth has been associated with (or caused by) expansion in gross domestic capital formation, which in turn has been partly fed by gross national savings. One can see that capital formation has been comparable among the ASEAN economies with the exception of the Philippines. Moreover, these rates have been short of the savings rates available domestically. Hence, for them, foreign savings have been additional sources of capital formation.

It seems obvious that for the five ASEAN countries their foundations have been strong. Yet, in spite of their sound "fundamentals", they suffered currency attacks that eventually led to a state of economic decline. This aspect of the crisis requires a separate discussion. It suffices to say that the real side of the trade (as opposed to the asset side) fundamentals have been showing a deterioration, indicating distortions that require policy actions (for example, the dramatic slowdown in merchandise export growth in 1996 and the overvaluation of currencies, among others). Although several other fundamental weaknesses have been raised, such as weak financial systems, lack of prudent regulations, non-transparent governance, and corruption, these have been at *status quo* since before the onset of the crisis.

There are therefore mechanisms in place for early recovery through which the ASEAN economies can grow and trade out of the crisis. This, of course, assumes that the appropriate policies are made that recognize the need for the viability of the trade sectors in addition to the recapitalization of financial institutions, which is particularly necessary for some countries (for example, Thailand). The mechanisms that have been spelled out provide a fundamentally sound foundation for recovery, compared to the situation if the devastation had taken place without this strong economic history.

The Philippines, however, does not seem to fit squarely into this pattern of strong "fundamentals" in part because its performance has been different from the other ASEAN countries. For example, the Philippine's manufacturing behaviour, national savings, and domestic capital formation rates do not converge with the other four countries. That it has been equally vulnerable to the crisis (though to a lesser degree) suggests that strong fundamentals in the above sense do not provide automatic immunity (see Alburo, forthcoming). More concretely, what the crisis has left behind in the affected economies is the immediate capacity to rebound, given the right policy mixes. But the behaviour and the seeming exception of the Philippines does not suggest a train of causality one way or the other.

Both own-country and third-party forecasts of growth for the ASEAN economies affected by the crisis tend to show a "bottoming out" and 1999 was expected to show positive but feeble growth rates (see Figure 3.1). The Asian Development Bank's (ADB's) outlook is that the ASEAN economies are on the way to recovery. In the case of the most severely affected countries, Indonesia and Thailand, the forecast was zero growth rates for 1999. All, however, would achieve positive growth rates for 2000, with both the Philippines and Singapore hitting 4 per cent GDP growth rates.

Figure 3.2 shows the growth rates of exports for the ASEAN countries which were positive with the exception of the Philippines, which seems to decline over the period 1999–2000. The turnaround began from negative growth rates or close to zero export growth rates, as in the case of Indonesia in 1998. The converse of the trade figures is even more telling. Imports have increased significantly across all the ASEAN countries that were hit by the crisis. These import surges have been in two critical areas: capital goods and intermediate imports. The former indicates a domestic demand that is now reflected in the market, while the latter indicates export recovery as these intermediate imports are for inputs into export production. Moreover, there is now an overall increase in the demand for electricity in these ASEAN economies, which show that the crisis may have bottomed out in terms of domestic behaviour and export markets.

With regard to the financial part of the crisis, however, there remains several snags. There is the large overhang from the exposure of the ASEAN countries' banking systems to the huge private debts accumulated prior to the crisis. In Thailand and Indonesia, the magnitudes of the non-performing loans require substantial infusion of funds to recapitalize the banking sector. To the extent that there are varying views on the involvement of the government in the recapitalization exercise, recovery may be delayed. Institutional reforms to improve bank supervision and other prudential regulations are important for all the ASEAN economies. The governments should also reconcentrate their resources in private sector activities. This implies a considerable set of tasks that have yet to be completed and thus, this sector is far from recovery. It is in this context then that foreign direct investment in the *post-crisis* period will play a vital role. It can bring in much needed foreign capital while relieving government budgetary constraints. It can also boost technological capacities required to sustain the recovery without substantial costs. Even if FDI is small initially, it will invite confidence from the rest of the investment world and thus contribute to greater stability of the countries.

This FDI approach to sustain economic recovery is supported by large Japanese transnationals, and while investments (into the region) may not be as smooth as in the past, they will continue to increase, as the currency devaluations, massive surplus of undervalued assets, and long-term reductions in the cost of doing business in Asia provide opportunities for investment (Kobe 1998). This long-term perspective may not be shared by all Japanese firms. Small and medium-sized firms may find it easier to relocate their production back to Japan in response to declining costs triggered by the depreciation of the year. Such decisions, however, may have to be weighed against the larger context of the long-term scenario in the region and the behaviour of the larger Japanese firms, which dictate production and supply transactions. Indeed, there are indications, for example, that Japanese FDI in the Philippines has been going lately into input supplies and further backward integration (Philippine Export Development Plan 1999). This is consistent with the notion that Japanese overseas operations are now the backbone of Japanese industry. What has been overlooked is the rise of FDI coming from the United States to replace the vacuum left in part by Japanese and Asian capital in the recent past. Given the unprecedented American growth experience, there are indications that American capital and corporations are coming in to take advantage of the opportunities created by the crisis (Kim 1998). And as foreign investment laws are modified in the Asian countries, the options for more sectoral presence become wider. Of course, the European countries are also likely to take advantage of equity participation and acquisitions arising from the crisis. Though debt capital is not likely to be forthcoming from any of the major capital sources, FDI is another matter altogether. In all, the combination of re-flows of capital towards FDI, the configuration of Japanese production relations, the likely positive response from U.S. investors and other sources, indicate that FDI will continue to flow, however modest. Some of these flows may not turn out to be new money but conversion of private debt capital into equity. The continued vigour of FDI (though there was in fact some slowing down early in the crisis) has been an important source of support for the recovery process, especially in the wake of the difficulties in the turnaround of the financial sector. The expanded participation of more investors (significantly beyond traditional Japanese sources) has also helped boost domestic confidence in the recovery of their economies in ways that would otherwise have been difficult to achieve. Despite the apparent difficulties in the financial sector's adjustments, foreign capital has been instrumental in gearing it into more effective modalities (for example, encouraging more collaboration between domestic and foreign banks). In this sense, the sector's recovery can also eventually rely on private sector capital.

Issues in Sustaining Growth

The previous section argued that there are signs that the ASEAN economies hit by the crisis have indeed "bottomed out" and are on the way to recovery and a return to growth. That the region was able to recover quickly is not surprising, given what has been described as a growth foundation built over the years prior to the crisis. Indeed, the speed of the recovery is somewhat surprising, and indicates its critical importance.

How sustainable is this recovery is a different, though related, question. The uneven speed of the adjustment processes suggests, offhand, that there is no assurance of sustainability. For example, the demands of the financial sector may impinge on the other sectors' ability to maintain their recovery. The early recovery itself (since the necessary conditions for the growth are there) can be attributed to several factors. One is the easing of government budgetary behaviour in the light of the crisis. It must be remembered that early into the crisis, the infusion of multilateral resources carried with it the conditions of budgetary surplus. What is redeeming is the realization that the ASEAN countries had prudent fiscal pictures and further tightening would only exacerbate the crisis. Therefore, a reversal of budgetary behaviour into active fiscal policies would avert a downward spiral of the economies. Government-led or continuing deficits are not likely to be sustained because the demands from other factors (such as banking sector reforms) will also have to be met. Another is the ability of the ASEAN economies to look outwards to generate economic activities. For sure, they were helped along by the sharp currency depreciations throughout the period of the crisis. Trade has been particularly helpful to the countries in generating foreign exchange and keeping the export sectors active despite difficulties in financial support (for example, export credits that were short because of related banking problems).

Yet it was clear that exchange rates actually experienced overshooting early on, and currencies have appreciated. Figure 3.3 (which is the Real Effective Exchange Rate Indices for Asian countries hit by the crisis) readily indicates that export markets are not assured, given the rebound of the exchange rates. We must look into the competitiveness of ASEAN trade among themselves and with the rest of the world. Finally, new capital inflows (FDI and non-debt capital) have responded to the sales of assets and other forms of foreign ventures (helped along by the sharp currency depreciation). While for some countries, this will continue for some time as financial restructuring takes place, liquidated assets are clearly finite. The recovery that is apparent now is therefore fragile and needs nurturing towards sustainability. The financial sector reforms and restructuring have to be closely synchronized with other sectors. Even more important is likely policy complacency as growth results lull determination.

But what is more threatening to any recovery and growth from the crisis, which is often neglected in discussions about it, is that the crisis may have eroded the very foundations of the growth process. The economic and social structures of these foundations have, of course, not been constant throughout the crisis. These have been disturbed and thus the ability to keep the foundations for growth may have been eroded. This would vary in individual countries depending on the initial condition prior to the crisis, which would in turn have been defined by its growth experience in the past. In any case, the threats to sustainability and long-term growth are real and have to be considered.

The contraction of the economy triggered by immediate currency depreciation has raised unemployment rates and worsened related indicators. For a country like the Philippines, which may not have been at the eye of the crisis but which has had high unemployment rates, the condition has actually worsened. The increase in unemployment has set off a chain reaction throughout the economic system, unleashing more adverse effects. The incidence of poverty has risen as fixed income earners and other vulnerable groups have been affected by loss of livelihood and increases in prices. The affected groups in turn respond by cutting down on expenditures, forgoing further education of their children, postponing consumption of medical and related services, and other amenities. In one sense, these impacts are the direct results of the crisis. On the other hand,

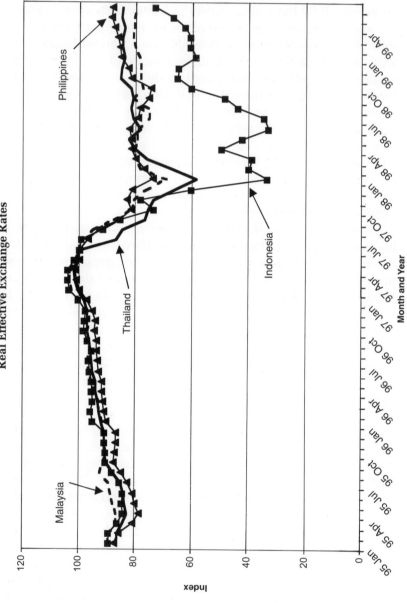

FIGURE 3.3
Real Effective Exchange Rates

the way policies have reacted to the crisis has also created social conditions which either aggravate the initial effects or muffle them. To the extent that national governments curtail expenditures that starve basic economic, social, and physical infrastructure, the crisis will worsen and threaten long-run growth. For example, in the Philippines, the initial attempts to reduce deficits at the height of the crisis led to mandatory cuts in essential expenditures, which were later reversed. However, there was a time lag in carrying out the reversed policies. How extensive is this threat to sustainability for the other ASEAN economies need to be examined. Needless to say, the strength of the economies *before* the crisis is important in this consideration. A sharp rise in inflation rates can wipe out achievements in poverty alleviation overnight and cannot be corrected in the same length of time. While multilateral institutions have realized this important factor, reversals are often difficult to manage, and it is inevitable that some damage is done.

Indeed, the competitiveness of the region, which started with gains through exchange rate depreciation, rests on improvement in productivity, which in turn is conditioned by social and physical environments, as noted above. In composite competitiveness rankings by the World Economic Forum (among 59 countries), Singapore topped the ASEAN countries (ranked 7), followed by the Philippines (ranked 39), Malaysia (ranked 40), Thailand (ranked 49), and Indonesia (ranked 52). This kind of ranking, however, is not helpful in terms of understanding the likely sustainability of achieved competitiveness.

Table 3.1 extracts some indicators from a World Bank database on competitiveness among the ASEAN countries. Five indicators have been selected: (a) annual growth rates of gross domestic investments (average for 1990–96), (b) foreign direct investments (as percentage of GDP for 1996), (c) annual growth rate of real GDP per worker (average between 1980 and 1990), (d) high technology goods exports (as percentage of manufactured goods exports in 1996), and (e) science graduates (as average percentage of total graduates between 1988 and 1990). Several points are worth noting from the table. First, real productivity growth rates among the ASEAN countries show how many cushions they can have with lost competitiveness from the exchange rate. Here, the Philippines cannot rely on productivity improvements since its record was negative in the eighties. On the other hand, Singapore and Thailand

TABLE 3.1
Some Competitiveness Indicators

	Indonesia	Malaysia	Philippines	Singapore	Thailand
Annual Growth of Gross Domestic Investment (1990–96)	9.9	16.0	4.7	9.0	10.3
FDI (percentage of GDP) 1996	3.5	4.5	5.9	10.0	1.3
Average Annual Growth of Real GDP per worker (1980–90)	3.9	2.7	−0.7	4.9	4.7
Hi-tech Exports (percentage of manufactured exports) 1996	18.0	67.0	62.0	71.0	36.0
Science Graduates (percentage of total graduates) Average 1988–90	11.0	28.0	30.0	53.0	18.0

SOURCE: World Bank.

have comparable growth rates, which means that they can compensate for some currency appreciation. The events leading up to the crisis and the crisis itself may have altered the pattern of productivity growth for all the ASEAN countries and thus their competitiveness.

Secondly, the importance of FDI to productivity is highlighted by how much flow into the country. The crisis may have encouraged significant inflows but the task is in capitalizing on those flows to improve technological capacities, marketing networks, and production techniques. Where the FDI is manifested only in mergers and acquisitions, it would be another matter to ascertain if they contribute to long-term sustainability for domestic affiliates.

Finally, the threat of the economic and social effects of the crisis on long-term sustainability of growth can be seen not only in real productivity per worker but also in the wave of future global trade concentrating on high technology products and research and development-intensive goods. These could partly be developed by boosting domestic capacities for producing these goods by increasing the supply of science graduates.

Conclusions

This chapter has argued that whichever of the theoretical constructs that have been proposed are valid, the fact of the matter is that the countries of the ASEAN region that were hit by the economic crisis have experienced early recovery. The degree of recovery, however, varies from country to country. The more important point argued here is that the early recovery, especially among those directly hit by the crisis, has been determined, in large part, by the strength of the underlying fundamentals of the individual economies. While it is true that the global environment may have helped in the quick rebound of the crisis-hit countries, there is no doubt that without the resiliency of the fundamentals (which did not evaporate with the crisis), recovery could have been protracted.

The initial policy stance, tied to the bail-out support from multilateral institutions, among the affected countries in the aftermath of the crisis — that is, fiscal and monetary tightening — exacerbated rather than diminished the adverse effects. Although this was eventually reversed, some damage to the fundamentals may have occurred. This aspect of the recovery process, however, needs to be further analysed empirically.

However, the recovery described in this chapter has not been even across the region, or broad-based within countries. In particular, it was shown that financial markets (such as exchange rates) quickly recovered although not to their pre-crisis levels. Stock markets also rebounded. As a result, the real sector gained ground from the severe contraction in 1998. On the other hand, bank and corporate restructuring still has to take root in the affected countries. The region's banking crisis had sharply increased non-performing ratios, curtailing the sector's ability to deliver effective financial intermediation. Although the ratios started to fall by the latter half of 1999, the slow recovery of the sector has put a drag to the overall recovery process. Similarly, corporate restructuring also needs to take strong roots in the region. Moreover, social recovery has yet to take place in the affected countries, and to the extent that the initial fiscal tightening had threatened the behaviour of the basic fundamentals, the region's competitiveness has likewise been threatened.

Beyond the recovery of the region from the crisis is the critical question of its competitiveness, and whether the countries' capacities to meet global competition have been affected. The chapter has argued that some of the policy mistakes early in the crisis may have altered some of the fundamentals. After all, the initial recovery was a product of the exchange rate overshooting, but the chapter has shown that some appreciation has returned. It has also been shown that, based on other studies on competitiveness, several factors are deemed important to a nation's competitiveness, namely, the growth rate of real gross domestic investments, growth rate of FDI, growth rate of real GDP per worker, high technology goods exports, and science graduates, among others. In the final analysis, it is whether the crisis has affected these factors that will influence the course of competitiveness in the region. Whether the initial policy mistakes made in responding to the crisis created some damage to the fundamentals remains to be seen, although there is some evidence that a number of fiscal-tightening measures had adverse impacts on long-term capacities through the educational infrastructure.

The Asian crisis has affected the ASEAN economies, as described in the previous sections. Though not across all the countries nor to the same degree, the impact has been to alter either their competitiveness directly or their potential to remain competitive. Consequently, ASEAN's growth sustainability has likewise changed.

NOTES

1   The empirical question is whether there has been a rise in "corruption" and decline in "governance" in Asia prior to the crisis or whether this has remained the same and thus cannot have been a major reason for the crisis. For an interesting debate on this, see Columbia Business School (1998).
2   Even if economic fundamentals are there, the political environment may not be there. So Indonesia is often used as an example of a country that has the economic fundamentals right but not in other areas.

REFERENCES

Alburo, Florian. "Economic Turmoil in Asia: Prospects for FDI Flows". *Philippine Review of Business and Economics* (December 1998).
———. "The Asian Financial Crisis and Philippine Responses: Long Run Considerations". *The Developing Economies*. Forthcoming.
Columbia Business School. *Challenges and Opportunities of the Southeast Asian Crisis.* New York: Columbia University Business School, 1998.

Glick, Reuven. *Thoughts on the Origins of the Asia Crisis: Impulses and Propagation Mechanisms.* Center for Pacific Basin Studies Working Paper PB98-07. Federal Reserve Bank of San Francisco (FRBSF), 1998.

Glick, Reuven, and Andrew Rose. "How Do Currency Crises Spread?". *Economic Letter.* FRBSF, 1998.

Ichimura, Shinichi, William E. James, and Eric D. Ramstetter. "On the Financial Crisis in East Asian Economies". *ICSEAD Working Paper Series Vol. 98–14.*

Institute of International Finance (IIF). "Capital Flows to Emerging Market Economies". Washington, D.C., 1998.

Kim, Joseph. "Statement". In *Challenges and Opportunities of the Southeast Asian Crisis*, pp. 11–13. New York: Columbia Business School, 1998.

Kobe, Yoshinori. "Statement". *Challenges and Opportunities of the Southeast Asian Crisis.* pp. 25–27. New York: Columbia Business School, 1998.

Krugman, Paul. "What Happened to Asia". Manuscript, 1998.

McKinnon, Ronald, and Huw Pill. "International Overborrowing: A Decomposition of Currency and Credit Risk". *World Development.* July 1998.

Montes, Manuel F. *The Currency Crisis in Southeast Asia.* Singapore: Institute of Southeast Asian Studies, 1998.

Moreno, Ramon. "What Caused East Asia's Financial Crisis?" FRBSF *Economic Letter No. 98–24.* FRBSF, August 1998.

Moreno, Ramon, Gloria Pasadilla, and Eli Remolona. "Asia's Financial Crisis: Lessons and Policy Responses". In *Asia: Responding to Crisis.* FRBSF Economic Studies WP PB 98-02. Tokyo: ADB Institute, 1998.

Nomura Asia Pacific Research Group. "Asia's Bubble Crisis: No Instant Cure". Hong Kong, 1999.

Philippine Export Development Plan. "Main Report" (Draft). Philippines Department of Trade and Industry, 1999.

4

ASEAN Free Trade Area: Progress and Challenges

NATTAPONG THONGPAKDE*

ASEAN Free Trade Area (AFTA) in Retrospect

ASEAN Economic Co-operation Before AFTA

Since the establishment of ASEAN in 1967 by the five founding members — Singapore, Malaysia, Indonesia, the Philippines, and Thailand — the political view was carried through as the centre of co-operation for a decade. During the early days of the establishment of ASEAN, there were a number of factors causing political instability in the region, including an ideology revolution, internal tensions, conflicts between some countries in the region, tensions arising from the Vietnam War, as well as the threat of an expansion of communism. Hence, the formation of a regional grouping was a means of solving conflicts among members and to sustain peace within the ASEAN region. "At that time, political instability in the region was the driving force behind ASEAN, and it has been argued that much of the attraction of regional economic integration was merely its use as a 'cover' for political co-operation, in particular, *vis-á-vis* instability in Indochina."[1] Later, economic co-operation was promoted in the mid-1970s, at the first two summits.

Co-operation among the ASEAN members during the first decade (1967–76) was clouded by differences among them. The progress of integration was significantly slow except for a number of political agreements. At the end of the Vietnam War in 1975, the ASEAN countries were concerned about the spread of the Marxist-Socialist system. This led to the first summit in Bali, in 1976, with the aim of strengthening co-operation in the region. The main discussion at the first summit still focused on political co-operation but a few points on economic collaboration were included, which became the framework for trade co-operation and led to the establishment of the Preferential Trading Arrangement (PTA) to stimulate trade among the ASEAN members.

The Preferential Trading Arrangement, launched in 1977, was the principal instrument for economic co-operation. The PTA was applied to basic commodities by providing preferential tariff rates, or margin of preferences (MOP). There were weaknesses in the implementation, resulting in difficulties in increasing intra-ASEAN trade. In the early stages, the MOP was applied as a product-by-product scheme with an exclusion list including important products that had high trade values. The MOP started at only 10 per cent for products that were either wholly produced in ASEAN or with local content of at least 50 per cent in value. Another weak point was the bureaucractic process to verify MOP eligibility, because it increased the costs of importers and made the scheme less attractive.

"As the PTA progressed through time, these weaknesses were reorganized and policy pronouncements were made to improve the mechanisms. In 1980, the product-by-product scheme was substituted with an across-the-board approach where preference would automatically be given to items below a certain import-value ceiling."[2] The level of MOP was raised in several stages. Finally, it was raised to a maximum of 50 per cent. The number of products on the exclusion list was reduced as a proportion of the products on the list was put on the PTA. Even though the PTA was revised from time to time, it was not sufficient to speed up trade among the ASEAN members. From 1970 to 1975, intra-ASEAN trade, as a percentage of total ASEAN trade, was between 12 and 16 per cent, which was the same level as in the late 1960s.

Besides the PTA, ASEAN also initiated other economic co-operation schemes. They included the ASEAN Industrial Complementation (AIC), the ASEAN Industrial Joint Ventures (AIJV), and the ASEAN Industrial Projects (AIP).

The ASEAN Industrial Projects scheme, introduced in 1976, aims to establish large-scale individual industrial projects by the founding five ASEAN members to respond to regional demand and to ensure more efficient use of regional resources. The ASEAN Industrial Complementation scheme (established in 1981), and its variant, the Brand to Brand Complementation scheme (BBC, established in 1988), are schemes for private sector projects concerned with the production and exchange of automotive components to facilitate horizontal specialization in the production of these products in the region. These initiatives have encouraged automotive brand owners to take advantage of economies of scale by exchanging approved automotive parts and components for specified brand models through tariff rate preference. Furthermore, the ASEAN Industrial Joint Venture was launched in 1983. The scheme is more flexible and covers a wider group of industries. The objective is to encourage greater investment into and within the region, and to increase industrial production through resource pooling and market-sharing activities.

Industrial co-operation among the ASEAN countries was not viable for a number of reasons. First, the original members of ASEAN were more or less at the same pace and level of development, and they produced the same tradable goods. Thus, their manufacturing sectors were more competitive than complementary. Secondly, both resource allocation and industries could be predetermined by policy-makers. Thirdly, the government in some member countries did not provide adequate attention and support to the scheme, especially when the regional projects conflicted with national industrial projects.

Lack of attention from the private sector was another factor. The evidence is that only eighteen products under the AIJV programme were accredited during 1983–90. Later, the AIJV was phased out and replaced with the ASEAN Industrial Co-operation scheme. Another example was the AIP's diesel project to complement the automotive industry, on which agreement could not be reached because of the problem of market sharing.

Establishment of AFTA

During the early 1990s, there was considerable progress in regional co-operation. The United States and Canada had reached a bilateral agreement in 1989, and the enlargement to the North American Free Trade Agreement (NAFTA) to include Mexico, was discussed and became effective in 1994. The Asia-Pacific Economic Co-operation (APEC) was also preparing the framework for a Free Trade Area (FTA), which reached agreement at the APEC summit meeting in Seattle in 1993. In addition, the economic integration of the European Community, which became the European Union with the aim of integrating into a single market, gave the best example of regional co-operation.

The Regional Trading Arrangement (RTA) has impacts on member as well as non-member countries. First, the RTA is intended to stimulate governments to be concerned about economic reform and also to provide a guideline for freer trade in the domestic market and to guard against protectionism. Secondly, small countries in particular, by participating in the RTA, can gain access to a larger market. Thirdly, member countries can stimulate trade within the RTA, and build a trading block against other countries. Among the member countries, the tariff rates have to be reduced to some extent but they can be kept at a higher level for non-member countries. Thus, the imported goods from member countries can gain a competitive edge. Finally, the small economies in the RTA will gain greater economies of scale and increased efficiency in production. Consequently, the RTA members will attract foreign investment.

With regional co-operation and trade negotiations intensifying in the Uruguay Round, the ASEAN members had to review its progress on co-operation. This led the ASEAN members to launch concrete economic co-operation measures. In the Fourth Summit in Singapore (1992), the ASEAN Free Trade Area (AFTA) was formed under the Common Effective Preferential Tariff (CEPT) scheme.

The primary objective of AFTA is to enhance ASEAN's competitiveness in the world market. The aims are also to expand intra-ASEAN trade and to gain economies of scale and specialization to further deepen economic co-operation. Finally, it is anticipated that greater foreign direct investment will flow into the region as a result of ASEAN economic integration.

AFTA Framework

The Common Effective Preferential Tariff scheme is the vehicle to achieve the ASEAN Free Trade Area (AFTA). The CEPT provides a means for harmonizing internal tariff rates. The traded goods under the CEPT programme, defined by the Harmonized System (HS) 6-digit level, include all manufactured products and processed agricultural products, excluding agricultural products. Through the CEPT scheme, the tariffs for products in the Inclusion List have two schedules — the normal track and the fast track. According to the original schedule, ASEAN agreed to reduce tariff rates in the normal track to 0–5 per cent within fifteen years, starting from 1 January 1993. For products on the fast-track list, the tariff reduction would be completed by the year 2003.

Owing to the spread and deepening of regionalism around the world, ASEAN decided to accelerate the AFTA timetable to ten years instead of the initial fifteen years. Thus, by the year 2003, the reduction of tariffs under the normal track will be completed. The fast track was also accelerated to seven years (year 2000) from ten years. Furthermore, agricultural products were brought under the CEPT and products in the Temporary Exclusion List (TEL) would have to be phased into the Inclusion List (IL).

In 1997, although the ASEAN members were facing the devastating regional economic crisis they decided to speed up the CEPT timetable. According to the Bold Measure from the Hanoi Summit in 1998, the six original ASEAN members agreed to accelerate the CEPT schedule for the products under the normal track by one year from 2003 to 2002, and set a target to achieve a minimum of 90 per cent of tariff lines within 0–5 per cent by 2000.

Owing to the difference in their economic structure from the original members and the later date of membership accession, the four new members presented different deadlines for the CEPT scheme. The deadline for the reduction of CEPT tariff lines to between 0–5 per cent was 2006 for Vietnam and 2008 for Laos and Myanmar. With the Bold Measure, the CEPT programme for the new member countries was also accelerated to 2003 for Vietnam and to 2005 for Laos and Myanmar. Cambodia, the latest ASEAN member, submitted its CEPT package on 1 January 2000, and will complete its AFTA commitment in 2010.

TABLE 4.1
Summary of CEPT Acceleration

	ASEAN-6		Vietnam	Laos & Myanmar	Cambodia
	Fast Track	*Normal Track*			
Original Plan (1992)	2003	2008			
AEM Meeting (1994)	2000	2003	2006	2008	
Bold Measure (1998)	2000	2002	2003	2005	2010
Zero Tariff Rate (1999)	2015	2018			

SOURCE: ASEAN Secretariat.

To achieve the ultimate target of AFTA of deepening economic integration, ASEAN also provided for the further reduction of tariff rates under the CEPT to 0 per cent and the acceleration of the transfer of products in the Temporary Exclusion List to the Inclusion List. By initial agreement, the six original members would achieve zero tariff rates by 2015, and for the new members by the year 2018. With this framework, 60 per cent of tariff lines would be reduced to 0 per cent by 2003 (see Table 4.1).

AFTA-plus Initiatives: Deepening Co-operation

Tariff reduction is only part of the liberalization process. At the multilateral and regional levels, other issues have been negotiated, such as trade in services and intellectual property rights. The EU has integrated into a single market with freer movement of investment and goods, and harmonized customs. APEC has also moved to other areas besides tariff reduction, including sector liberalization, and trade facilitation. Hence, ASEAN has launched the economic initiatives to deepen co-operation among member-countries. The following sections will discuss other important areas of co-operation, which are trade in services, ASEAN investment area, customs harmonization, and growth areas.

Trade in Services

ASEAN has recognized the importance of the services sector in enhancing investment and competitiveness. In 1995, a working group on Co-operation in Services was established. It explored the possibility and mechanisms needed to open up the services sector among the ASEAN members. The agreement on trade in services was then adopted at the ASEAN Summit in Bangkok in December 1995. ASEAN countries would negotiate intra-regional liberalization of services in seven sectors: namely, financial services, tourism, telecommunications, maritime transport, air transport, construction, and business services. Of these sectors, there was agreement at the Summit that the process of negotiations in telecommunications, financial services, and tourism would be concluded within eighteen months.

The objectives of the member states under the ASEAN Framework Agreement on Services are:

1. to enhance co-operation in services among the member states in order to improve efficiency and competitiveness, diversify production capacity and supply, and distribution of services within and outside ASEAN;
2. to reduce substantially restrictions to trade in services among member states; and
3. to liberalize trade in services by expanding the depth and scope of liberalization beyond those undertaken by member states under the General Agreement on Trade in Services (GATS) with the aim of realizing a free trade area in services, also known as GATS-plus offer.

The ASEAN Agreement on Services is made up of two parts. The first part involves measures to enhance co-operation in services, which include the improvement of infrastructure, research and development, exchange of information and technologies, and joint marketing and purchasing arrangements. The second part consists of liberalization measures requiring members to abide by the principles of GATS in the elimination of all market access limitations and prohibition of the emergence of new forms of market discrimination.

An initial package of offers was originally scheduled for June 1997. However, owing to the inability to reach agreement in all areas, this package was not tabled until the ASEAN Economic Ministers Meeting in October 1997. There were also several obstacles causing a delay in the liberalization as not all countries submitted offers, and offers in construction and financial services were also delayed until the end of 1998. The offers made by each country are listed in Table 4.2. Apart from these offers, Cambodia, the latest member of ASEAN, also made offers in several areas: namely, tourism, financial services, business services, and air transport.

The offers involved all modes of service supply, including cross-border supply, consumption abroad, commercial presence, and movement of persons. Moreover, a significant number of offers made involved the opening-up of new service sectors or activities that had not previously been included in the GATS, mostly in the area of air transport, business services, and tourism.

An initial package of commitments was completed as scheduled in 1998. The ASEAN Economic Ministers, who also signed the Protocol to Implement the Initial Package of Commitments, endorsed it. The second package of commitments was concluded and approved at the 30th ASEAN Economic

TABLE 4.2
The Initial Offers, by Country and Sector

	Sector				
Brunei	Air transport				Tourism
Indonesia			Maritime transport		Tourism
Laos					
Malaysia	Air transport		Maritime transport		Tourism
Myanmar					
Philippines		Business services			Tourism
Singapore	Air transport				Tourism
Thailand			Maritime transport		Tourism
Vietnam				Telecommunications	Tourism

SOURCE: World Bank.

Ministers Meeting. To further liberalize this sector, ASEAN members initiated another round of negotiations covering all service subsectors and modes of supply. This round commenced in 1999 and will end in 2001.

ASEAN Investment Area

The concept of an ASEAN Investment Area (AIA) was approved at the ASEAN Summit in Bangkok in December 1995. The aim of the AIA is to enhance the competitiveness of the region through stimulating investment inflows to ASEAN members from either ASEAN or non-ASEAN investors. With the AIA scheme, the barriers to intra-ASEAN investment would be reduced and removed, and the regulations would be reasonable, consistent, and transparent.

ASEAN agreed to complete the AIA by the year 2010. The AIA involves four main activities: firstly, co-ordinating ASEAN investment co-operation and facilitation programmes; secondly, co-ordinating promotion programmes and investment awareness; thirdly, opening up all industries immediately, with some exceptions; and finally, providing immediately national treatment for ASEAN members, with some exceptions. To reach the AIA goal, ASEAN agreed to the process of unilateral action, with some flexibility.

The industrial sectors, under the AIA agreement, are also grouped in the Temporary Exclusion List and the Sensitive List. With the flexibility approach, different timetables for each country are allowed because of the diversity in the levels of economic development and the late entry of the new members. The original ASEAN members decided to eliminate the TEL by 2010. Vietnam will phase out the TEL by 2013, and Laos and Myanmar by 2015. The TEL and AIA implementation programmes will be reviewed every two years.

Customs Harmonization

ASEAN has moved forward in regional integration, of which the agreement on customs harmonization is a part. Harmonization is an effort to simplify trade transactions and to facilitate trade among the members. The Director-General's Meeting in 1995 emphasized that customs co-operation was an essential ingredient for any free trade arrangement and would contribute towards sustaining and enhancing economic growth and dynamism in ASEAN.[3] In 1997, the ASEAN Customs Vision 2020 was adopted. It stressed the commitment to harmonize customs procedures and to develop customs practices to world-class standards of efficiency, professionalism, and services. The principal objective is to promote trade and investment in the region.

Three main aspects of customs harmonization are tariff nomenclature, customs valuation, and customs procedure. For the new members, mutual assistance such as technical assistance between customs administrations will be provided.

To realize the ASEAN Customs Vision 2020, the ASEAN Customs Policy Implementation and Work Programme (PIWP) was finalized. It is a collection of action plans which covers fifteen customs elements, such as tariffication, cargo processing, customs valuation, transparency enhancement, mutual assistance, and partnership with the business community.

To stimulate intra-ASEAN trade flow, the special arrangement for ASEAN members on customs procedures was adopted. The Green Lane System for CEPT products was launched in 1996. It expedited the clearance of CEPT-eligible products at customs check-points in ASEAN. This is an important step towards AFTA implementation, which allows freer movement of goods within ASEAN's border. Since the Green Lane System was implemented in 1996, the customs processing time for CEPT products is now shorter than non-CEPT products by 40 per cent in Thailand, and 60 per cent in Malaysia.[4] However, the utilization rate of this scheme is still low since many companies are not aware of the agreement.

Growth Areas Development

Growth areas can be seen as a form of sub-regional economic co-operation based on encouraging specific and limited linkages of complementary economic activities across borders. AFTA, like the North American Free Trade Area and the EC, is the formal vehicle for strengthening economic co-operation and integration at the national level, which requires fundamental changes in national institutional and administrative arrangements. However, growth areas operate with less institutional formality linking adjacent areas with different factor endowments and comparative advantages to form a sub-region of economic growth that is driven by market dynamism. Growth areas can also be viewed as a pragmatic response to problems accrued from such national integration since they involve simply adjacent areas within countries that have complementary capabilities and resources. In addition, a basic rationale for economic co-operation is that it can support the development process beyond national limits. It allows the relaxation of domestic supply and demand side constraints on individual economies by expanding access to key inputs and by enlarging the effective market accessible to participants.

Although sub-regional co-operation is primarily market-driven, in which the private sector plays an important role in providing capital, technology, training, and marketing channels, the government's role as a catalyst should not be overlooked. Infrastructure is seen as an essential factor to transform geographic proximity to economic linkages. In addition, investment and institutional frameworks need to be facilitated by the government to anchor and sustain sub-regional co-operation. This includes the legal, regulatory, and policy frameworks, and transborder agreements involving customs, immigration, foreign exchange transactions, and investment guarantees.

Within ASEAN, sub-regionalism has emerged as a new phenomenon. An example is the Singapore-Johor-Riau (or SIJORI) Growth Triangle, also known as the Southern Growth Triangle. There are two other growth areas in this region: the Northern Growth Triangle or the Indonesia-Malaysia-Thailand Growth Triangle (IMT-GT), and the East ASEAN Growth Area (EAGA) which is comprised of Brunei, Indonesia, Malaysia, and the Philippines. This form of co-operation, if successful, will strengthen integration of the ASEAN members.

ASEAN Enlargement: Broadening Co-operation

ASEAN co-operation at the start had been aimed at establishing peace and prosperity in the region. The ASEAN members remained the same number for more than twenty-five years after its founding in 1967. Then in 1984 ASEAN expanded to include the new country, Brunei Darussalam, after its independence. Brunei is a small country in the region, located between Malaysia and Indonesia, but is an important oil exporter to the world.

The initial endeavor of ASEAN was to form a group of Southeast Asian countries. According to the ASEAN Declaration, "the Association represents the collective will of the nations of South-east Asia to bind themselves together in friendship and co-operation and, through joint efforts and sacrifices, secure for their peoples and for posterity the blessings of peace, freedom and prosperity". Thus, ASEAN took a giant step to reach this goal with Vietnam's admission in July 1995.

A decade after the admission of Brunei Darussalam, ASEAN admitted Vietnam as the seventh member. Vietnam has a different political system from the six older members. It has just developed a market economy with economic restructuring, called *doi moi* or reform programme, since 1986. The market approach under *doi moi* contributed to high and sustainable growth between 1988 and 1996. The economy grew at an average annual rate of more than 5 per cent in 1988–90, increasing to more than 8 per cent in 1991–96.[5] The level of income and living standards have improved and the share of the manufacturing sector in gross domestic product (GDP) has also risen. As Vietnam had been prepared for economic openness, its trade volume expanded rapidly and there was an influx of foreign direct investment, mainly from Taiwan, and Korea, as well as from ASEAN investors. By joining ASEAN, Vietnam signalled its willingness and strength to shift its strategic outlook for greater regional co-operation.

The vision of ASEAN-10 came closer to being achieved when Cambodia, Laos, and Myanmar, named as the CLM countries, revealed their intention to join ASEAN.

The Lao People's Democratic Republic (PDR) and Vietnam had attended ASEAN meetings as observers since 1992. The admission of Vietnam inspired the Lao PDR to accelerate its plan to join ASEAN. In 1995, the Lao PDR, Cambodia, and Myanmar (CLM) proposed to join ASEAN. With the large difference in the level of economic development and political systems from the older members, the ASEAN Standing Committee (ASC) was set up as a working group to offer the CLM countries policy guidelines, consultations, and briefs for facilitation.

The formal report at the special meeting in Malaysia stated that "the CLM countries were all technically prepared to join ASEAN and had given satisfactory written undertaking of fulfilling all obligations of membership and commitment under various ASEAN agreements".[6] The special meeting advised that the CLM would be admitted in July 1997.

Owing to unstable political circumstances in Cambodia, its admission was delayed. Myanmar and the Lao PDR joined the ASEAN community on schedule, on 23 July 1997. Even though the admission of Myanmar raised conflicts between ASEAN and its third partners, such as the United States and the European Union (EU), the enlargement process proceeded. The ASEAN view of regional co-operation can be summed up by Tan Sri Noordin Sopiee's statement "The purpose of ASEAN is not to bring nice guys into a club. The purpose of ASEAN is to live at peace among ourselves".[7]

When the political situation in Cambodia stabilized, ASEAN officially accepted Cambodia as the tenth ASEAN member in April 1999. Thus, ASEAN achieved its ultimate goal of co-operation among the Southeast Asian countries.

The integration of the CLM countries and Vietnam will benefit ASEAN in many ways. First, the economies of the newcomers are highly complementary with the original members. The Lao PDR and Cambodia share a border with Thailand and also with Vietnam on the other side. Their trade partners are dominated by the ASEAN countries, mostly by Thailand. Most foreign direct investment in the CLM countries also come from ASEAN investors. Moreover, the different economic structures among the new and the original members also enhance the linkage between the groups. The new members have abundant labour at low wages available to the original members for labour-intensive production. In addition, the newcomers, especially the CLM countries, have very poor infrastructure that may be supported by the original members. In the longer term, integration among the Southeast Asian countries will enhance the competitiveness of the region through lower production costs and expansion of the share of exports in the world market (Thongpakde Nattapong 1997).

The second benefit of ASEAN enlargement is the political stability in the region as the structure of regional co-operation allows the setting up of consultation networks on many levels, from officials to leaders of states. Within this structure, the issues and disputes among members can be discussed, tension reduced, and confidence enhanced. Finally, ASEAN will improve its position in international fora. The four new ASEAN members will increase the size of ASEAN's GDP by about 6 per cent, to about US$650 billion, in 1995 prices, which is equivalent to approximately nine-tenths of China's economy.[8] (For details, see Table 4.3.)

TABLE 4.3
Social Economic Indicators

		Brunei	Cambodia	Indonesia	Laos	Malaysia
Land Area	(sq.km)	5,765	181,035	1,919,317	236,800	329,758
Population (1999)	(million)	0.2	10.9	209.3	5.3	21.8
Labour force (1996)	('000)	138	n.a.	78,300	2,030	8,200
GDP per capita						
(1997)	(US$)	17,890	159	1,055	348	4,665
Literacy rate (%)	men	93.1	n.a.	89.7	69.4	89.4
	women	84.6	n.a.	77.8	44.4	79.4
Life expectancy at	men	73.4	51.5	63.3	52	69.9
birth (years)	women	78.1	55	67	54.5	74.3

TABLE 4.3 *(cont'd)*

		Myanmar	Philippines	Singapore	Thailand	Vietnam
Land Area	(sq.km)	676,577	300,000	648	514,000	330,955
Population (1999)	(million)	45.1	74.5	3.5	60.9	78.7
Labour force (1996)	('000)	26,860	29,733	1,802	32,800	34,700
GDP per capita						
(1997)	(US$)	274	1,151	28,107	2,576	330
Literacy rate (%)	men	88.2	94.4	95.5	96.3	94.7
	women	77.7	93.8	86.1	92.0	87.7
Life expectancy at	men	58.5	66.5	74.9	65.8	64.9
birth (years)	women	61.8	70.2	79.3	72	69.6

SOURCE: *www.un.org/Depts/unsd/social/*; Department of Foreign Affairs and Trade, East Asia Analytical Unit, "The New ASEANs: Vietnam, Burma, Cambodia and Laos (Canberra, 1997); Ing Barings, Indochina Research, *Cambodia & Laos Review*, (Bangkok, February 1997).

AFTA: Achievements and Shortcomings

Achievements of AFTA

AFTA has been a significant accomplishment of ASEAN co-operation. ASEAN has been established for more than three decades, but the success of its economic co-operation efforts in the first two decades was insignificant. However, just eight years after the establishment of AFTA, trade and economic co-operation among the member countries has become visible and concrete, with a clear direction. The following highlights some important achievements of AFTA.

Integration of all Southeast Asian Countries

As mentioned above, when ASEAN was established, the political environment in the region was unstable and at the beginning the organization was more concerned with political rather than economic issues. The major objective of ASEAN's formation then was to pursue peace and stability in Southeast Asia. With differences in ideology, economic and political systems, and ongoing wars, it was beyond the imagination of most people that the goal would be realized. However, one year before the new millennium, ASEAN had integrated all the Southeast Asian countries. This ASEAN enlargement is a demonstration to the world that, after a long period of instability and hostility, the region is now at peace, in harmony and unity. Former socialist countries in the region are ready to integrate into the global economic system. ASEAN enlargement, thus, strengthens its position in the international fora.

Furthermore, incorporating all Southeast Asian countries into ASEAN can induce foreign investment, which is a major objective of AFTA. The enlargement is evidence that the region is stable and safe for foreign investors to conduct their business. It increases the size of the regional market, which now includes 500 million people occupying a land area of 4.5 million square kilometres. Besides a larger market, the new members provide new opportunities for investment with diversified resource endowments, a large labour force, and low cost of operation.

There is also a geographic dimension to ASEAN enlargement. The ASEAN-10 have an expanded territory stretching to the borders of the southern part of China and to the eastern part of South Asia. Thus, it is in a location that can connect with China and South Asia by land. This provides greater opportunities for ASEAN to strengthen economic ties with these neighbouring countries.

Tariff Reduction

The success of the CEPT scheme can be assessed from the pace and scope of product coverage in the agreement. ASEAN originally set up a moderate goal of tariff reduction to be completed in the year 2008. With the successful conclusion of the Uruguay Round and emerging regionalism that has speeded up the process of liberalization, ASEAN decided to accelerate tariff reduction. It shortened the deadline by five years to 2003 for products under the normal track. The tariff for products under the fast track will be reduced to 0–5 per cent in 2000. For the new members, the deadlines have been extended according to the date of accession. Each new member has ten years to meet the target.

Products on the Temporary Exclusion List were to be reviewed within eight years of the implementation of the CEPT. However, ASEAN has speeded up the liberalization by phasing in products in the TEL into the CEPT scheme in five equal instalments beginning on 1 January 1996, and ending on 1 January 2000.

Moreover, in 1994 ASEAN decided to include unprocessed agricultural products into the CEPT scheme. Initially, the CEPT covered only manufactured and processed agricultural products. Liberalization in agricultural trade is always a sensitive issue for trade negotiations in every forum; therefore, reaching this agreement should be considered a great success. A total of 1,358 tariff lines (out of 1,995 tariff lines) were phased into the Inclusion List (IL) in 1996. However, 402 tariff lines of agricultural products were put on the TEL. These products have been phased into the CEPT scheme in seven instalments from 1997 to 2003. The rest were classified as sensitive or highly sensitive products for which a special arrangement had to be implemented (Teh 1999).

With this scheme, in 1999, 85.4 per cent of tariff lines was on the IL, while 12 per cent of the product list was on the TEL. There was 1.48 per cent and 0.55 per cent in the General Exception List,[5] and Sensitive List, respectively (Table 4.4). Table 4.5 presents the CEPT package for the ASEAN-6, and Cambodia for the year 2000. The percentage of products on the IL will increase to 98.4 per cent and the TEL will include only 0.13 per cent of the product list. In 1995, there was 7.4 per cent of the product list on the TEL. In the year 2000, about half of the product lists of new members will be in the IL.

TABLE 4.4
1999 CEPT Package

Country	Inclusion List			Temporary Exclusion List	Sensitive List	General Exception List	Total
	Normal Track	Fast Track	Total				
Brunei	3,691	2,495	6,186	90	203	14	6,493
Indonesia	4,852	2,105	6,957	180	72	4	7,213
Laos	1,247	0	1,247	2,126	90	88	7,213
Malaysia	5,518	3,193	8,711	318	63	85	9,177
Myanmar	1,691	665	2,356	2,987	108	21	5,472
Philippines	4,403	1,028	5,431	174	28	68	5,701
Singapore	3,532	2,207	5,739	—	0	120	5,859
Thailand	5,613	3,443	9,056	63	0	7	9,126
Vietnam	1,472	246	1,718	1,153	127	17	3,015
ASEAN	32,019	15,382	47,401	7,091	811	304	55,607
Share in Total	57.58	27.66	85.24	12.75	1.46	0.55	100.00

NOTE: As of 11 February 1999
SOURCE: ASEAN Secretariat.

TABLE 4.5
CEPT Product List of the ASEAN-6 and Cambodia for the Year 2000

Country	Inclusion List	Temporary Exclusion List	Sensitive List	General Exception List	Total
Brunei	6,276	—	14	202	6,492
Cambodia	3,114	3,523	50	134	6,821
Indonesia	7,158	21	4	69	7,252
Malaysia	9,092	—	73	63	9,228
Philippines	5,571	35	62	27	5,695
Singapore	5,739	—	—	120	5,859
Thailand	9,103	—	7	—	9,110
ASEAN	42,935	56	481	160	43,636
Share in Total	98.40	0.13	1.10	0.37	100.00

SOURCE: ASEAN Secretariat.

TABLE 4.6
Average CEPT Tariff Rates, by Country

Country	1999	2000	2001	2002	2003
Brunei	1.30	1.00	0.97	0.94	0.87
Indonesia	5.29	4.57	4.36	4.10	3.69
Laos	5.00	5.00	5.00	5.00	5.00
Malaysia	3.00	2.57	2.40	2.27	1.97
Myanmar	4.45	4.38	3.32	3.31	3.19
Philippines	6.54	5.27	4.79	4.53	3.62
Singapore	0.00	0.00	0.00	0.00	0.00
Thailand	9.75	7.40	7.36	6.02	4.64
Vietnam	3.90	3.38	2.97	2.72	1.78
ASEAN[1]	4.59	3.74	3.54	3.17	2.63

[1] Regional CEPT tariff rates as a weighted average, with the number of tariff lines in IL for 1998 used as the weights.
SOURCE: ASEAN Secretariat.

With the CEPT, the average tariff rate of ASEAN was 4.59 per cent in 1999, and will be reduced to 2.63 in 2003 (Table 4.6).

During the economic crisis, ASEAN took the bold measure to shorten the timeframe of the CEPT by one year, to end in 2002. Furthermore, while the original target of AFTA was to reduce CEPT tariff rates to 0–5 per cent, the thirteenth AFTA Council Meeting in September 1999 set the new goal of zero tariff rate. The Council agreed that the target date would be the year 2015 for the old members and 2018 for the new members. The target has been set to eliminate tariffs for 60 per cent of ASEAN's products by the year 2003. As mentioned in Teh (1999), the schedules for achieving zero tariff will not be a problem for Brunei and Singapore who already meet the target, but Malaysia and Indonesia will have about 55 per cent of their products with zero tariff. Thailand and the Philippines will have to reduce tariffs for a considerable amount of products to meet the target. This task is more difficult for the new members than for the older members because of the larger portion of tariff lines in their TEL.

The one-year accelerated schedule may not make such a great difference in economic impact. However, this declaration coupled with the zero tariff target reveals that officially, ASEAN still pursues trade and investment liberalization. Moreover, it reveals the confidence of ASEAN in the prospects for economic recovery in the region and for the countries in crisis in the process of getting back on track to a normal development path.

Increase in Intra-ASEAN Trade

The share of intra-ASEAN exports rose from 18.7 per cent in 1990 to about 23 per cent in 1996. With the slow-down of economic growth in the countries in the region, the share of intra-ASEAN export declined to 22.1 and 20.6 per cent in 1997 and 1998 respectively (Table 4.7). The tariff reduction under the CEPT will further increase trade among ASEAN. Thus, ASEAN enlargement will reinforce ASEAN trade. Not only will the enlargement increase the market size of ASEAN but it will also enhance its resource diversification. The structures of the economies of the older members are similar; thus, the scope of exchange among them is limited. They compete in some industries. Factor endowment and the production structures of the new members are different from the older ones; the former are rich in natural resources and labour, while the latter have more skilled labour and capital. These factors are complementary and would enhance trade opportunity (Thongpakde 1997).

TABLE 4.7
Intra-Regional Export Shares, 1990–98

	1990	1991	1992	1993	1994	1995	1996	1997	1998
NAFTA	41.4	42.2	43.7	45.8	48.0	46.2	47.6	49.1	51.0
EU	59.0	58.7	59.5	56.2	56.8	63.5	62.8	62.1	62.5
MERCOSUR	8.9	11.1	14.0	18.5	19.2	20.3	22.7	24.8	24.8
ASEAN	18.7	19.3	19.1	20.0	22.7	23.0	22.9	22.1	20.6
Andean Community	3.8	5.8	7.8	9.8	10.5	11.8	10.4	10.0	10.0

SOURCE: International Monetary Fund, *World Economic Outlook*, October 1999.

Setting Clear Objectives and Direction in Economic Co-operation

At the early stage of ASEAN, the political objectives and half-hearted liberalization had undermined economic progress. Since the establishment of AFTA, ASEAN has forged ahead with economic co-operation. AFTA has set a clear statement that ASEAN is liberalizing trade among members. AFTA has also initiated concrete measures and a framework to reach the target of tariff reduction and elimination of trade barriers. Other ASEAN initiatives, mentioned above, and ASEAN's Vision 2020 provide direction that ASEAN will liberalize not only trade but also investment and movement of persons. The clear direction and framework will guide ASEAN to reach the objective and alleviate protection pressure.

Enhancing Trade Negotiation Capability

The ASEAN members have been active in trade forums at the multilateral and regional level. During such fora, the spirit of co-operation and consultancy help members in negotiation. In the Uruguay Round, the ASEAN negotiators agreed that they would support one another by taking their counterparts' side, although they might not have an interest in that issue. This collaboration among members shows unity and makes the negotiation position stronger. A small country can be overlooked in trade negotiations, but a small country with the support of a group of 500 million population can make a difference.

Fostering Unilateral Liberalization

Trade and investment liberalization always faces resistance from producers who fear competition. With AFTA, policy-makers in the ASEAN countries commit to deregulate the economy within the region, so it is difficult to turn back to a protective regime. Furthermore, consent to regional liberalization is easier than comprehensive liberalization, and the competition among members can be viewed as practice for ASEAN producers to cope with inevitable global competition. AFTA also familiarizes people with the concept of liberalization. All of these factors, to some extent, foster the process of further liberalization of trade and investment.

Shortcomings

Modest Intra-regional Trade

While data in Table 4.7 show that intra-ASEAN trade has been rising since the establishment of AFTA, the shares are much smaller than those of the two powerful regions, the EU and NAFTA. Intra-NAFTA export accounted for 51 per cent of its total export in 1998, and intra-EU export was 62.5 per cent in the same year. The share of intra-ASEAN export was 20.6 per cent in 1998, even less than that of the MERCOSUR, which was 24.8 per cent.

ASEAN does not include super economic powers such as the United States, Japan, or other G-7 countries. Therefore, members have to depend on outside markets. Their exports, thus, compete with each other in the major markets. The drawback is that regional tariff preferential treatment that reduces tariffs within the region can cause trade diversion from non-member countries, and cancel the welfare gain from trade creation. Low intra-regional trade also weakens the significance of AFTA and limits the scope of integration. It is beneficial to ASEAN members to unilaterally reduce tariffs for non-members and to uphold ASEAN agreements in a spirit of open regionalism.

Difference in the Stage of Economic Development of the Members

Even the older members of ASEAN are not homogeneous. The members have differences in size, level of income, and industrialization, historical, and political backgrounds. Incorporating the new members widens the differences in their characteristics further. Consider socio-economic indicators: one can see that the new members are far behind the older members with regard to income, health, education and infrastructure development. Differences in per capita GDP among the ASEAN countries are wider than those in the EU, and the United States, as presented in Table 4.8. Laos' per capita GDP was only one-third of Indonesia's and one per cent of Singapore's in 1997. The coefficient of variation for per capita GDP, where the higher number indicates a larger discrepancy, was 1.69 for ASEAN, while the corresponding numbers for the EU and the United States were 0.31 and 0.70 respectively.

TABLE 4.8
Per Capita GDP, 1997
(In US$)

ASEAN		EU		NAFTA	
Brunei	17,890	Austria	25,465	Canada	20,082
Cambodia	159	Belgium	23,948	Mexico	4,265
Indonesia	1,055	Denmark	30,718	United States	28,789
Laos	348	Finland	23,309	Average	17,712
Malaysia	4,665	France	23,843	Standard	
Myanmar	274	Germany	25,468	Deviation	12,432.6
Philippines	1,151	Greece	11,181	Coef. of	
Singapore	28,107	Ireland	20,603	Variation	0.70193
Thailand	2,576	Italy	19,962		
Vietnam	330	Luxembourg	37,785		
Average	5,655.5	Netherlands	23,270		
Standard		Portugal	10,269		
Deviation	9,553.21	Spain	13,412		
Coef. of		Sweden	25,718		
Variation	1.68919	United			
		Kingdom	21,921		
		Average	22,458.1		
		Standard			
		Deviation	7,095.91		
		Coef. of			
		Variation	0.31596		

SOURCE: Data from *www.un.org/Depts/unsd/social*

The wider differences can affect consensus building and co-operation. For the new members, social and infrastructure development may get higher priority than industrial and trade liberalization. Reduction in tariffs also affects those governments that do not implement proper tax system reform as this may have an impact on other development projects. Thus, there is always a concern about tariff reduction on the part of some officials from the new member countries. So far, there is agreement on tariff reduction according to the AFTA timeframe; however, one should be aware of possible problems in the future.

While the CEPT scheme covers only tariff reduction, other AFTA-plus initiatives, such as trade in services and the AIA, require changes in domestic regulations and institutions. Thus, the scope of adjustment is larger than in the case of the CEPT and involves more groups of people than in the case of tariff reduction. On the optimistic side, the agreements will facilitate adjustment to the market mechanism comparable with the reform plans in the countries concerned. On the pessimistic side, agreements may be harder to conclude, since, with differences in economic structure, some may think that rules and regulations should be different in each country, and some may not clearly realize the gains from liberalization.

Weakened Prospects of Economic Growth as a Result of the Crisis

The last decade has been one of growth in GDP and exports for the East Asian countries. However, just before the financial crisis, the slowdown of exports from the region, over-investment in some heavy industries, and fragile financial institutions revealed the weakness of the economies. These countries need to restructure their industries and reform their financial sectors to sustain competitiveness.

The financial and economic crisis caused a severe recession in ASEAN. Just a couple of years ago that situation was beyond imagination. Now ASEAN faces problems of slow growth rates, rising public debt, high unemployment, and weak financial institutions.

It will take time for ASEAN to go back to the prosperity environment of the period before the crisis. It has been forecast that it would take six years from now for the GDP per capita of Thailand to reach the level of 1997, just before the crisis (Sussangkarn 1999).

While reforms are needed, it is more difficult to implement them under these circumstances. The resources are limited. Owing to many constraints, it is anticipated that the growth rates of income will be moderate. Furthermore, there are a number of social problems to be tackled. These issues may distract industrial restructuring and liberalization reforms for sustainable competitiveness. Moreover, the situation may raise protective pressure.

Challenges

The progress of AFTA has been impressive; however, AFTA needs to adjust to the changing international environment. To discuss the challenges facing AFTA, it is important at the outset to review the prospects of the global environment.

The successful conclusion of the Uruguay Round has strengthened the set of multilateral rules of trade with a wider coverage to encompass trade in goods, services, intellectual property rights protection, and dispute settlement. The achievements of the Uruguay Round include substantial reduction of tariffs, and integration of textile and clothing trade and agricultural products under GATT disciplines. After the Round, negotiations under the World Trade Organization (WTO) continued and liberalization in financial services, basic telecommunication services, and the Information Technology Agreement were accomplished. With the establishment of the WTO, the momentum of trade liberalization at the multilateral level has continued.

The next multilateral trade negotiation under the WTO is around the corner. Agreement was reached at the conclusion of the Uruguay Round that the negotiation on the built-in agenda would resume no later than the year 2000. These include liberalization of trade in agriculture and trade in services, review of major WTO agreements such as Trade-related Investment Measures (TRIMs), Trade-related Aspects of Intellectual Property Rights (TRIPs), and Dispute Settlement Understanding.

During the last five years, trade issues have been raised and discussed, such as trade and investment, competition policy, government procurement, trade facilitation, electronic commerce and non-tariff barriers (NTBs). The WTO will consolidate the proposals in these issues and present them for adoption at the WTO Ministerial Conference in December 2000. The proposals would constitute the mandate for the new Round and for future work programmes of the WTO (IMF 1999a).

Therefore, at the multilateral negotiation, liberalization in trade and investment will continue to be pursued, and international agreements will have a strong influence on domestic regulation and policy. Tariff reduction will not be sufficient. Furthermore, international markets will be more competitive. The agreement on textiles and clothing is a good example as that agreement will intensify competition. It will abolish textile and clothing quota in the year 2005 and competitive exporters will be able to expand their markets without quantity restrictions. ASEAN will have to face competition from very strong exporters like China, India, and Mexico which have indicated their comparative advantage in these products (Thongpakde and Pupphavesa 1999).

Regional Trading Arrangements (RTAs) have been expanded in number and scope of integration. By 1999, there were more than 100 RTAs in effect. The EU has been successful in creating a single market and a single currency. It has also expanded the scope of its free trade area to immediate neighbours, including Central and Eastern European countries and countries in the Mediterranean basin. Under these agreements, the EU trades duty-free, and without quota restrictions, with the signatories. In the American continent, there is an agreement to establish the Free Trade Area of the Americas (FTAA), including 34 countries. The goal is to create a free trade area by the year 2005. In 1991, Argentina, Brazil, Paraguay, and Uruguay established MERCOSUR, setting a goal to be a full customs union by the year 2000. The Andean Community aims to be a common market by 2005 (IMF 1999a).

RTAs can have a positive effect by stimulating and facilitating members to implement appropriate structural reforms and reduce trade barriers among members and outsiders. However, rules and regulations can be trade barriers for non-members and tariff preference can divert trade from non-members. The strict rules of origin in NAFTA favours Mexico's exports in textiles and clothing at the expense of East Asian countries.

It is surprising that the economic crisis did not cause overall protection pressure. A *World Economic Outlook* (1999b) study found that according to the index of trade restrictiveness during 1998, 24 countries out of 173 increased their openness, resulting in an improvement of the overall index. The countries whose trade systems were classified as open had increased from 79 countries in 1997 to 87 countries by 1998. This indicator implies that most countries stuck with their liberalization policy. The number of anti-dumping petitions initiated by the WTO in 1997 and 1998 increased only moderately. Therefore, there is no clear sign of protection employing the anti-dumping scheme. Some countries had increased tariffs during the crisis but this was more for the purpose of increasing fiscal revenue than to protect industries. The case of protection is clearer in the case of steel industries in the industrial countries, and protection measures were introduced in Latin American countries in response to declining commodity prices and the crisis in Brazil. However, the trend of overall liberalization in the Latin American countries has not been reversed.

The study warned, however, that the factors and risks that underlie protection pressure remains. These include the pace of recovery of the crisis-affected countries, slowdown in world growth, rising trade deficits in many countries, and declining commodity prices. These will affect the prospects of export and economic growth and thus could be employed to justify protective measures.

During the last decade, the ASEAN countries were attractive to foreign investors because of many factors, such as high GDP growth rates, low operating costs, economic and political stability, and good fundamentals. The crisis has shown the weakness of their economies, increased instability in exchange rates, and the weak prospect of economic growth. As foreign investment is one of the major factors for economic growth, ASEAN needs to rebuild foreign investors' confidence and make the environment conducive for their investment again.

With a more competitive international environment, export competition is intensifying as a result of liberalization and RTAs while the threat of protection still persists. Consequently, trade regulations and negotiations will be more complex. ASEAN needs to adjust to this environment to be relevant and to be able to enhance its members' competitiveness. The following are challenges that the member countries will have to overcome.

Make a Comeback from the Crisis with Sustained Growth and Stability

ASEAN significantly struggled as a result of the economic crisis. However, there are signs of recovery with stable and strong exchange rates, low interest rates, and higher growth rates of exports and GDP, but there are still persistent problems of bank recapitalization, corporate debt restructuring, excess capacity in heavy industries, higher public debt, high unemployment, and rising social problems. Therefore, it is vital to seriously solve these problems although the priority, focus, and mechanisms used will be different among the member countries. The main task is to restructure the financial and industrial sectors and to reduce social tension.

Many studies have concluded that excessive capital inflow, especially short-run capital flow and lack of good governance in the public and private sectors, were the main factors causing the crisis. Transparency and accountability are critical to strengthen financial, corporate, and public management in order to restore business confidence and induce needed foreign investment. There should also be measures to control short-term capital movement. These require the reform of institutions and regulations to cope with the problems.

Avoiding Protection Pressure

The above discussion indicates that there is no significant sign of widespread protection pressure. However, at the AFTA Council Meeting of 1999, there were indications not favourable for AFTA. Malaysia proposed to put off the phasing-in of automotive CBU/CKD packs from the TEL to the IL by January 2000. Thailand and the Philippines also expressed difficulties in the phase-in of some products. The Council decided that the issue would be considered again at the informal AEM in November 1999. The products under review would be limited to automotive products, petrochemicals and palm oil.

This was the first incident that threatened to delay the CEPT schedule. The problem was not caused by the economic crisis but by domestic pressure. This incident shows that despite the success of the CEPT, there is potential danger of protection sentiment. It is important to settle the issue in such a way that it will not be a precedent for other members to delay tariff reduction.

Besides the proposal to delay tariff reduction for some products at the AFTA Council Meeting, there has been no serious problem in tariff reduction. However, non-trade barriers still obstruct trade, and much needs to be done to eliminate NTBs. Table 4.9 presents the list of NTBs compiled by the ASEAN Secretariat, based on a survey of firms in ASEAN. The complaints included, for example, customs valuation, customs processes, licensing standards, and import restrictions. The problems are mainly from the implementation of regulations rather than the regulations themselves. To facilitate the free flow of trade, these unjustified NTBs have to be removed.

Besides tariff reduction, anti-dumping regulations have been used to protect industries. The petitions against anti-dumping have increased since the establishment of the WTO. ASEAN should restrain from employing this measure against members, especially

TABLE 4.9
Non-Tariff Issues in ASEAN

No.	Country	Non-Tariff Issues Under Discussion
1.	Brunei Darussalam	Differing product specifications for vehicles
		Inconsistent and non-automatic licensing for telecommunications equipment
		Lengthy procedures for licensing approvals
		Inconsistent customs classification
		Difficulties with temporary importation
		Differing office hours at common customs borders
2.	Indonesia	Privileges provided to selected companies (e.g. oil)
		Non-automatic licensing
		Facilitation fees at customs
		Import restrictions
3.	Lao PDR	Inconsistent customs classification
		Inconsistent customs valuation
4.	Malaysia	Local sourcing policy
		Non-automatic licensing
		Lengthy procedures for approvals for pharmaceutical products
		Quota restrictions
		Problematic and inconsistent customs classification
		Facilitation fees at customs
		Problematic labelling requirements
		High uplifts on customs valuation
5.	Philippines	Cumbersome procedures for import licences
		Problematic testing and inspection requirements
		Slow customs classification process and lack of classification expertise
		Non-transparent customs valuation uplifts
		Problems with PSI
		Import quotas and bans
6.	Singapore	Problematic requirements on standards
7.	Thailand	Lengthy procedures for import licences
		Inconsistent and non-transparent customs classification
		Customs valuation uplifts
		Facilitation fees at customs
		Problematic quota restrictions
		Problematic labelling requirements
		Stringent inspection requirements
8.	Vietnam	Cumbersome application for quotas
		Non-transparent licensing procedures
		Non-publicized frequent regulatory changes
		Inconsistent and problematic customs classification
		Import restrictions
		Additional surcharges

SOURCE: ASEAN Secretariat, *Report of the Thirteenth Meeting of the ASEAN Free Trade Area (AFTA) Council*, 29 September 1999.

because of the excess capacity of heavy industries. Raising the issue will weaken the solidarity of members and the spirit of liberalization.

Speeding Up Liberalization

If indeed Vision 2020 is to benefit ASEAN as a region and each ASEAN member, there is a need to commit and initiate mechanisms to reach the goal. However, the target of creating a free flow of goods, services, and investment, and a freer flow of capital is too far away for ASEAN to achieve that goal. APEC has also set the year 2020 to be a free trade area for developing country members. ASEAN with a smaller number of members and close relations should do better than APEC. Some RTAs also aim to be free trade and investment areas before 2020. ASEAN has already brought forward the target date for tariff reduction; therefore, it should be more ambitious and consider shortening the time-frame for achieving Vision 2020. With strong commitment, the accelerated deadline for free trade and investment will stimulate unilateral liberalization.

While ASEAN should consider a faster pace of liberalization, it should also be aware that the task is more difficult than in the past. Liberalization involving a larger number of members and complicated issues beyond tariff reduction make agreements harder to conclude. There is the possibility that some conflict among members, such as territory dispute, may undermine co-operation. Consensus-building will not be an easy task. Siazon Domingo (1999) suggests that the "ASEAN way", which consists of the principles of consensus, consultation, and non-interference, instead of relying on an institutional and legalistic approach, had succeeded in the past. However, in practice there is a need to adapt the principles of the ASEAN way for a faster decision-making process among members.

Strengthening Trade Negotiation Capability

Since intra-ASEAN trade is small compared to external trade, it is vital that the world market is open for ASEAN exports. As mentioned above, the international environment will be more competitive and trade issues will be more complex. There may be new issues that are barriers to ASEAN trade, such as product standards, RTAs, trade and environment, and trade and labour rights. There may also be some issues that can expand ASEAN markets, such as trade in agriculture. Negotiations will have a strong impact on ASEAN trade.

ASEAN unity will improve trade negotiation power. ASEAN is not homogeneous, and some issues may not interest all members. Members may even have differences in opinion on some issues, but they should not have different stands on trade issues. It is too early to conclude whether ASEAN should negotiate as one economy or not. If so, ASEAN needs to develop its Secretariat or some other institution representing ASEAN to conduct negotiations. The mechanism must be realistic and differences in members' opinions should be taken into consideration.

NOTES

* The opinions expressed in this chapter are those of the author only, and do not necessarily reflect the view of the Thailand Development Research Institute (TDRI). The able research assistance of Jarunee Termpaiboon, Chirath Isarangkun Na Ayuathaya, and Panidta Puapunwattana is appreciated. The author is grateful to Dr Srawooth Paitoonpong who read and commented on the chapter.

1 Seiji F. Naya, and Michael G. Plummer, "Economic Co-operation after 30 Years of ASEAN", *ASEAN Economic Bulletin* 14, no. 2 (November 1997): 119.

2 ASEAN Secretariat, *ASEAN Economic Co-operation Transition & Transformation* (Jakarta, 1997), p. 43.

3 ASEAN Secretariat, "Joint Press Statement of the Third Meeting of the ASEAN Director-General of Customs", Hanoi, Vietnam, 27–28 November 1995. (*http://www.aseansec.org/economic/customs/jpsdg03.htm*)

4 ASEAN Secretariat, "Joint Press Statement of the Fourth Meeting of the ASEAN Director-General of Customs", Jakarta, Indonesia, September 1996 (*http://www.aseansec.org/economic/custom/jpsdg04.htm*)

5 Department of Foreign Affairs and Trade, *The New ASEAN: Vietnam, Burma, Cambodia & Laos* (1997), p. 40.

6 ASEAN Secretariat, "History and Evolution of ASEAN", at *http:\\www.aseansec.org/history/asn_his2.htm*

7 Charles E. Morrison, "ASEAN: Forum, Caucus, and Community", *ASEAN Economic Bulletin* 14, no. 2 (November 1997): 156.

8 Department of Foreign Affairs and Trade, East Asia Analytical Unit, *The New ASEANs : Vietnam, Burma, Cambodia & Laos* (1997), p. 309.

9   The General Exception List was reviewed and it was discovered that some
products did not comply with the CEPT scheme. The 13th AFTA Council
meeting in September 1999, after a line-by-line review of each country's
list, agreed to transfer 230 tariff lines out of the General Exception List.

REFERENCES

ASEAN Secretariat. *ASEAN: An Overview*. Jakarta: ASEAN Secretariat, 1996.
————. *ASEAN Economic Co-operation: Transition and Transformation*.
Singapore: Institute of Southeast Asian Studies, 1997.
————. *Report of the Thirteenth Meeting of the ASEAN Free Trade Area
(AFTA) Council: 27 September–2 October 1999*. Singapore, 1999.
East Asia Analytical Unit, Department of Foreign Affairs and Trade. *ASEAN
Free Trade Area: Trading Bloc or Building Block?* Canberra: AGPS Press
Publication, 1994.
————. *The New ASEANs: Vietnam, Burma, Cambodia, and Laos*. Canberra:
AGPS Press Publication, 1997.
Garnaut, R. "ASEAN and the Regionalization and Globalization of World
Trade". *ASEAN Economic Bulletin* 14, no. 3 (1998): 215–23.
Imada, P., and S. Naya, eds. *AFTA: The Way Ahead*. Singapore: Institute of
Southeast Asian Studies, 1992.
International Monetary Fund. *International Financial Statistics Yearbook*.
Washington, D.C.: IMF, 1998.
————. *Direction of Trade Statistics Quarterly* (June). Washington, D.C.: IMF,
1999.
————. *World Economic Outlook* (October). Washington, D.C.: IMF, 1999a.
————. *World Economic Outlook* (May). Washington, D.C.: IMF, 1999b.
Morrison, C. E. "ASEAN: Forum, Caucus, and Community". *ASEAN Economic
Bulletin* 14, no. 2 (1997): 150–58.
Naya, S. F., and M. G. Plummer. "Economic Co-operation after 30 Years of
ASEAN". *ASEAN Economic Bulletin* 14, no. 2 (1997): 117–26.
Paitoonpong, S., W. Pupphavessa, N. Thongpakde and N. Poapongsakorn.
*Development in the Greater Mekong Subregion and Thailand's
Development Strategy: Final Report*. Bangkok: TDRI, 1996.
Petri, P. A. "AFTA and the Global Track". *ASEAN Economic Bulletin* 14,
no. 2 (1997): 190–201.
Philippines Institute for Development Studies and ASEAN Secretariat.
"ASEAN Economic Co-operation for the 1990s". Report prepared for the
ASEAN Standing Committee, Philippines, 1992.
Rieger, H. C. *ASEAN Economic Co-operation Handbook*. Singapore: Institute
of Southeast Asian Studies, 1991.
Siazon, D. L. "Moving ASEAN beyond AFTA." Paper prepared for the seminar-
workshop on "Beyond AFTA and Towards an ASEAN Common Market".
Manila, 1999.

Singh, D. A. "Towards One Southeast Asia". *ASEAN Economic Bulletin* 14, no. 2 (1997): 127–30.

Smith, A. L. "The AFTA-CER Dialogue: A New Zealand Perspective on an Emerging Trade Area Linkage". *ASEAN Economic Bulletin* 14, no. 3 (1998): 238–52.

Sussangkarn, C. *Economic Crisis and Recovery in Thailand : The Role of the IMF*. Bangkok: Thailand Development Research Institute, 1999.

Teh, Robert. "Completing the CEPT Scheme for AFTA". Paper prepared for the seminar-workshop on "Beyond AFTA and Towards an ASEAN Common Market". Manila, Philippines, 1999.

Thongpakde, Nattapong. "Impacts and Implications of ASEAN Enlargement on Trade". *TDRI Quarterly Review* 12, no. 4 (1997): 20–29.

Thongpakde Nattapong and Wisarn Puppavesa. "Returning Textiles and Clothing to GATT Disciplines." Paper prepared for the East Asia Conference on "Options for the WTO Negotiations", organized by PECC/TPF and the World Bank, Manila, Philippines, 1999.

5

ASEAN Investment Area: Progress and Challenges

NICK J. FREEMAN*

FDI in South-East Asia (ASEAN 10) decreased by 23 per cent in 1998. The share of these countries as a group in total FDI in Asia has declined by nearly one tenth during the 1990s.[1]

Introduction

The Association of Southeast Asian Nations (ASEAN) has been through rough times in the last couple of years. A vicious currency crisis in Thailand during mid-1997 mutated into a financial crisis, which then spread to the other currencies and financial markets of Southeast Asia, before mutating again into a more virulent regional economic downturn across much of East Asia. Depicted by one observer as the "bonfire of the certainties", the Asian economic crisis knocked (formerly ebullient) *subjective* business confidence across the region, which further exacerbated the damage already being done to more *objective* business activity. Previously bold commercial banks took fright, as over-leveraged corporates in several countries began to default on loans, *en masse*. Banks' loan books were frozen, credit became scarce, interest rates climbed precipitously, and the business environment became extremely hazardous. In those countries worst affected, good and bad firms alike found themselves in life-threatening situations. Some countries even saw the economic fallout from the crisis making an impact in their political arenas. The value of ASEAN's various local currencies came under downward pressure, as did the prices of most asset classes, from shares to property. Many forms of business endeavour were adversely impacted, including trade and investment. For almost anyone involved in business in ASEAN during 1997–99, the experience was decidedly unpleasant. Perhaps the only net winners so far have been corporate lawyers and accounting firms.

For most of those with operational investments in ASEAN, the period since mid-1997 has been extremely disappointing, as both the value of these investments, and the earnings to be derived from them, have shrunk fairly substantially. Conversely, for those seeking to enact new investments in Southeast Asia, the period since mid-1997 has been quite exciting. Not only can some operational businesses now be bought at levels commensurate with their distressed condition, but post-crisis liberalization reforms are allowing foreign investors to acquire assets that were previously off-limits (in formerly protected sectors). This state of affairs has also dovetailed with new trends apparent in the field of international business, particularly with regard to a burgeoning of mergers and acquisition (M&A) activity, and strategic alliances. Global over-capacity has brought down prices for a wide spectrum of services, products and commodities, thereby squeezing corporate profit margins.[2] Major corporates have responded by trying to derive efficiency gains from intra-industry consolidations ("bulking up") and introducing new technology, among various other strategies, in a bid to maintain positive earnings.

While these new trends have been most apparent in the industrialized countries, their growing impact on the developing world — including much of Southeast Asia — should not be under-estimated. A major re-evaluation of emerging markets' comparative advantages is under way, as are notions of what makes an attractive host country environment. Looking ahead, for example, the skill levels of the local work-force are likely to be of increasing importance, at the expense of the low labour rates of the local work-force (a traditional bulwark of emerging markets).[3] Similarly, the digital infrastructure of a host country, and/or its record on intellectual property rights, is likely to be of greater relevance to foreign investors than its ability to provide greenfield sites or export processing zones for yet more conventional "smoke-stack" industrial plants. A full-blown business revolution may not be under way, but a paradigm shift in international business is occurring, and this poses new challenges for all those Southeast Asian countries seeking to attract foreign capital.[4] Simply getting back to the way things were before the "wheel came off" in mid-1997, and before the Asian crisis rudely interrupted the sustained economic growth trajectory that Southeast Asia had been enjoying, is not an option for the region. Instead, the region must prepare for the global business environment of the future, and it is in this forward-looking context that we should view the ASEAN Investment Area (AIA) initiative.

Brief Background to the ASEAN Investment Area

The tangible evolution of the AIA can be traced back to the Fifth ASEAN Summit, held in December 1995, at which the proposal for establishing a regional investment arrangement — subsequently to become known as the ASEAN Investment Area — was approved, in a bid to "enhance ASEAN's attractiveness and competitiveness for promoting direct investments".[5] However, the AIA's roots lie even further back in ASEAN's history, as far as the ASEAN Agreement for the Promotion and Protection of Investments of 1987 (amended in a 1996 protocol), and the Framework Agreement on Enhancing ASEAN Economic Co-operation, of early 1992. The AIA initiative also exists in company with the ASEAN Free Trade Area (AFTA) and ASEAN Industrial Co-operation (AICO) scheme, both of which also seek to promote increased foreign direct investment (FDI) within a region that encompasses half a billion people. Far from existing in a vacuum, the AIA must dovetail with various other tangential ASEAN initiatives, such as the Hanoi Plan of Action[6] and the ASEAN Framework Agreement on Services.[7] In particular, the AIA and AFTA should be regarded as two supporting pillars in a regional strategy to "develop ASEAN into a highly competitive and conducive investment area by providing investors with greater opportunities for economies of scale, synergies and [a] lower transaction cost environment".[8] But with specific regard to foreign investment activity in ASEAN, the AIA "is now the key instrument governing and promoting FDI flows in the region".[9]

The AIA took concrete form following the signing of the Framework Agreement on the AIA, in Manila in October 1998, and actually came into force in mid-June 1999. Although still "in short trousers", the AIA has made some fairly considerable first steps, at least in terms of designing a road map for its future development.

Progress Defining the ASEAN Investment Area

> Together with the AFTA programme, the AIA will give investors, existing and new, a framework highly conducive for regional integrated production activities, procurement, manufacturing and resources based investment activities.[10]

The enactment of the AIA by ASEAN takes the region into pioneer territory, as no other regional grouping has previously attempted to create such an integrated and comprehensive investment-supporting environment.[11] The AIA pertains to direct investment activity in the manufacturing, agriculture, mining, fishery, and forestry sectors, as well as services incidental to these sectors, within ASEAN (that is, Southeast Asia). The mandate of the AIA does not extend to portfolio investment. The ultimate goal of the AIA is quite simple: to permit the free flow of investment within ASEAN by 2020. The framework agreement broadly sets out how this goal is to be achieved, and includes the following elements:

- a programme of investment co-operation initiatives, intended to generate increased investment flows within ASEAN, from both intra- and extra-ASEAN sources;
- national treatment to be granted to ASEAN investors by 2010, and to all investors by 2020;
- all industries to be open to ASEAN investment by 2010, and to all investors by 2020;[12]
- the corporate sector to play a greater role in the AIA development process;
- co-ordinated investment promotion initiatives to raise awareness of FDI opportunities in ASEAN;
- greater transparency in investment regimes and policies, as well as more streamlined investment procedures;
- and promoting a freer flow of capital, skilled workers, and technology among ASEAN members.[13]

The AIA strategy is a two-stage process, aiming for a more liberal investment environment by January 2010 for intra-ASEAN investment activity, and a wholly liberal investment regime across the Southeast Asian region by 2020, in conformity with "ASEAN Vision 2020".[14] Among the other features of the framework agreement (see Article 4) is an attempt to better co-ordinate investment co-operation within ASEAN, in a bid to stimulate greater FDI inflow activity, both from within ASEAN and beyond the regional grouping. The corporate sector is expected to play a major role in this co-operation effort, and the AIA initiative will also seek to generate a freer flow of capital, skilled labour, and technology within ASEAN.

Achieving some of the above may not be as easy as it first appears. It should be understood that this is a very demanding strategy, albeit necessary for what is an equally lofty ultimate goal. This is particularly true for some member countries of ASEAN that remain slightly suspicious of overseas investors in general, and somewhat ambivalent on the virtues of foreign capital in particular. Partly for this reason, the AIA framework agreement provides for the temporary exclusion of some sectors.

An AIA Council, at ministerial level, has been established to oversee the framework agreement. The AIA Council is made up of the ASEAN Secretary-General, ministers responsible for investment, and heads of investment agencies in member countries. However, ASEAN member countries are expected to develop their own AIA action plans, which are to be reviewed every two years by the AIA Council.[15] Other obligations for the ASEAN signatories include undertaking "appropriate measures to ensure transparency and consistency in the application and interpretation of their investment laws, regulations and administrative procedures in order to create and maintain a predictable investment regime in ASEAN".[16] Members must also seek to "enhance the attractiveness of the investment environment … for direct investment flows", and "take such reasonable actions as may be available … to ensure observance of the provisions of [the framework agreement] by the regional and local governments and authorities within their territories".[17] For some ASEAN countries, such improvements in their FDI regimes are very necessary, and if successfully enacted, will be welcomed by foreign investors.

As noted above, under Article 7 of the framework agreement all members of the AIA are committed to opening up all industries to

ASEAN investors immediately, and are to provide ASEAN investors with what is often termed "national treatment".[18] However, each member can submit a Temporary Exclusion List (TEL), and a Sensitive List (SL) of industries or measures affecting investments for which national treatment to ASEAN investors cannot yet be granted.[19] The Temporary Exclusion List is to be reviewed every two years, with the aim of being completely phased out by 2003 for the ASEAN-6 and Myanmar; and 2010 for Cambodia, Laos and Vietnam.[20] The Sensitive List is to be reviewed in January 2003, and periodically after that date. It is anticipated that most members' Sensitive Lists will be fairly short, as the terms of AFTA provide for tariffs to be below 5 per cent in most sectors by 2002. In such a situation, it would be illogical to have certain industries protected from the AIA by their inclusion in the Sensitive List, while at the same time being exposed to almost zero tariffs under AFTA.[21] This is a good example of the extent to which the AIA and AFTA arrangements should be regarded as working in tandem (at least) and/or in harmony (at best).

There is one other important caveat on the issue of national treatment. Although no member state may preferentially treat an ASEAN investor from one country ahead of another, Article 8 also states that nothing will prevent a member "from conferring special treatment or advantages to adjacent countries under growth triangles and other sub-regional arrangements between member states". Article 13 of the framework agreement also allows members to divert from the terms of the agreement if they do not concur with measures "necessary to protect national security and public morals", among others. Under Article 15, the threat of "serious balance of payments and external financial difficulties" can also be cited by a member country as reason to "adopt or maintain restrictions on investments on which it has undertaken specific commitments".[22] Quite clearly, the AIA framework agreement — in its current form — is a flexible product, but if members meet the deadlines for phasing out some of these exclusion areas, the AIA should become more rigid in the future.

The first ASEAN Joint Investment Promotion Missions, or roadshows, are scheduled to take place during the first half of 2000, with Malaysia leading a mission to Japan, Singapore leading a mission to the United States, and Thailand leading a mission to Europe.[23] The primary objective of the roadshows is to "show that ASEAN is on the road to recovery and to provide ASEAN the opportunity to market the countries collectively".[24] Although not strictly part of the AIA initiative *per se*, these roadshows are likely to include presentations on the AIA, and marketing the countries can be viewed as an element in the AIA's strategy of jointly promoting the region as a host for foreign investment.

To summarize, progress on the AIA since its inception can be outlined as follows:

- all ASEAN members have ratified the framework agreement, which came into force in June 1999;
- a Temporary Exclusion List for the manufacturing sector has been prepared, and similar TELs for the agriculture, forestry, fishery and mining sectors are expected by the end of 1999;
- interpretative notes to the framework agreement have been drafted and made public;
- a series of comparable FDI statistics for ASEAN countries have been generated;
- a 1999 ASEAN Investment Report will be launched;
- and a work programme for the AIA, between 1999 and 2003, has been developed.[25]

The compilation of comparable FDI statistics for each of the member countries is important to enable the AIA — and ASEAN as a whole — to better respond to emerging trends in foreign investment activity. (Future FDI statistics should also provide some indication on whether the AIA is generating positive results.) It is also important here to briefly look at FDI trends in Southeast Asia.

Recent Trends in ASEAN's Foreign Direct Investment Flows[26]

... FDI has become the most dynamic component of international resource flows to developing countries ...[27]

Southeast Asia has been a major recipient of foreign direct investment since about the mid-1980s, and FDI has played an important part in the economic development of the region, as well as becoming a significant element in the overall corporate profile of most ASEAN economies.[28] The significant role that foreign investors, and multinational firms in particular, have played in the economic development and industrialization of the ASEAN region should not be under-estimated, as it is greater than is implied by the raw figures for FDI as a proportion of total capital formation in these host countries.[29] Together with foreign capital, multinational firms have "imported" into Southeast Asia a range of economic and production capabilities that have fed into, and brought sustenance to, the host countries' economies. Dunning asserts that "[We] have seen that the economic growth and prosperity of nations has become increasingly dependent on their ability to upgrade their indigenous resources and capabilities by human resource development, innovations and improved organisational efficiency; and ... the wherewithal for doing this frequently resides in the competencies of MNEs".[30]

It is important to note that Southeast Asia's commendable inflows of foreign investment during the last twenty years or so have not been completely unique — the steady and significant rise in FDI inflows to Southeast Asia has been in conformity with a world-wide increase in FDI activity during the same period, far out-pacing global growth in both trade and output.[31] For the transitional countries of Southeast Asia, which opened their doors to FDI for the first time in the late 1980s, they have had the pleasurable experience of being able to "surf" on a high tide of foreign investment in emerging markets, at least until quite recently. Much of this FDI into Southeast Asia has been oriented towards assembly and manufacturing capability, particularly for exports to the industrialized markets, as well as some domestic and regional market servicing. Tables 5.1 and 5.2 provide country-by-country data for FDI inflows and outflows within Southeast Asia, in the period between 1993 and 1998.

Until the onset of the Asian crisis, the region's FDI inflow growth trend was fairly sustained, from just under US$16 billion in 1993 to slightly less than US$28 billion in 1997 (see Table 5.1). Although this growth rate was undoubtedly commendable, it was only in tandem with global growth in FDI inflows, and inflows into developing countries as a whole. Since around 1993, the growth trajectory was lower than China was recording for its FDI inflows.[32] Indeed, in the early 1990s it appeared as if Southeast Asia was starting to lose out to China, India (and Indochina, to a lesser extent) on new FDI inflows, as its share of cumulative Asian foreign investment began to contract.[33] The resurrection of Latin America as a business prospect, after its debt crisis of the 1980s (and buoyed by MERCOSUR), also started to pose some competition for Southeast Asia in attracting finite FDI inflows in the 1990s. This state of increasing competition helped prompt ASEAN to undertake a

TABLE 5.1
Southeast Asia's Foreign Direct Investment Inflows, 1993–98
(In US$ million)

	1993	1994	1995	1996	1997	1998
Brunei	14	6	13	11	5	4
Cambodia	54	69	151	294	204	140
Indonesia	2,004	2,109	4,346	6,194	4,673	−356
Laos	36	59	88	128	86	45
Malaysia	5,006	4,342	4,178	5,078	5,106	3,727
Myanmar	149	91	115	38	124	40
Philippines	1,238	1,591	1,478	1,517	1,222	1,713
Singapore	4,686	8,550	7,206	7,884	9,710	7,218
Thailand	1,805	1,364	2,068	2,336	3,733	6,969
Vietnam	1,002	1,500	2,000	2,500	2,950	1,900
SE Asian total	15,994	19,681	21,643	25,980	27,813	21,400
China	27,515	33,787	35,849	40,180	44,236	45,460
Developing countries	78,813	101,196	106,224	135,343	172,533	165,936
World	219,421	253,506	328,862	358,869	464,341	643,879
S E Asia as % of world total	7.3	7.8	6.6	7.2	6.0	3.3
S E Asia as % of developing world	20.3	19.4	20.4	19.2	16.1	12.9
S E Asia compared to China	58.1	58.3	60.4	64.7	62.9	47.1

Source: UNCTAD (1999).

number of initiatives designed to improve the general allure of Southeast Asia — as a regional market — to foreign investors, including AFTA and later the AIA.[34] Following the onset of the Asian crisis, figures for Southeast Asia's FDI inflows in 1998 suggest that inflows dropped by about 23 per cent over the previous year, thereby halving the region's share of global FDI inflows, from 7.2 per cent in 1996 to just 3.3 per cent in 1998. Similarly, as a proportion of developing countries' cumulative FDI inflows, Southeast Asia's share dropped from 20.4 per cent in 1995 to 12.9 per cent in 1998. Whether or not this recent dip in FDI inflows to Southeast Asia (since 1996) can wholly be attributed to the Asian crisis — and whether it is the product of a cyclical downturn or something more structural — the ASEAN countries would be remiss if they did not try to stem this decline.[35] At least in part, the AIA initiative should be seen as a policy response to this declining trend in FDI inflows during the 1990s, and particularly since the recent regional economic downturn,

TABLE 5.2
Southeast Asia's Foreign Direct Investment Outflows, 1993–98
(In US$ million)

	1993	1994	1995	1996	1997	1998
Brunei	50	—	20	40	10	10
Cambodia	2	—	—	—	—	—
Indonesia	356	609	603		178	44
Laos	—	—	—	—	—	—
Malaysia	1,464	2,591	3,091	4,133	3,425	1,921
Myanmar	—	—	—	—	—	—
Philippines	374	302	399	182	136	160
Singapore	2,152	4,577	6,281	6,274	4,722	3,108
Thailand	232	492	887	931	447	122
Vietnam	—	—	1	—	—	—
SE Asian total	4,578	8,57	11,261	12,120	8,908	5,355
China	4,400	2,000	2,000	2,114	2,563	1,600
Developing countries	39,756	42,600	52,089	58,947	65,031	52,318
World	247,425	284,915	358,573	379,872	475,125	648,920
S E Asia as % of world total	1.9	3.0	3.1	3.2	1.9	0.8
S E Asia as % of developing world	11.5	20.1	21.6	20.6	13.7	10.2

SOURCE: UNCTAD (1999).

although the AIA arrangement quite clearly dates from before the commencement of the Asian crisis in July 1997.

The major flows of FDI activity in the Southeast Asian region in the twentieth century have tended to come in a series of, sometimes overlapping, waves. Between 1900 and 1930, the Southeast Asian countries received the majority of their foreign investment inflows from their respective "metropolitan mother country", with France dominating FDI across all of Indochina; Britain the major investor in Burma, Malaya, and (non-colonial) Thailand; the Dutch in Indonesia; and the United States in the Philippines.[36] After the end of colonialism, firms from the United States and Europe continued to invest in the region, albeit along less clearly defined colonial lines. The 1980s saw the rise of investment by Japan, and then the Asian newly industrializing economies (NIEs) — Hong Kong, Taiwan, South Korea — seeking in part low-cost assembly and manufacturing platforms to export goods, among various other locational attributes.[37] However, these latter flows have recently declined substantially, primarily as a result of the Asian crisis, and the date of their return – in meaningful numbers — remains unknown.

The 1990s saw the rise of intra-regional FDI flows within Southeast Asia, in addition to the more well-established flow lines of FDI activity from the industrialized countries to the immediate north and further west.[38] Malaysia and Singapore in particular — together with Indonesia and Thailand to a lesser extent — have had relatively substantial FDI outflows in the last decade, as can be seen in Table 5.2.[39] In the period between 1994 and 1996, Southeast Asia was the source of about 3 per cent of global FDI outflows, or 20 per cent of outflows from developing countries. While some of these outflows went beyond Southeast Asia, a fair proportion were directed at neighbouring Southeast Asian countries. Indeed, in the years immediately prior to the Asian crisis, fellow ASEAN members were the premier foreign investors in the four transitional countries of the region: Singapore was the top foreign investor in both Myanmar and Vietnam; Malaysia leading in Cambodia; and Thailand dominating FDI activity in Laos. But this intra-regional FDI trend has not been confined to Indochina, as evidenced by fairly substantial Singapore investments in Malaysia and Indonesia, and in Thailand to a lesser extent. Although the Asian crisis has rudely interrupted this developing pattern in intra-regional FDI activity, one might expect this trend to recommence in the medium-term, should Southeast Asia see a sustained recovery on both the macroeconomic and micro-corporate levels. To that extent, the AIA should be regarded as a platform to help stimulate and support a return to pre-crisis FDI flow patterns in Southeast Asia.

In terms of FDI stock in Southeast Asia, Table 5.3 shows that this grew considerably during the 1980s and 1990s, from less than US$24 billion across the region in 1980 to almost US$234 billion in 1998 — roughly a tenfold increase. The inward stock of FDI in Southeast has been roughly 5–6 per cent of total global FDI stock, over the same period, and around 20–22 per cent of FDI stock in the developing world. Measured as a percentage of gross domestic product (GDP), Southeast Asia's inward FDI stock has risen steadily during the last two decades, from under 10 per cent in 1980 to just over 28 per cent in 1997. (Table 5.5 provides a breakdown of Southeast Asia's stock of FDI, as a percentage of GDP. Tables 5.4 and 5.6 provide breakdowns of Southeast Asia's outward FDI stock, in figures and as a percentage of GDP.)

TABLE 5.3
Southeast Asia's Inward Foreign Direct Investment Stock, 1980–98
(In US$ million)

	1980	1985	1990	1995	1997	1998
Brunei	19	33	30	68	84	88
Cambodia	—	—	—	498	925	1,065
Indonesia	10,274	24,971	38,883	50,601	61,475	61,116
Laos	2	2	14	212	426	471
Malaysia	5,169	7,388	10,318	27,094	37,278	41,005
Myanmar	5	5	173	937	1,099	1,139
Philippines	1,225	2,601	3,268	6,086	8,420	10,133
Singapore	6,203	13,016	28,564	59,582	78,637	85,855
Thailand	981	1,999	8,209	17,452	13,009	19,978
Vietnam	7	38	294	5,569	11,019	12,919
SE Asian total	23,885	50,053	89,753	168,099	212,372	233,769
China	57	4,305	18,568	131,241	215,657	261,117
Developing countries	132,945	237,239	370,644	769,262	1,055,656	1,219,271
World	506,602	782,298	1,768,456	2,789,585	3,436,651	4,088,068
S E Asia as % of world total	4.71	6.40	5.08	6.03	6.18	5.72
S E Asia as % of developing world	17.97	21.10	24.22	21.85	20.12	19.17

SOURCE: UNCTAD (1999).

TABLE 5.4
Southeast Asia's Outward Foreign Direct Investment Stock, 1980–98
(In US$ million)

	1980	1985	1990	1995	1997	1998
Brunei	—	—	—	—	—	—
Cambodia	—	—	—	—	—	—
Indonesia	—	49	25	1,295	2,073	2,117
Laos	—	—	—	—	—	—
Malaysia	414	1,374	2,671	11,143	12,725	14,645
Myanmar	—	—	—	—	—	—
Philippines	171	171	155	1,209	1,527	1,687
Singapore	7,808	7,808	7,808	35,050	44,522	47,630
Thailand	13	16	404	2,173	1,951	2,073
Vietnam	—	—	—	—	—	—
SE Asian total	8,406	9,418	11,063	50,870	62,798	68,152
China	—	131	2,489	15,802	20,479	22,079
Developing countries	13,392	28,096	73,069	236,596	341,552	390,911
World	513,105	685,753	1,714,147	2,840,216	3,423,433	4,117,144
S E Asia as % of world total	1.64	1.37	0.65	1.79	1.83	1.66
S E Asia as % of developing world	62.77	33.52	15.14	21.50	18.39	17.43

SOURCE: UNCTAD (1999).

TABLE 5.5
Southeast Asia's Foreign Direct Investment Inward Stock,
As % of GDP, 1980–97

	1980	*1985*	*1990*	*1995*	*1997*
Brunei	0.4	1.1	0.8	1.4	1.7
Cambodia	—	—	—	18.0	32.8
Indonesia	14.2	28.6	36.6	25.6	28.6
Laos	—	0.1	1.6	12.0	24.3
Malaysia	21.1	23.7	24.1	31.8	38.1
Myanmar	0.1	0.1	0.7	0.9	0.6
Philippines	3.8	8.5	7.4	8.2	10.2
Singapore	52.9	73.6	78.2	71.2	81.6
Thailand	52.9·	5.1	9.6	10.5	8.5
Vietnam	0.1	0.6	4.5	27.3	55.8
S E Asian average	14.6	14.1	16.4	20.7	28.2
China	—	1.5	5.2	18.8	23.5
Developing countries	5.9	9.8	10.5	14.1	16.6
World	5.0	6.9	8.7	9.9	11.7

SOURCE: UNCTAD (1999).

TABLE 5.6
Southeast Asia's Foreign Direct Investment Outward Stock,
As % of GDP, 1980–97

	1980	*1985*	*1990*	*1995*	*1997*
Brunei	—	—	—	—	—
Cambodia	—	—	—	—	—
Indonesia	—	—	—	0.7	1.0
Laos	—	—	—	—	—
Malaysia	1.7	4.4	6.2	13.1	13.0
Myanmar	—	—	—	—	—
Philippines	0.5	0.6	0.4	1.6	1.9
Singapore	66.6	44.1	21.4	41.9	46.2
Thailand	—	—	0.5	1.3	1.3
Vietnam	—	—	—	—	—
S E Asian average	6.9	4.9	2.9	5.9	6.3
China	—	—	0.7	2.3	2.2
Developing countries	0.8	1.4	2.3	4.7	5.8
World	5.3	6.3	8.4	10.2	11.9

SOURCE: UNCTAD (1999).

   Finally, another FDI trend in Southeast Asia worthy of mention
is that multinational investors tend to turn away from multiple
subsidiaries churning out similar products towards vertically
integrated production networks. As Dunning points out,
multinational firms are moving from a system of "overseeing a group
of fairly autonomous foreign affiliates each more or less replicating
the activities of the parent companies, ... to one in which each
affiliate is part of a regional or global network of inter-related
intra- or inter-firm activities ...".[40] Although this has been apparent
in the industrialized countries for some time, it is also now becoming
increasingly evident in various parts of the developing world,
including Southeast Asia. A major implication of this trend is a
marked change in what foreign investors require from a host country
(discussed further, below), shifting away from cheap factor inputs
and towards better human and physical resources. As UNCTAD has
stated:

> A striking feature of the new environment is how transnational
> companies shift their portfolios of mobile assets across the globe
> to find the best match with the immobile assets of different locations.
> ... The ability to provide the necessary immobile assets thus becomes
> a critical part of an FDI — and competitiveness — strategy for
> developing countries. While a large domestic market remains a
> powerful magnet for investors, transnational companies serving global
> markets increasingly look for world-class infrastructure, skilled and
> productive labour, innovatory capacities, and an agglomeration of
> efficient suppliers, competitors, support institutions and services.[41]

Impact of the Asian Crisis on FDI in Southeast Asia

As noted above, the impact of the Asian crisis on foreign investment
activity in Southeast Asia appears to have been fairly considerable.
This should come as no surprise. With local currencies going into
tail-spins, interest rates and imported inflation rising rapidly,
domestic demand wilting, corporate debt reaching critical levels,
loan portfolios haemorrhaging, and asset values tumbling, it would
have been bizarre if we had not seen some sort of reaction in FDI
activity. Intra-regional investment activity slowed down
considerably, as did FDI sourced from North Asia. However, FDI
flows from the West — and the increasingly important community

of multinational firms — remained roughly net-constant; for every U.S. or European investor that decided not to go ahead with a planned investment in the region, as a consequence of the crisis, it seems there was another prepared to "take a speculative punt" by picking up some domestic business assets at distressed price levels.[42] This echoes an Asia-wide trend that has seen intra-Asian investment "replaced by large purchases of Asian firms by investors from non-Asian OECD countries, particularly by American, British, Dutch and Swiss firms".[43] According to UNCTAD, transnational firms pumped US$85 billion into the wider Asia-Pacific region during 1998 — an 11 per cent decline from 1997, but US$3 billion more than in 1996.[44] While most Asia-Pacific countries saw a downward trend in their FDI inflow figures in 1998, year-on-year, China, the Philippines, South Korea, and Thailand registered foreign investment inflow increases. These rises helped to offset declines registered in Indonesia (which actually saw a net outflow of FDI in 1998), Malaysia, Singapore, and across all of Indochina.

Although domestic sentiment in most crisis-hit countries has been against the predatory attacks of Western investors swooping down on what are often regarded as defenceless local firms, policy-makers — cognizant of the need to attract substantial foreign investment in order to recapitalize their domestic banking and corporate sectors — in most countries have accelerated their business liberalization programmes, and thereby supported this behaviour.[45] For example, foreign investors have been able to gain direct entry into Thailand's domestic banking sector for the first time. In the case of ASEAN, the Bold Measures Statement — issued at the Hanoi Summit in December 1998 — invites all foreign investors (both within ASEAN and beyond) to take advantage of special incentives *in the manufacturing sector*, through a series of short-term measures aimed at enhancing ASEAN's investment climate.[46] Although different for each member country, the incentives include various measures, such as 100 per cent foreign equity, income tax exemptions, duty-free import of capital goods, domestic market access, rapid customs clearance, industrial land use, employment of expatriates, and so on.[47]

Far from diverting attention away from the AIA initiative, the Asian crisis has served to underline its importance, and — like the recent acceleration of the AFTA deadlines — added a greater sense of urgency to the whole project. This was evidenced at the first meeting of the AIA Council, in March 1999, where a decision was made to expand the remit of the framework agreement to include manufacturing services, and open national treatment to ASEAN investors in the manufacturing sector immediately.[48] Further evidence of accelerated implementation includes the bringing forward of various deadlines by which members of the AIA must have completely phased out their Temporary Exclusion Lists (from 2010 to 2003 for the ASEAN-6 and Myanmar). As noted above, the foreign-invested sector is now an important element in almost all of the ASEAN member economies, and the recent weakening in inflow trends is an issue worthy of not inconsiderable concern by policy-makers. The *raison d'être* for the AIA would have been valid even if the Asian crisis had not occurred, but the fact that the region has been through a severe economic downturn has provided additional emphasis to its utility. Countries like Indonesia and Thailand have little prospect of getting back on their feet without the injection of substantial quantities of foreign funds to refinance their banks and recapitalize their major corporates. While FDI is only one of several conduits for such an inflow of foreign funds, it is one of the most important nonetheless.[49] And if this is to happen on terms other than a distressed assets "fire sale", then these economies will have to provide a business environment that is stimulating to foreign investors. While the individual ASEAN member countries could go it alone, a co-ordinated regional drive would be far more convincing in the short-term, and probably more fruitful in the long-term.

The AIA Arrangement: Its Place in the Bigger Scheme of Things

The AIA was designed prior to the Asian crisis, enacted after the crisis, and will be tested in the new millennium. In the global market-place, competition to attract FDI has become increasingly fierce, particularly among developing countries. Consequently, countries have sought to improve their relative attractiveness to foreign capital by offering a range of incentive measures to foreign investors. With the exception of the short-term measures aimed at enhancing the ASEAN investment climate, the AIA has sensibly avoided getting too engrossed in incentive schemes and various other "bells and whistles" that investment promotion initiatives often pursue. While investors will obviously welcome measures that provide them with additional tax breaks or other inducements, the extent to which such bonuses actually attract investment inflows that would otherwise not have arrived is, in this observer's view, mixed. A substantial price can be paid for such incentive measures by the host economy, if they heavily distort the domestic market, adversely affect resource allocation, or result in economic inefficiencies.[50] An incentive scheme can actually back-fire if foreign investors find the array of subsidies to be overly complex, or worry that incentives will be withdrawn at a later date. It is far better to seek an investment regime — whether it be national or regional — that is simple, transparent, efficient, and constant over time. In general, the AIA appears to be striving to achieve precisely this.

With policy-making resources often limited in some ASEAN countries, it is important that the AIA does not overlap with similar regional initiatives. Such a scenario would not only pose the danger of burdensome policy duplication, but also the peril of regulatory contradictions. Perhaps the regional initiatives with which both the AIA and AFTA will be most commonly compared — and has the potential for greatest overlap — is APEC's strategy for improving the investment regimes within the latter's own, wider regional remit.[51] The Asia-Pacific Economic Co-operation (APEC) forum is primarily conducting this through a series of Individual Action Plans (IAPs) — under the Manila Action Plan — that member economies submit annually, but which are broader than just being FDI-specific, as well as being voluntary and non-binding. Perhaps the nearest comparison to the AIA within APEC's spectrum of work is the APEC Non-Binding Investment Principles, signed in Jakarta in November 1994.[52] Under these *non-binding* investment principles, APEC member economies "aspire" to various principles relating to: transparency, non-discrimination between home countries of investors, national treatment, investment incentives, performance requirements, expropriation and compensation, repatriation and convertibility, dispute settlement, entry and sojourn of personnel, avoidance of double taxation, investor behaviour, and removal of barriers to capital exports. AIA primarily differs in that it is a *binding* agreement — or at least, a deadline-drive agreement — among all members to liberalize their FDI regimes (including opening up sectors to foreign equity participation and granting national treatment) by a set of incremental dates, and unlike the IAPs, is specific to foreign direct investment.[53] The AIA also differs in that its strategy includes an aim for member countries to jointly promote FDI within ASEAN through a co-ordinated programme of initiatives. As a result, the AIA certainly has the *potential* to become a more proactive and focused investment liberalization and promotion arrangement than currently envisaged by APEC.[54] But it is wholly conceivable that APEC will seek to upgrade its initiatives in the field of investment in the future, possibly using the investment section of the Osaka Action Agenda as a "jumping off" point.[55] The ultimate objective here is for the APEC economies to "achieve free and open investment in the Asia-Pacific region", through a process of medium-term refinements in "APEC's understanding of free and open investment", and a longer-term assessment of "the merits of developing an APEC-wide discipline on investment".[56] It is not hard to envisage such a process ultimately resulting in an AIA-style of arrangement across the Asia-Pacific region, albeit in the long-term.

In the field of applied business, making a clear distinction between trade and investment activity — and the policy frameworks that govern both activities — can be a difficult exercise. So much of world trade is now conducted "within" vertically integrated multinational firms, as goods are passed from one subsidiary to another. Similarly, numerous investment projects will import a substantial proportion of their inputs, and operate in order to generate products for export, necessitating that a host country or region not only has a liberal FDI regime, but also a liberal external trade regime. In the case of ASEAN, this is evidenced by the development of both AFTA and the AIA. Although the WTO and the Uruguay Round focus on trade issues, a number of agreements stemming from this body do have some bearing on FDI activity, including the Agreement on Trade-Related Investment Measures (TRIMs); the Agreement on Trade-Related Apects of Intellectual Property Rights (TRIPs); government procurement; and trade in services.[57] In the case of TRIMs, the WTO does not oppose investment incentives *per se*, but is against investment measures that might hinder free trade; for example, through discriminatory measures such as export restrictions or national treatment of imports. Prior to its recent demise, a *partially* overlapping initiative with the AIA might have been the OECD's proposed Multilateral Agreement on Investment (MAI) project, although this danger now seems to have evaporated with the virtual abandonment of the MAI proposal. First unveiled by the United States in 1995, the MAI initiative —

which envisaged a global arrangement for FDI, albeit primarily
focused on issues relating to foreign assets and their expropriation
— was never able to attain a sufficient degree of acceptance from
even within the OECD, let alone the developing country community,
and various other pressure and lobby groups.[58] As a result,
Washington effectively "threw in the towel" on this proposed
arrangement in late 1998.

Challenges Facing the AIA: Practical and Policy Dilemmas in Going Forward

> ... Asian economies should seek to spur growth by promoting
> productivity growth. This means more open and freer financial, goods,
> and labour markets as well as liberal trade and exchange systems ...
> At the same time, substantial investment in education will be required
> for [Asian] economies to keep pace with, and reap the maximum
> benefit from, worldwide technological advances.[59]

The first anniversary of the Framework Agreement on the AIA
occurred in October 1999, and actually came into force less than
six months before. With the AIA initiative still new, it is perhaps
too early to assess its progress. However, it is never too early to make
an assessment of the challenges that lie ahead. Ultimately, the AIA
initiative will be tested, not on its applicability to the conditions of
Southeast Asia — and the global business environment in general
— in 1998–99, but on its applicability to the region — and the
demands of foreign investors — in the first two decades of the next
century. Therefore, as a forward-looking policy instrument, the AIA
needs to be "ahead of the curve", delivering the sort of strategy that
will stimulate the next generation of foreign investment activity
within ASEAN.

If the primary aim is for ASEAN to maximize FDI activity within
the Southeast Asian region, then the AIA appears to be an excellent
starting point, by tackling the broad policy frameworks behind the
investment regimes in each of the host countries. This should
generate results for each member country, and the region as a whole.
However, the current remit of the AIA alone is not guaranteed to
buoy FDI activity within Southeast Asia. UNCTAD recently noted
that as developing countries all trend towards improved host country
business regimes, diminishing returns are now setting in.[60]

Consequently, the grounds on which host countries compete to attract investment is moving into tangential areas, as foreign investors become more discerning about what they want from developing countries in terms of a platform for an investment project.[61] If every country provides an equally liberal FDI regime, then competition shifts to other arenas of comparative advantage, such as quality of infrastructure, general skill levels, financial sector support, political stability, macroeconomic stability, and so on.[62] Mallampally and Sauvant take this argument one step further:

> The challenge for developing countries is to develop a well-calibrated and, preferably, unique combination of factors determining FDI location and to match those determinants with corporations' strategies. Policies intended to strengthen national innovation systems and encourage the spread of technology are central because they underpin the ability to create assets."[63]

For this reason, the AIA should not operate in isolation, but seek to work in tandem with other ASEAN initiatives aimed at improving elements of members' economies, from the "harder" issues like finance, infrastructure, and communications, to "softer" issues like education and property rights.[64] For example, if the consensus view is that much of the next generation of global FDI activity is going to be driven by technological advances and innovation, then the AIA should seek to work in tandem with pertinent regional initiatives that can focus on providing a "techno-friendly" Southeast Asia, such as the "e-ASEAN Initiative".[65] One caveat to the above assertion is that the sort of FDI activity that each of the AIA member countries might be seeking to attract, and can realistically support, will tend to differ. Malaysia may wish to attract foreign capital into its multi-super corridor project, whereas Laos may seek to encourage foreign capital in eco-tourism projects, or coffee processing. Similarly, the level of hi-tech industry that Singapore's economy can support is going to be ahead of what Vietnam can realistically expect to attract, at least in the short-term. That said, all the ASEAN countries are seeking to attract the highest quality of FDI possible, and should always aim to maximize the value-added that their domestic economies can derive from such investment.

As noted above, trade and investment should not be regarded as two wholly distinct business activities. Similarly, AFTA and the AIA will not operate in capacities that are wholly divorced from each other. Arguably, the AIA cannot function without the presence of AFTA, as foreign investors would not be convinced of a Southeast Asian drive towards greater FDI activity within the region if significant tariff barriers continued to exist between the member countries.[66] For transnational companies seeking to have integrated operations in the region, such trade barriers are a major problem.

Quite sensibly, the AIA allows for a series of temporary exclusions and sensitivities to be phased out over the next decade or so. If "the proof is in the pudding", then we will have to see if member countries are able to adhere to the timetable, and completely phase out these various "let-out clauses" on national treatment by the deadlines given. In this regard, the AIA should really be viewed as a process. One can foresee that the ability of individual ASEAN members to meet these deadlines will be varied, with some countries likely to find it harder than others, as both economic and political factors play a determining role in setting the pace. For example, the AIA will pose very substantial challenges for the transitional countries of ASEAN (Cambodia, Laos, Myanmar, and Vietnam), solely in terms of economic factors.[67] Gearing up to comply with their individual AFTA deadlines is already a major task for some of these countries, let alone the additional demands that come from being a signatory to the AIA (see Appendix). They recognize that complying with AFTA and the AIA necessitate making changes that will radically alter their domestic business environments, and in so doing will herald "chill winds" for various elements of the local business community. Where such elements have lobbying power, pushing through with liberalization measures is not going to be "a stroll in the park". Some commentators have already intimated that for these countries, AFTA and the AIA are regarded as economic prices to be paid for joining ASEAN, rather than an attraction. Indeed, the leaderships of some transitional countries may regard the AIA as a liability, rather than an asset, of belonging to ASEAN. And if their domestic economies are insufficiently prepared, they could well be right.

But this is not to suggest that the transitional countries of ASEAN should avoid complying with the AIA; quite the contrary. A failure to create an investment environment that is broadly in line with the AIA benchmark is likely to doom a country to insignificant levels of FDI inflows, and for countries that lack adequate domestic resources of capital, technology, and expertise, this is not an option but a necessity. Quite clearly, the transitional countries of ASEAN do lack these resources, in spades. Therefore, care has to be taken in seeking to ensure that they are able to meet the AIA deadlines. This in turn means that emphasis must be placed on the AIA as a *process*, in order that the transitional countries are able "to get from here to there". Care must also be taken to ensure that the AIA process does not duplicate, or contradict, similar development initiatives across the transitional countries of the region, and the Asian Development Bank's (ADB's) Greater Mekong Sub-Region initiative in particular.[68] Beyond this, it should be recognized that implementing the AIA will also pose a challenge for ASEAN as a whole, and perhaps the ASEAN Secretariat in particular. Given the limited resources available to the regional grouping, and the competing demands put on the relatively small staff, getting the AIA to 2020 will be a fairly demanding exercise.

Perhaps some of the seemingly less strident aspects of the AIA initiative have the potential to reap the greatest rewards, as well as posing the greatest challenges: the input of the corporate sector; and the freer flow of capital, skilled workers, and technology. In a sense, these are some of the key elements in the AIA as a process, through which the "headline" goals and deadlines will need to be achieved. As APEC has discovered, there is a need for private sector input in regional initiatives that pertain to business. How can policy-makers in government ministries be expected to have a grounded appreciation of the real factors that determine trade and investment flows? It is far better not only to consult the corporate sector, but also to get the corporate sector actively involved in the policy formulation process. Indeed, this may become increasingly important as the pace of technological innovation accelerates and corporate sector views on what is an ideal host country foreign investment regime undergo a seismic re-think. Besides, although government agencies can assist in promoting investment flows, it is the corporate sector that will actually *drive* investment activity. Therefore, not to have the corporate sector actively involved in the AIA initiative would be like staging "Romeo and Juliet" without the balcony scene. That said, it remains a challenge as to how ASEAN will bring the corporate sector actively into the AIA arrangement, at a policy-making level. The freer flow of financial and human capital, as well as technology, is another important pillar of the AIA initiative, particularly when the arrangement is seen as a process. Arguably,

all the best foreign investment laws and regulations in the world —
including national treatment — are somewhat superfluous if foreign
investors are unable to remit capital in and out of overseas projects.
Yet at present, some ASEAN countries do not host business regimes
that allow overseas investors to freely remit profits, for example.
Indeed, in some Southeast Asian countries hit hard by the Asian
crisis, foreign investors must currently create their own foreign
exchange earnings, which compel investors to enact fairly complex
countertrade deals. Not surprisingly, such host country conditions
deter many more potential overseas investors from even considering
an investment.

Although wholly unintentional, one peril for the AIA might
come from any future perception — right or wrong — that certain
ASEAN members are deriving greater benefits from the arrangement
than others, or even at the expense of others. While wholly in the
realm of speculation, one could perhaps conceive of scenarios
whereby the intended development of a regional framework for
integrated production activities allows some host countries to gain
better leverage from this situation than others. A similar danger
would exist if the newer members of ASEAN felt that the AIA —
and/or its sequential introduction of Temporary Exclusion Lists —
benefited the main industrial sectors in the core countries, ahead of
those sectors which are strongest in the transitional countries, at
which point, the volition of the newer members to stick by
commitments could weaken. However, such a scenario is by no
means unavoidable. If one looks at the track record of the European
Union's internal market initiative, although the core countries have
continued to digest a large proportion of the "FDI pie", some of the
more peripheral and low-income members of the EU have also
enjoyed some success in attracting new foreign investment inflows.
Another area for potential peril — and open to perceptions, either
right or wrong — is if non-ASEAN investors come to regard the AIA
as a regional arrangement that makes their capital "second class".
Although the AIA aims to open the region fully to foreign investment
by 2020, ASEAN investors will enjoy these privileges a full decade
before investors from outside the region. This issue also brings us
to the difficulty of defining what is an ASEAN or a non-ASEAN
investor, as the recent rise in transnational companies, strategic
alliances, and complex cross-shareholding arrangements make the
identification of a particular firm's "origins" or national character
hard to achieve satisfactorily.[69]

The point was made earlier that the AIA must be an arrangement tailored for the region in the next millennium, rather than for an ASEAN of 1997, or even 1999. For that reason, the AIA must also have the capability to embrace the types of investment activity that are likely to be in the ascendant on the other side of Y2K, as well as more traditional areas of business activity. The global growth sectors of late have tended to be in areas such as banking and insurance, telecommunications and information technology (IT), chemicals and biotechnology, Internet-related businesses, and so on. The AIA should therefore seek to ensure that it is capable of promoting such sectors, and not allow the Temporary Exclusion Lists to become ghettos where member countries try to protect domestic firms in high growth areas. An AIA that is only pertinent to FDI in plantations and power generation, or shoes and textiles, is probably not the right way to proceed, and will fail in its objectives if foreign investors display disinterest.

Where foreign investment activity growth is perhaps most apparent is in the burgeoning services sector. (Tables 5.7 and 5.8 provide a breakdown of FDI inflows and stock in 1998, by sector, for developed countries, developing countries, and South and East Asia.) This has been driven in large part by the leaps being made in technological innovation, which in turn is driving the deregulation of various service industries, as foreign firms — with such technology as proprietary assets — have gained greater leverage through their "enhanced ownership-specific advantages". Investment in the services sector necessitates a differing — and often more demanding — host country environment, providing a more advanced platform of human as well as physical inputs, resources, and logistical support. This is a notion that Singapore has acknowledged, and which drives in large part its move towards greater human resource training, "technopreneurship", and a "knowledge-based economy". Even outside the services sector, product life-cycles have been shrinking, inventory is becoming a thing of the past, and those locations best able to support just-in-time operations are going to be ahead of the game. As multinational firms move towards increasingly complex integrated production strategies (in a bid to maximize profit margins within an increasingly competitive business environment), host countries will need to offer even more conducive platforms and resources. This brings us back to the fact that the AIA will probably be less successful if it is used in isolation, and must work together with other ASEAN initiatives to upgrade the host

TABLE 5.7
FDI Inflows by Industry Sector, 1998

	Developed countries		Developing countries		South, East and Southeast Asia		Global	
	Value (US$m)	Share (%)	Value (US$m)	Share (%)	Value (US$m)	Share (%)	Value (US$m)	Share (%)
Primary	8,577	9.2	1,787	6.7	1,044	5.7	10,364	8.6
Manufacturing	34,974	37.5	17,802	66.8	14,140	76.6	52,776	44.0
– electric machinery	2,785	3.0	2,066	7.7	1,873	10.2	4,850	4.0
Services	39,999	42.9	6,654	25.0	2,994	16.2	46,653	38.9
– finance	12,639	13.6	857	3.2	253	1.4	13,497	11.3

TABLE 5.8
FDI Inflow Stock by Industry Sector, 1998

	Developed countries		Developing countries		South, East and Southeast Asia		Global	
	Value (US$m)	Share (%)	Value (US$m)	Share (%)	Value (US$m)	Share (%)	Value (US$m)	Share (%)
Primary	86,443	11.9	11,549	10.3	5,730	8.4	97,992	11.7
Manufacturing	277,763	38.2	69,649	62.1	42,192	61.7	347,412	41.4
– electric machinery	26,856	3.7	11,674	10.4	8,879	13.0	38,530	4.6
Services	324,226	44.6	30,579	27.2	19,983	29.2	354,805	42.3
– finance	119,714	16.5	10,695	9.5	8.597	12.6	130,409	15.5

SOURCE: UNCTAD (1999).

country business environments in the region. The AIA, ASEAN and the member countries must also be entrepreneurial in their approach to attracting foreign investment, and responsive to emerging trends in international business. One such global trend that Dunning and others have highlighted is the move towards spatial clustering of related businesses, including those enacted by foreign investors. Although this is perhaps more in the remit of single countries, and even regional authorities within host countries, the AIA could play a supporting role.[70]

Taking one step further, the anticipated explosion in e-commerce activity (including e-commerce investment) will probably have major implications for external trade and global foreign investment.[71] If so, e-commerce will also have major implications for regional economic arrangements, like AFTA, NAFTA, the EU and the AIA, in a business world that is seemingly moving towards a single, global economy and market-place.[72] As Drucker recently pointed out, "the competition is not local anymore — in fact it knows no boundaries ... in e-commerce there are neither local companies nor distinct geographies."[73] The full implications of e-commerce for existing forms of regional business arrangements have probably not yet become apparent.

Portfolio Investment and Capital Flows within the AIA

Article 2 of the Framework Agreement on the AIA clearly states that the AIA initiative does not pertain to portfolio investment. On the one hand, this is perhaps a good thing, as an agreement that also seeks to cover portfolio investment activity in ASEAN would almost certainly necessitate a markedly different framework agreement. Besides, flows of portfolio investment within ASEAN have yet to develop into levels commensurate with intra-regional FDI flows (with the possible exception of Singapore). Rather, the current profile of foreign portfolio flows within ASEAN tends to echo FDI flows prior to the mid-1980s, with much of the investment stemming from outside the Southeast Asian region. Nevertheless, cumulative portfolio investment activity is yet to rival the scale of FDI activity in the region. As Table 5.9 shows, net flows of portfolio equity in the Asia-Pacific region as a whole have not been more than 43 per cent of total net equity flows since 1996, were less than 10 per cent in 1998, and are expected to be only 31 per cent in 1999. (Table 5.10 shows the same figures, for global emerging markets.)

TABLE 5.9
Asia-Pacific Financial Flows

	(In US$ billion)					(As % of private and official flows)				
	1996	1997	1998E	1999F	2000F	1996	1997	1998E	1999F	2000F
Net private flows	**174.3**	**71.0**	**8.6**	**39.3**	**26.8**	100.0	100.0	100.0	100.0	100.0
Equity investment	64.6	57.1	58.4	64.9	55.0	37.1	80.4	679.1	165.1	205.2
– direct equity	45.4	51.1	53.4	49.6	45.9	26.0	72.0	620.9	126.2	171.3
– portfolio equity	19.1	6.0	5.0	15.2	9.1	11.0	8.5	58.1	38.7	34.0
Private creditors	109.7	13.9	–49.8	–25.6	–28.3	62.9	19.6	–579.1	–65.1	–105.6
– commercial banks	75.6	–8.3	–52.2	–21.9	–24.5	43.4	–11.7	–607.0	–55.7	–91.4
– non-bank private creditors	34.2	22.2	2.4	–3.7	–3.8	19.6	31.3	27.9	–9.4	–14.2
Net official flows	**3.6**	**35.5**	**28.7**	**8.5**	**12.4**	100.0	100.0	100.0	100.0	100.0
– int. financial institutions	0.2	24.7	21.4	–1.5	5.1	5.6	69.6	74.6	–17.6	41.1
– bilateral creditors	3.4	10.8	7.3	10.0	7.3	94.4	30.4	25.4	117.6	58.9

SOURCE: Institute of International Finance Inc. (1999).

TABLE 5.10
Emerging Market Financial Flows

	(In US$ billion)					(As % of private and official flows)				
	1996	1997	1998E	1999F	2000F	1996	1997	1998E	1999F	2000F
Net private flows	**334.7**	**265.9**	**136.1**	**135.5**	**155.0**	100.0	100.0	100.0	100.0	100.0
Equity investment	127.3	141.8	126.8	141.9	130.9	38.0	53.3	93.2	104.7	84.5
– direct equity	92.8	113.1	120.2	117.3	107.4	27.7	42.5	88.3	86.6	69.3
– portfolio equity	34.5	28.7	6.6	24.6	23.5	10.3	10.8	4.8	18.2	15.2
Private creditors	207.4	124.1	9.3	–6.4	24.1	62.0	46.7	6.8	–4.7	15.5
– commercial banks	118.4	34.1	–45.4	–29.5	–14.3	35.4	12.8	–33.4	–21.8	–9.2
– non-bank private creditors	88.9	90	54.7	23.1	38.4	26.6	33.8	40.2	17.0	24.8
Net official flows	**5.3**	**35.9**	**53.0**	**22.1**	**14.7**	100.0	100.0	100.0	100.0	100.0
– int. financial institutions	6.7	28.1	35.8	8.5	9.6	126.4	78.3	67.5	38.5	65.3
– bilateral creditors	–1.5	7.8	17.3	13.6	5.1	–28.3	21.7	32.6	61.5	34.7

SOURCE: Institute of International Finance Inc. (1999).

On the other hand, making a clear distinction between FDI and portfolio investment is becoming an increasingly difficult exercise in the world of international business, as the actual "mechanics" of direct investment activity become increasingly complex, and FDI deals increasingly employ capital market instruments. Elements of FDI activity, notably in the ascendant field of mergers and acquisitions (M&A), now rely in large part on portfolio investment tools, and the depth and complexity of a host country's capital markets can have an indirect — but nonetheless substantial — impact on its FDI inflows. Given the current level of global and regional over-capacity across a spectrum of products and commodities, "greenfield" FDI activity is on the wane. This decline is inversely proportional to the global rise in M&A activity (see Tables 5.11 and 5.12), as firms seek to offset growing pressure on profit margins by consolidating, taking equity stakes in rivals, entering strategic alliances, and in its most extreme form, buying out competitors' market share.[74] Therefore, an AIA that is oriented towards the conventional type of "greenfield" investment activity may be of limited utility on the other side of the millennium.[75] Conversely, an AIA that is able to provide a more conducive environment for M&A activities may be able to stimulate FDI activity in the region considerably. (Table 5.13 provides details of M&A activity in Southeast Asia during the 1990s.)

Given the increasingly convoluted world of foreign investment (both FDI and portfolio) and capital flows in general (for example, commercial bank lending), there may also be some utility in seeking to extend the remit of the AIA — or create an additional framework agreement that dovetails with the AIA — to cover related capital market and financial flow issues.[76] Without wishing to get into the current debate on the virtues and vices of "hot money", and the perils of excessive foreign currency lending, it is undoubtedly true to say that a host country's relative attraction to foreign direct investors is determined in part by the standard and scale of its financial system. From the perspective of a foreign investor, an extremely liberal foreign investment law is fine, but can be significantly discounted by an inadequate domestic financial infrastructure and banking sector.[77] From the perspective of a host country, the volatility of capital flows or a flimsy financial system can do much to undermine the good work done in improving other elements of the domestic business environment in a bid to attract

TABLE 5.11
Global Cross-border Mergers and Acquisitions, 1991–98

		1991	1992	1993	1994	1995	1996	1997	1998
Global M&A sales	US$bn	85.28	121.89	162.34	196.37	237.18	274.61	341.65	544.31
M&A sales in developing countries	US$bn	10.66	32.17	48.67	60.98	52.75	83.4	95.62	67.76
M&A sales in developing countries	% of total	12.50	26.39	29.98	31.05	22.24	30.37	27.99	12.45
Majority-owned M&A deals									
– Global	US$bn	49.06	73.77	66.81	109.55	140.81	162.69	236.22	410.70
– Developing countries	US$bn	1.42	8.46	9.65	9.30	9.17	18.44	41.03	45.64
– Developing countries	% of total	2.89	11.47	14.44	8.49	6.51	11.33	17.37	11.11
Revenue from FDI activity in privatizations in developing countries	US$bn	5.50	6.00	6.40	6.40	6.40	5.60	21.10	—

SOURCE: World Bank, *Global Development Finance 1999* (New York: World Bank, 1999).

TABLE 5.12
Top Ten Industries for Global M&A Deals in 1998

	No. of deals	US$bn
Oil and gas	98	76.2
Automotive	144	50.9
Banking and finance	317	50.8
Telecommunications	231	50.0
Paper products, printing and publishing	232	40.9
Utilities	111	39.6
Insurance	124	37.9
Business services	853	37.7
Chemicals	349	24.3
Retail	152	18.0

SOURCE: KPMG Corporate Finance.

TABLE 5.13
Cross-border M&A Deals in Southeast Asia, by Seller, 1991–98
(In US$ million)

	1991	1992	1993	1994	1995	1996	1997	1998
Brunei	—	—	—	—	—	—	667	—
Cambodia	—	—	—	30	667	63	—	—
Indonesia	275	2,287	1,421	6,507	4,125	2,654	4,312	1,705
Laos	—	—	10	—	—	2	—	—
Malaysia	1,004	1,197	541	393	821	4,497	2,361	1,693
Myanmar	5	—	15	104	632	134	6	—
Philippines	123	576	679	1,824	2,966	2,708	2,835	2,238
Singapore	127	450	2,071	1,145	597	1,692	1,208	548
Thailand	152	2,556	330	605	2,963	2,063	1,405	1,820
Vietnam	49	227	2,329	2,894	1,975	1,300	901	88

SOURCE: UNCTAD (1999).

more FDI inflows.[78] While smaller, "niche" investment companies may be willing to adopt very flexible strategies in order to conduct profitable projects in developing markets with weak financial systems, major multinational firms — with the advantage of global reach, and therefore global choice — tend to have lower levels of tolerance in this field.[79] And with major multinationals now the source of a majority of FDI activity — as well as two-thirds of global trade — most developing countries cannot afford to rely solely on niche investors. A discussion of what elements should be included in such an additional ASEAN framework agreement on financial flows and markets is probably worthy of a separate paper altogether. However, its broad thrust could be parallel to that of the AIA, in assisting member countries to move towards more open, mature financial markets, ideally by given deadlines. Tangible projects could also be parallel to those under the AIA, such as in the field of accurate data collection, interpretation and analysis, as well as assisting pertinent regulatory bodies and government agencies to upgrade their institutional capacities.[80]

Conclusion

> The policies of ASEAN governments, and of ASEAN itself, ... [need] continual modification and fine tuning in the light of technological, financial and political developments now emerging in the global economy ... [Although] much of the responsibility for creating and maintaining the right economic and political ambience for the wave of FDI now being attracted to ASEAN rests with individual host government, ... [it is clear] that this also requires an active and entrepreneurial stance by ASEAN itself to ensure an uninterrupted flow of both intra-ASEAN FDI and trade, and that of investment by non-ASEAN firms in ASEAN countries.[81]

Although the AIA has yet to gain real momentum, and details of its implementation have yet to be fully ironed out, this observer is reservedly optimistic about its chances of delivering greater FDI activity into the Southeast Asian region. While it is relatively easy to cite pertinent issues that the AIA fails to cover, as done here, there is little doubt that the AIA arrangement does provide a binding and relatively uniform framework for member countries to apply to their investment regimes. If the volition is there, within each member country, the AIA will provide a blueprint for what should subsequently become a platform for the free flow of investment within the Southeast Asian region. That in itself would be a major feat. Undoubtedly, this is where a regional drive to increase investment should probably commence.

The above notwithstanding, the AIA arrangement in itself does not guarantee a substantial pick-up in FDI activity within ASEAN, and there are various initiatives that ASEAN should explore, either as add-ons to the AIA or as parallel projects. Moves to upgrade the quality of FDI data in the ASEAN region is a good example, and a potentially important one, particularly now that M&A activity is on the rise in the region. Fine-tuning the AIA will not be possible unless policy-makers can gain a genuine appreciation of what is happening in terms of FDI flows and trends, and that in turn requires much better quality investment data (rather than the investment propaganda that some ASEAN countries persist with). Both Chia and Mirza have identified some of the major deficiencies in Southeast Asian FDI data, including: the omission of re-invested earnings and inter-company loans, the use of cumulative approval and/or pledges data over actual inflows, double counting in projects with multiple foreign investors from differing countries, failure to discount capital contributions by local partners in foreign joint ventures, and so on.[82] To be fair to ASEAN, Southeast Asia does not have a monopoly on this problem, as it tends to be apparent in much of the developing world, but this does not lessen the argument for dealing with the issue.[83]

Armed with improved data on FDI flows and trends, the AIA should also develop an ethos of entrepreneurial responsiveness to emerging trends and developments, ideally with a significant degree of input from the corporate sector. An AIA that can spot new trends, and then harness them, in a bid to increase the flow and quality of foreign investment would be an arrangement that could reap added dividends, and send a positive signal to foreign investors in general about Southeast Asia's appetite for foreign capital. Collaboration between the AIA, the ASEAN Surveillance Process, and other areas of financial sector capacity-building would also be a boon at a time when FDI activity is increasingly calling upon financial resources to enact deals. Although the AIA is now the main pillar of ASEAN's policy towards investment in the region, it is one element of a bigger picture in Southeast Asia. Besides, ASEAN is presumably not only seeking to attract larger cumulative quantities of FDI (although that alone would be nice), but also to harness foreign investment in a way that maximizes its benefits. To achieve this, ASEAN's investment agenda must go beyond the confines of the AIA's defined remit and also work on areas pertaining to human resource development, research and development, financial markets, the environment, and so on.

Not only will the AIA's success be dependent in large part on the commitment of the ten member countries, but the AIA arrangement will be no substitute for the ASEAN countries unilaterally enacting additional FDI-friendly policy measures of their own. As noted above, although the sorts of policies contained within the AIA framework agreement are necessary to attract FDI interest in Southeast Asia, some member countries will need to improve various other elements of their host country business regimes if they are to successfully attract foreign investment inflows.

We should also not underestimate the challenges that the AIA will pose for a few Southeast Asian countries. With some of the newer members of ASEAN already hardpressed to meet the fairly onerous commitments of membership, if only in terms of officials attending the myriad meetings that ASEAN hosts each year, it is important that the AIA does not cause an unduly large additional burden on their limited resources. It is also important that the AIA delivers real dividends. The incremental rolling out of the AIA — along with AFTA — over the next decade or so will pose significant challenges for some of the existing sub-regional arrangements in Southeast Asia, such as the various growth triangles and Greater Mekong initiatives. Will a wholly AIA- and AFTA-compliant ASEAN need such sub-regional arrangements in the medium term, at least in their current form? The answer is probably not. Although the likely evaporation, or re-engineering, of the latter are no concern of the AIA *per se*, it would be beneficial if ASEAN seeks a way to do this in a manner that causes least distress or misunderstanding.

There will always be a temptation to view the AIA as a static goal, to which ASEAN is striving to reach, according to a series of staggered deadlines. Although true in part, successful implementation of the AIA should also be regarded as a *process* that members will be undertaking, and that process will be more challenging for some countries than others. The transitional countries in particular will probably find the road to AFTA- and AIA-compliance an uphill struggle. More specifically, the policy-makers in the transitional countries will find it an uphill struggle to cajole ambivalent — and sometimes hostile — leadership and public opinion not to veto the sorts of economic reforms that are necessary to comply with AFTA and the AIA.[84] Therefore, ASEAN — and perhaps the AIA Council in particular — will face some additional challenges in helping the transitional countries of Southeast Asia through this process. For the AIA, it is no longer a case of "talking the talk", because now is the time to begin "walking the walk".

APPENDIX
The AIA Timetable in Context

1987	ASEAN Agreement for the Promotion and Protection of Investments
1992	Framework Agreement on Enhancing ASEAN Economic Co-operation
1996	Protocol to Amend the 1987 ASEAN Agreement for the Promotion and Protection of Investments.
	Protocol on ASEAN Dispute Settlement Mechanism
October 1998	AIA Framework Agreement signed in Manila
June 1999	AIA came into force
End-1999	A Temporary Exclusion List for AIA to be drawn up
2000	ASEAN-6 to have 0–5 per cent of tariffs on a minimum of 90 per cent of tariff lines, under AFTA
2002	ASEAN-6 to have 0–5 per cent tariffs on all products, under AFTA
2003	First review of the AIA Sensitive List
	Temporary Exclusion List for ASEAN-6 and Myanmar to be completely phased out
	Vietnam to have 0–5 per cent tariffs, under AFTA
2005	Laos and Myanmar to have 0–5 per cent tariffs, under AFTA
2010	National treatment for ASEAN investors
	All industries open to ASEAN investment
	Temporary Exclusion List for Cambodia, Laos and Vietnam to be completely phased out
	Cambodia to have 0–5 per cent tariffs, under AFTA
2020	National treatment for all investors
	All industries to be open to all investors
	A free flow of investments in ASEAN

NOTES

*   The author wishes to acknowledge the input of Hafiz Mirza and Listijani Sasmito in the provision of data and material for various elements of this chapter.

1   UNCTAD, *World Investment Report 1999*, p. 58.

2   Lester Thurow estimates that current global production potential exceeds expected consumption by at least a third. See "Building Wealth", *Atlantic Monthly*, June 1999.

3   A recent (post-Asian crisis) Singapore survey of retail-oriented multinational companies with operations in Southeast Asia, found that an inadequate supply of skilled labour was the most severe barrier to FDI activity in the region (with 59 per cent of respondents ranking this barrier as severe or very severe), ahead of increasing costs of production (58 per cent), political instability (55 per cent), unclear host country policies (48 per cent), infrastructure problems (36 per cent), and so on. Survey conducted by Frank Bartels and Nick Freeman, the full results and analysis of which are forthcoming.

4   As U.S. Federal Reserve Chairman Alan Greenspan noted in May 1999: "... newer technologies and foreshortened lead times apparently have made capital investment distinctly more profitable, enabling firms to substitute capital for labour and other inputs far more productively than they could have a decade or two ago. Capital ... has deepened significantly since 1995". If Greenspan is right, on a global scale, capital flows chasing lower labour unit costs in emerging markets may become a thing of the past, and countries that provide a conducive platform on which foreign investors can generate sustained productivity gains will steal a march on those that cannot. See Greenspan (1999).

5   ASEAN, "Framework Agreement on the AIA", p. 1.

6   The Hanoi Plan of Action is intended as a strategy towards fulfilling the ASEAN Vision 2020, encompassing the period from 1999 to 2004. The main elements of the Hanoi Plan of Action are: strengthening macroeconomic and financial co-operation; enhancing greater economic integration (including the AIA initiative); promoting science and technology development and developing IT infrastructure; promoting social development and addressing the social impact of the Asian crisis; promoting human resource development; protecting the environment and promoting sustainable development; strengthening regional peace and security; enhancing ASEAN's role as a force for peace in the Asia Pacific; promoting awareness of ASEAN; and improving ASEAN's own structures and mechanisms. See *http://www.aseansec.org/summit/6th/prg_hpoa.htm*.

7   The scope of the AIA framework agreement has been expanded to cover services incidental to manufacturing, agriculture, forestry, fisheries, and mining. Joint Press Statement, 2nd Meeting of the AIA Council, 29 September 1999, p. 3. The ASEAN Secretariat identifies 28 other relevant agreements that pertain to operating and investing in the ASEAN region. A full list can be found in Annex A of ASEAN's *Handbook of Investment Agreements in ASEAN*, pp. 69-71.

8   ASEAN, *Handbook of Investment Agreements in ASEAN*, p. 3. Making a clear distinction between trade and investment in the applied world of international business can be quite hard, as it poses additional challenges to policy-makers. For example, an extremely liberal foreign investment

regime may attract scant FDI inflows if the trade regime (for example, tariff structure) remains particularly harsh.

9   ASEAN, *Handbook of Investment Agreements in ASEAN*, p. 3.
10 Ibid., p. 9.
11 Mirza et al. (1997), p. 1.
12 "Opening up" means both granting access to the domestic market and removing restrictions on foreign equity participation. See interpretative notes to the framework agreement on the AIA.
13 The full text of the AIA framework agreement can be found at: *http://www.aseansec.org/economic/aem/30/frm_aia.htm.*
14 The text of ASEAN Vision 2020 can be found at: *http://www.aseansec.org/summit/vision97.htm.*
15 See Article 6 of the AIA framework agreement.
16 Article 5 of the AIA framework agreement.
17 Article 5 of the AIA framework agreement.
18 "National treatment" broadly means that foreign investors should receive no less favourable conditions than domestic investors. In the specific case of the AIA, Article 7 of the framework agreement states that "each member state shall ... accord immediately to ASEAN investors and their investments, in respect of all industries and measures affecting investment including but not limited to the admission, establishment, acquisition, expansion, management, operation and disposition of investments, treatment no less favourable than that it accords to its own like investors and investments".
19 A Temporary Exclusion List for the manufacturing sector had already been agreed, while similar lists for agriculture, forestry, fishing, and mining were expected to be ready by end-1999.
20 These deadlines to end the exclusion have recently been brought forward. The initial deadlines were 2010 for the ASEAN-6, 2013 for Myanmar and Vietnam, and 2015 for Laos.
21 Such logic is less appropriate for the newer members of ASEAN, which have deadlines for compliance with AFTA that are much later than those for the ASEAN-6 countries.
22 Article 15 of the framework agreement goes on to state: "It is recognised that particular pressures on the balance of payments of a Member State in the process of economic development or economic transition may necessitate the use of restrictions to ensure, *inter alia*, the maintenance of a level of financial reserves adequate for the implementation of its programme of economic development or economic transition". In such cases, the AIA Council has to be notified within two weeks. Measures to safeguard balance of payments should "avoid unnecessary damage to the commercial, economic and financial interests of any other Member State", should "not exceed those necessary to deal with the circumstances", and be temporary. Consultations between a member country adopting balance of payments measures and the AIA and other members must begin within 90 days from the date of notification.

23 Details can be found on page 4 of the "Joint Press Statement of the 31st ASEAN Economic Ministers Meeting", 30 September 1999, Singapore.

24 Ibid., p. 4. Although ASEAN obviously seeks to attract FDI inflows from all points on the globe, there may be some utility in focusing on specific regions. Similarly, the AIA may wish to promote itself in those regions where it can expect to attract the greatest interest. Albeit a rather subjective view, this observer would suggest that Europe should be one of the regions to focus on, given the room for potential "up-side" on European investment in Southeast Asia.

25 Joint Press Statement, 2nd Meeting of the AIA Council, 29 September 1999, Singapore. The "task force" responsible for generating the comparable FDI statistics was recently upgraded into a working group, "to address all FDI statistical issues and to monitor the flow of FDI in ASEAN". The AIA Council's *1999 ASEAN Investment Report* was to be launched at the Informal Summit, in Manila, on 28 November 1999. The report was said to contain an assessment of the size and trends of FDI flows in Southeast Asia, and also examined the impact of the recent Asian crisis on ASEAN's ability to attract FDI.

26 Foreign direct investment is defined by UNCTAD as "an investment involving management control of a resident entity in one economy by an enterprise resident in another economy. FDI involves a long-term relationship reflecting an investor's lasting interest in a foreign entity." Other definitions of FDI are sometimes used, usually relating to the proportion of equity and/or control of assets that a foreign investor has in a local company.

27 UNCTAD Press Release TAD/INF/2819, 27 September 1999. *http://www.unctad.org/en/press/pr2819en.htm*

28 This includes providing employment opportunities, contributing to fiscal revenues, generating foreign exchange earnings, etc. FDI projects by multinational firms have also been a major motor in the export-driven growth of the Southeast Asian region. See Thomsen (1999).

29 Lindblad asserts that: "Singapore constitutes perhaps the most 'pure' illustration of how FDI can make a decisive contribution towards attaining rapid economic growth." See Lindblad (1998), p. 166. Singapore policy-makers have deliberately sought to integrate the country's economy with the production networks of major multinational firms.

30 Dunning (1997).

31 Mallampally and Sauvant (1999), p. 1.

32 Of course, any country's aggregate FDI inflow data should be used with care since there is a tendency to inflate the actual size of foreign capital inflows. China is no exception to this rule. See Segal (1999), pp. 27–28.

33 For a brief discussion of FDI diverting from ASEAN to China, see Thomsen (1999), pp. 14–16.

34 Mirza et al. (1997), p. 1.

35 In terms of the cyclical versus structural debate, one should be aware that reasons for Southeast Asia's proportional decline in global FDI inflows may well have stemmed in part from problems in the home countries of traditional sources of foreign investment, in addition to bottlenecks within ASEAN. For example, the lengthy economic recession that Japan underwent during the 1990s — and its impact on the relative value of the yen — has caused a weakening in potential FDI inflows into Southeast Asia from this "major player".

36 See Lindblad (1998), chapter 2.

37 See Chia, "Foreign Direct Investment in Southeast Asia", pp. 37–40. Japanese outward FDI in particular accelerated after the Plaza Accord of 1985.

38 See Chia, "Intra-ASEAN Direct Investment: Present, Future Direction and Policy Implications". See also Tham Siew Yean (1998).

39 Table 5.6, which shows Southeast Asia's FDI outward stock as a percentage of GDP, indicates that Malaysia has FDI stock outside the country equal to 13 per cent of GDP, and Singapore has overseas FDI stock worth over 46 per cent of GDP, in 1997.

40 Dunning (1997).

41 UNCTAD (1999), pp. xxiv–xxv.

42 Although some foreign investors might validly argue that these sorts of investments are not "speculative punts", others have discovered that the cumulative level of undisclosed debt — which may not have been fully apparent during due diligence — in local firms can make the act of investing in post-crisis Asia a rather speculative exercise.

43 Miyake and Thomsen (1999), p. 117.

44 UNCTAD Press Release, 27 September 1999 (TAD/INF/2823). See *http://www.unctad.org/en/press/pr2823en.htm*.

45 The scale of activity, be they venture capitalists, "vulture funds", or normal investors, all seeking to buy distressed business assets in the countries worst hit by the Asian crisis, has not been as great as some had feared (and others had hoped). A major obstacle appears to have been persistent worries over the scale of — often hidden — debt attached to many distressed businesses in East Asia.

46 Statement on Bold Measures, 6th ASEAN Summit, Hanoi, 16 December 1998. The bold measures also include: bringing forward the AFTA deadline for the ASEAN-6 from 2003 to 2002; the Exclusions List of the AIA framework agreement will be brought forward from 2010 to 2003 for the ASEAN-6 and Myanmar, and from 2013 and 2015 for Vietnam and Laos, respectively, to 2010 for both.

47 Details of the short-term measures to enhance the ASEAN investment climate can be found at: *http://www.aseansec.org/economic/invest/meas_enh.htm*. The measures are initially expected to pertain to investment applications received between January 1999 and December 2000, in the manufacturing sector only.

48 See Joint Press Statement of the 1st Meeting of the AIA Council, 5 March 1999, Phuket.

49 FDI, unlike portfolio investment or lending, tends to be long-term in nature, is less volatile, and has the potential to bring with it a diverse spectrum of non-financial inputs. For this reason, FDI should be regarded as being at a premium to most other forms of foreign capital inflow. "Not only can FDI add to investible resources and capital formation, but, perhaps more importantly, it is also a means of transferring production technology, skills, innovative capacity, and organisational and managerial practices between locations, as well as of accessing international marketing networks". Mallampally and Sauvant (1999), p. 3.

50 For an analysis of the perils of FDI incentive schemes, see section 6 of PECC (1995), pp. 79–109. See also UNCTAD Press Release TAD/INF/2819 (*http://www.unctad.org/en/press/pr2819en.htm*), which warns of a "fiscal incentives competition race towards zero" in developing countries, as they compete to attract FDI through incentive schemes.

51 The potential for perceived overlap is greatest in those countries that are members of both APEC and ASEAN. However, it should be noted that not all ASEAN countries (for example, Cambodia, Laos, and Myanmar) are members of APEC. See also: *http://www1.apecsec.org.sg/*.

52 See: *http://www1.apecsec.org.sg/guidebook/annex-3a.html*.

53 Details of APEC economies' IAPs can be found at: *http://www1.apecsec.org.sg/iap/iap.html*.

54 It is important to stress the word "potential" here, as it remains to be seen whether the AIA will burgeon into a fully focused and proactive arrangement. This will be determined in large part by the extent to which member countries adhere to the AIA principles and work towards meeting the set deadlines.

55 The Osaka Action Agenda refers to 14 areas of business activity, of which investment is one, where there is a need to reduce the scale of impediments. APEC's work in this area is co-ordinated by its Committee on Trade and Investment (CTI), which was established by the Declaration on an APEC Trade and Investment Framework, of late 1993. The CTI is supported by an Investment Experts' Group, established in 1994.

56 Quotations taken from APEC's Osaka Action Agenda.

57 Indeed, even prior to the Uruguay Round, the WTO (nee GATT) had occasionally stepped into investment territory, such as the (unratified) Havana Charter of 1948, a 1955 resolution on investment by the GATT Contracting Parties, and a GATT panel ruling on Canada's 1984 Administration of the Foreign Investment Review Act.

58 Reports on the demise of the MAI can be found in the *Financial Times*, 20 and 21 October 1998. See also UNCTAD (1999), pp. 128–37; and *http://www.oecd.org//daf/cmis/mai/toronto.htm*

59 Stanley Fischer, "The Road to Sustainable Recovery in Asia", World Economic Forum, 18 October 1999, Singapore.

60 Dunning notes that of 599 recorded changes to FDI regulations, across 65 countries between 1991 and 1996, more than 95 per cent were pro-liberalization measures or related to investment promotion. See Dunning (1997). According to UNCTAD, a "... process of diminishing returns has set in [for the liberalization of FDI frameworks] and liberal FDI policy is increasingly losing its effectiveness as a locational determinant of FDI". UNCTAD, *World Investment Report 1998.*

61 A good diagrammatic representation of the various host country determinants of FDI can be found in Mallampally and Sauvant (1999), p. 3. The diagram is taken from UNCTAD's *World Investment Report 1998.*

62 The attraction of political stability may become of increasing importance to foreign investors in Southeast Asia — and East Asia as a whole — as the region goes through the post-crisis structural recovery process. Such a process is likely to put additional stresses and strains on the socio-political fabric of some countries.

63 Mallampally and Sauvant (1999), p. 5.

64 Various pertinent ASEAN initiatives are contained in the first five sections of the Hanoi Plan of Action, including: developing ASEAN capital markets, adopting new technologies, enhancing the private sector, co-operation on intellectual property rights, telecommunications interconnectivity, human resource development, and so forth. See *http://www.aseansec.org/summit/ 6th/prg_hpoa.htm.*

65 The "e-ASEAN Initiative" aims to create an "ASEAN e-space, in the world of information and communication technology, and to develop competencies within ASEAN to compete in the global market". See page 6 of the "Joint Press Statement of the 31st ASEAN Economic Ministers Meeting", 30 September 1999, Singapore.

66 As this chapter focuses solely on the AIA, the issue of non-tariff barriers within Southeast Asia is not discussed here, although it is worthy of note.

67 Political factors may also be a hindrance for those transitional countries that remain avowedly socialist and/or nationalist in terms of ideological stance. For such countries, notions of freer capital flows, and foreign investors enjoying national treatment, are scenarios not easy to digest.

68 Details of the ADB's Greater Mekong Sub-Region initiative can be found at: *http://www.adb.org/Work/GMS/default.asp.*

69 This is particularly true of Singapore, which acts as a regional hub for some of the world's largest multinational firms. If a subsidiary of such a multinational, based in Singapore, enacts an FDI project in another ASEAN country, should the investment be regarded as intra-ASEAN or extra-ASEAN?

70 Dunning depicts this trend as follows: "... material, product and production innovations are becoming increasingly interdependent of each other; and ... the ability of firms to upgrade their technological competencies and competitiveness is not just dependent on their own efforts, but on that of other firms supplying complementary technologies. This closer networking

of firms ... is a critical feature of "alliance" capitalism now emerging in the global economy; and is essentially a reflection of the need of firms to be both more specialized in the kinds of value-added activities in which they engage, yet, at the same time, be closely linked with critical suppliers, industrial customers and competitors." See Dunning (1997).

71   "E-commerce is to the Information Revolution what the railroad was to the Industrial Revolution ... [and] like the railroad 170 years ago, e-commerce is creating a new and distinct boom, rapidly changing the economy, society and politics." Drucker (1999b), p. 2.

72   Ibid., p. 3.

73   Ibid. He goes on to say: "What we call the Information Revolution is actually a Knowledge Revolution ... Increasingly, performance in these knowledge-based industries will come to depend on running the institution so as to attract, hold, and motivate knowledge workers." Drucker (1999c), pp. 4–5. And for "institution", also read "country".

74   The aggregate value of global M&A deals has risen steadily from US$85.3 billion in 1991 to US$544.3 billion in 1998; more than a sixfold increase over an eight-year period. M&A deals in developing countries have also risen substantially, from US$10.7 billion to US$67.8 billion over the same period; also more than a sixfold increase. The rates of growth are even higher for majority-owned M&A deals. See Table 5.9. In 1997, M&A deals accounted for 58 per cent of global FDI inflows. Table 5.10 profiles the top ten industries for global M&A deals in 1998.

75   If the world already has more than enough "widgits", then there is little utility in the ASEAN member countries having FDI regimes that promote the opening of new widget plants or widget-friendly export processing zones.

76   Such a framework agreement could evolve out of the ASEAN Senior Finance Officials Meeting (ASFOM) initiative, and the working group of ASFOM, and/or the ASEAN Central Banking Forum. See also *http://www.aseansec.org/economic/afc.htm*.

77   In Vietnam, the absence of local financial and capital markets hampers FDI inflows. See OECD (1998), p. 6.

78   Estimates suggest that East Asia witnessed a net outflow of a staggering US$100 billion in capital, in less than a year, during the Asian crisis. Tangentially, the damage done by commercial bank lending during — and since — the Asian crisis has not been given as much attention as portfolio investors in general, and hedge funds in particular. Table 5.8 shows quite clearly that it has been the commercial banks that have been aggressively withdrawing capital from the Asia-Pacific region since 1998, and will continue to do so during 2000, as they seek to reduce their loan exposure. This is in contrast to portfolio investors, who continue to be net importers of capital into the region, during and since the Asian crisis. Since a large part of the Asian crisis was caused by excessive lending to the corporate sector, much of which was in foreign currencies, the commercial banks have received surprisingly little "flack", compared to hedge funds, multilateral agencies, ratings agencies, etc.

79 One example of a flexible investor in ASEAN is a Thai firm that has a relatively substantial investment in Laos. The investment project makes and sells a product for purely domestic consumption, and receives revenues in local currency. But in order to remit any earnings, the Thai firm must first create its own foreign exchange. This is done by using the local currency revenue to buy Lao coffee, which the Thai firm then exports and sells on the international market. Such a strategy, with all the additional foreign exchange risks and administration involved, is unlikely to be acceptable to most major multinational firms.

80 Improved financial data collection and analysis is already receiving attention, under the ASEAN Surveillance Process, with support from the Asian Development Bank. See also *http://www.aseansec.org/economic/afc.htm.*

81 Dunning (1997).

82 See Chia, "Intra-ASEAN Direct Investment: Present, Future Direction and Policy Implications"; and Mirza (1999).

83 Annex Table A.I.1. in UNCTAD (1999) shows the fairly substantial divergence in FDI inflow figures for developing countries, as reported by UNCTAD, the World Bank, the IIF and J. P. Morgan (see p. 403).

84 The issue of woefully inefficient state enterprise sectors leaps to mind in this context. Were some of the transitional countries to comply with AFTA and the AIA tomorrow, the likely implications for state firms would be devastating. While compliance with AFTA and the AIA are not due by tomorrow, it is becoming increasingly evident that the economic and business liberalization programmes in the transitional countries are not moving at a very rapid pace. Therefore, to some extent at least, regional arrangements like AFTA and the AIA are driving state sector reform in the transitional countries of Southeast Asia.

REFERENCES

Alburo, Florian. "Towards APEC's Long-Term Trade and Investment Agenda: Developing Economy View". Paper presented at the APEC Study Centre Consortium Conference, May 1997.

APEC. *Guide to the Investment Regimes of the APEC Member Economies.* 4th edition. Singapore: APEC, 1999.

ASEAN. "ASEAN Economic Cooperation". [*http://www.aseansec.org/history/asn_eco2.htm*]

─────── . "ASEAN Finance Cooperation". [*http://www.aseansec.org/economic/afc.htm.*]

─────── . "ASEAN Vision 2020". [*http://www.aseansec.org/summit/vision97.htm*]

─────── . *Compendium of Investment Policies and Measures in ASEAN Countries.* Jakarta: ASEAN Secretariat, December 1998.

_____ . "Framework Agreement on the ASEAN Investment Area". [*http://www.aseansec.org/economic/aem/30/frm_aia.htm*]

_____ . *Handbook of Investment Agreements in ASEAN*. Jakarta: ASEAN Secretariat, December 1998.

_____ . "Hanoi Plan of Action". [*http://www.aseansec.org/summit/6th/ prg_hpoa.htm*]

_____ . "Joint Press Release, Inaugural Meeting of the AIA Council, 8 October 1998, Manila". [*http://www.aseansec.org/economic/aem/30/ eco_ai01.htm*]

_____ . "Joint Press Statement, 1st Meeting of the AIA Council, 5 March 1999, Phuket". [*http://www.aseansec.org/economic/aia01.htm*]

_____ . "Joint Press Statement, 2nd Meeting of the AIA Council, 29 September 1999, Singapore". [*http://www.aseansec.org/economic/aem/ 31/eco_aio2.htm*]

_____ . "Joint Press Statement of the 31st ASEAN Economic Ministers Meeting, 30 September 1999, Singapore". [*http://www.aseansec.org/ economic/aem/31eco_e31.htm*]

_____ . "Meeting of the 4th ASEAN Heads of Investment Agencies, 24 July 1998, Singapore". [*http://www.aseansec.org.economic.ahia98.htm*]

_____ . "Short-term Measures to Enhance ASEAN Investment Climate". [*http://www.aseansec.org/economic/invest/meas_enh.htm*]

_____ . "Statement on Bold Measures, 6th ASEAN Summit, 16 December 1998, Hanoi". [*http://www.aseansec.org/economic/invest/sum_bold.htm*]

Board of Investment (Thailand). "AIA: Mid-Summer Dream or No Way Out for ASEAN?". *BOI Investment Review* 8, no. 1 (31 March 1999). [*http:// www.boi.go.th/investreview/r080101.html*]

Chia Siow Yue. "Foreign Direct Investment in Southeast Asia". Paper presented at the Conference on Geoeconomic and Geopolitical Prospects in Southeast Asia, Turin, February 1996.

_____ . "Intra-ASEAN Direct Investment: Present, Future Direction, and Policy Implications". Paper presented at the Seminar on the Promotion of FDI in the Context of the ASEAN Investment Area, Bangkok, 23–24 May 1996.

_____ . "Towards Greater Coherence in Foreign Investment Policy". In *OECD and ASEAN Economies: The Challenge of Policy Coherence*, edited by K. Fukasaku, M. Plummer, and J. Tan, chapter 4. Paris: OECD, 1995.

Drucker, Peter. "Beyond the Information Revolution", *Atlantic Monthly*, October 1999. [*http://www.theatlantic.com/issues/99oct/9910drucker.htm*] [*1999a*] [*http://www.theatlantic.com/issues/99oct/9910drucker2.htm*] [*1999b*] [*http://www.theatlantic.com/issues/99oct/9910drucker3.htm*] [*1999c*]

Dunning, John H. "Strategy for Promoting Greater Integrated Networking Investment Activities in ASEAN". Paper given at the High Level Roundtable for the Formulation of Strategic Plans on Cooperation and Promotion of FDI in ASEAN, Kuala Lumpur, 24–25 February 1997. A version of this paper is forthcoming in Hafiz Mirza and Kee Hwee Wee, eds., *The Strategy, Objectives and Performance of Transnational*

Corporations in ASEAN: Country Studies. London: Edward Elgar, 2000.

Fischer, Stanley. "The Road to Sustainable Recovery in Asia". Speech made at the World Economic Forum in Singapore, 18 October 1999. [*http:// www.imf.org/external/np/speeches/1999/101899.htm*]

Freeman, Nick. "Impediments to Foreign Investment: The Complexities of a Changing International Business Environment". Paper presented at the ABAC-PECC Workshop on Impediments to Trade and Investment in APEC, 21 May 1999, Tokyo.

Greenspan, Alan. "The American Economy in a World Context". Speech given at the 35th Annual Conference on Bank Structure and Competition of the Federal Reserve Bank of Chicago, 6 May 1999. See *http:// www.bog.frb.fed.us/*

Hill, Hal, and Prema-chandra Athukorala. "Foreign Investment in East Asia". *Asian-Pacific Economic Literature* 12, no. 2 (November 1998): 23–50.

Institute of International Finance, Inc. "Capital Flows to Emerging Market Economies", 25 September 1999. [*http://www.iif.com/PublicPDF/ cf_0999.pdf*]

Lindblad, J. Thomas. *Foreign Investment in Southeast Asia in the Twentieth Century*. Basingstoke: Macmillan, 1998.

Mallampally, Padma, and Karl Sauvant. "Foreign Direct Investment in Developing Countries", *Finance and Development* 36, no. 1 (March 1999). [*http://www.imf.org/external/pubs/ft/fandd/1999/03/mallampa.htm*]

Mirza, Hafiz. "An Overview of FDI Data Collecting and Reporting in ASEAN: The Way Ahead". Paper presented at the Second Statistical Workshop on the Collection and Reporting of Statistics in ASEAN, Bali, 6–7 September 1999.

Mirza, Hafiz, Frank Bartels, Mark Hiley and Axele Giroud. "Foreign Direct Investment in ASEAN". Report submitted to the ASEAN heads of investment agencies, July 1997.

Miyake, Maiko, and Stephen Thomsen. "Recent Trends in Foreign Direct Investment". *Financial Market Trends*, no. 73 (June 1999): 109–26.

OECD. *Workshop on FDI Liberalisation, Financial Crises and Multilateral Rules for Investment*. DAFFE/IME/RD(8)2. Summary of workshop held in Bangkok, 9–10 November 1998. Paris: OECD, 1998.

Pacific Economic Co-operation Council (PECC). *Survey of Impediments to Trade and Investment in the APEC Region*. Singapore: PECC, 1995.

Segal, Gerald. "Does China Matter?", *Foreign Affairs*, September–October 1999, pp. 24–36.

Tham Siew Yean. "Competition and Cooperation for Foreign Direct Investment: An ASEAN Perspective". *Asia-Pacific Development Journal* 5 no. 1 (June 1998): 9–36.

Thomsen, Stephen. *Southeast Asia: The Role of Foreign Direct Investment Policies in Development*. Paris: OECD Working Papers on International Investment, 1999.

Thurow, Lester. "Building Wealth", *Atlantic Monthly*, June 1999. [*http://www.theatlantic.com/issues/99jun/9906thurow.htm*] [*http://www.theatlantic.com/issues/99jun/9906thurow2.htm*] [*http://www.theatlantic.com/issues/99jun/9906thurow3.htm*] [*http://www.theatlantic.com/issues/99jun/9906thurow4.htm*]

UNCTAD. *World Investment Report 1998: Trends and Determinants*. New York: United Nations, 1998.

UNCTAD. *World Investment Report 1999: Foreign Direct Investment and the Challenge of Development*. New York: United Nations, 1999.

Wee Kee Hwee. "Toward an ASEAN FDI Statistical System". [*http://www.aseansec.org/secgen/articles/wkw_fdi.htm*]

World Bank. *Global Development Finance 1999*. New York: World Bank, 1999. [*http://www.worldbank.org/prospects/gdf99/vol1.htm*]

6

Financial and Macroeconomic Co-operation in ASEAN: Issues and Policy Initiatives

RAMKISHEN S. RAJAN

Introduction

While the intellectual debate about the exact causes of the crisis in East Asia in 1997–98 and the appropriateness of various remedies rages on, one thing is clear: the boom-bust cycle in East Asia was caused by foreign bank lending. Indeed, the major part of the net US$130 billion outflow of capital from the four crisis-hit ASEAN economies (Indonesia, Thailand, Philippines, and Malaysia) and South Korea between 1996 and 1998 was due to reversals in net short-term lending by commercial banks. Reversals in portfolio equity investments roughly averaged about US$9 billion during this period (Table 6.1). Such large-scale capital withdrawals, curtailment in lending, and consequent sharp currency devaluations inevitably created major collateral damage and dislocations to the domestic financial sectors. Indeed, the closure of troubled financial institutions was a key element of the International Monetary Fund (IMF) programmes for the crisis-hit economies (Lane and Associates 1999). Table 6.2 provides some evidence of the dominance of banks (and "near-banks") relative to the bond and equity markets in East Asia. It is this heavy regional dependence on bank intermediation that contributed to the breadth, depth, and longevity of the crisis.

TABLE 6.1
Net Capital Flows to East Asia (Indonesia, Malaysia,
South Korea, Thailand and Philippines), 1995–99
(In US$ billion)

Type of Capital Flow	1995	1996	1997	1998[c]	1999[d]
Current account balance	−40.6	−54.8	−26.1	69.2	44.6
External financing	83.0	99.0	28.3	−4.2	7.8
Private flows	80.4	102.3	0.2	−27.6	0.3
Equity investment	15.3	18.6	4.4	13.7	18.5
Direct	4.2	4.7	5.9	9.5	12.5
Portfolio	11.0	13.9	−1.5	4.3	6.0
Private creditors	65.1	83.7	−4.2	−41.3	−18.2
Commercial banks	53.2	62.7	−21.2	−36.1	−16.0
Non-banks	12.0	21.0	17.1	−5.3	−2.3
Official flows	2.6	−35.3	28.1	23.4	7.6
Resident lending/others[a]	−28.3	−27.3	−33.7	−22.9	−21.0
Reserves (exc. gold)[a,b]	−14.1	−16.9	31.5	−42.1	−31.4

NOTES: [a] minus denotes increase
         [b] including resident net lending, monetary gold and errors and
             omissions
         [c] estimates
         [d] forecast
SOURCE: IIF (1999).

TABLE 6.2
Selected Indicators of Financial Sector Development
in East Asia, 1994–96
(% of GDP)

	Credit of Banking System (1995)	Bank Assets (1994)	Bank Share in Financial Intermediation (1994)[a]	Stock Market Capitalization (1996)	Bond Market Capitalization (1996)
Indonesia	50	57	91	10	6
S. Korea	70	75	38	43	24
Malaysia	132	100	64	33	56
Philippines	63	54	n.a.	n.a.	39
Thailand	137	110	75	4	14

NOTES: [a] Assets of banks as a percentage of the assets of banks and non-bank
             financial institutions
SOURCES: Rajan (1999b).

This being said, the aim of this chapter is not to revisit the origin and consequences of the crisis.[1] Rather, the focus here is threefold. First, the issue of "regional contagion" is briefly discussed. This provides the context within which the scope — if not the type — of regional co-operation in the financial and macroeconomic spheres may be considered. Secondly, the main policy initiatives in ASEAN in these areas are highlighted. Finally, concrete policy initiatives for regional co-operation in ASEAN and the larger East Asian region are tabled.

Rationale for Regional Co-operation in the Macroeconomic and Financial Spheres[2]

The currency crises of the 1990s, and particularly the one that hit ASEAN and the larger East Asian region in 1997–98, seem to be strongly suggestive of the relevance and pervasiveness of contagion or negative spillover effects that are largely regional in scope (thus, also referred to as "neighbourhood effects").

Following Masson (1998), we may describe "contagion" as a situation where a currency crisis in one economy leads to a jump to a "bad" equilibrium in a "neighbouring" economy. In other words, contagion refers to the simultaneous occurrence of currency crises among economies, with a currency collapse in one economy leading to a speculative attack on another (regional) currency. While there is a need to be very precise in defining the term "currency crisis" in empirical analyses, we take it here to involve an actual break of an exchange rate peg and concomitant currency depreciation, or speculative pressure which may not lead to an exchange rate depreciation but does lead to an international reserve depletion or an interest rate hike.

Thus, in the case of East Asia, while the crisis spread initially from Thailand (following the devaluation of the baht on 2 July 1997) to Indonesia, Malaysia, and the Philippines by the end of August that year, the South Korean won depreciated in November. This in turn had reverberations back to the rest of Southeast Asia. Singapore and Taiwan also experienced "modest" currency depreciations during September–October 1997, while Hong Kong's currency board came under severe pressures, resulting in a sharp interest hike to maintain the currency peg.

What is less clear are the channels which cause currency crises to be contemporaneous over time. Masson (1998) makes an important distinction between transmission channels that are related to investor sentiment or psychology (which he refers to as "pure contagion") and linkages between countries that are measurable/observable *ex-ante* (which he refers to as "spillovers" or "inter-relatedness"). He calls common external shocks that impact all regional economies "monsoonal" effects. Masson shows how it is conceptually possible for "pure contagion" to make an economy relatively more vulnerable to a currency crisis. The important point here is that there must exist a range or zone of weakness within which a currency is potentially vulnerable to a speculative attack in the first instance, with pure contagion increasing the zone of vulnerability. This is consistent with the escape-clause-based (ECB) second generation currency crises models pioneered by Obstfeld (1994), of which contagion models are a subset.

All ECB models stress that while speculative attacks are not inevitable (on the basis of underlying "fundamentals"),[3] neither are they arbitrary, random or undiscriminating (that is, unanchored by fundamentals). Rather, there must exist some weaknesses in the economic fundamentals of the economy for an attack to occur, as the credibility of the fixed exchange rate regime is less than perfect. If the economy is either very "good" or very "bad", it will respectively never or always be attacked. Within those two extremes — which imply unique equilibrium (that is, an attack with close to zero or one probabilities) — there is an intermediate range (grey area). Within this range, there may exist some weaknesses in the economy that are neither strong enough to completely preclude a speculative attack on the currency, nor sufficiently weak to make an attack unavoidable. Rather, there are a multiplicity of equilibra such that an economy remains on what seems to be a sustainable path ("superior equilibrium") until some trigger or evidently minor event coalesces market expectations to an "inferior" equilibrium, that is realized. Thus, shifts in market sentiments could lead to jumps between one equilibra and another, in the process introducing sharp volatility in financial markets.

Against this analytical background, it is revealing that in almost all crises experiences, the economies initially and worst affected by the crises were also the ones with the worst fundamentals to begin with. This is best illustrated in Table 6.3

TABLE 6.3
Summary of Economic Fundamentals of Selected East Asian Economies

Fundamentals	*Country Rankings*[a]						
	1	*2*	*3*	*4*	*5*	*6*	*7*
External							
International reserves[b]	P	I	M	T	K	H	S
Current account/GDP[c]	T	K	M	P	I	H	S
Debt/GDP[d]	T	P	I	M	S	H	S
Export slowdown[e]	T	S	M	K	H	P	I
Real exchange rate: deviation from PPP[f]	S	K	H	M	T	I	P
Banking Strength	K	T	I	M	P	H	S
Capital adequacy[g]	M	T	K	I	P	S	H
Non-performing loans[h]	I	K	T	P	H	M	S
Bank ratings[i]							
Liquidity Mismatches	P	M	T	I	S	K	H
Excess credit growth[j]	K	I	T	P	M	H	S
Short-term external debt/Reserves[k]	T	I	P	K	M	S	H
Broad Money/Reserves[l]							
Overall average[m]	T	I	K	P	M	S	H
Overall based on Thailand weights[n]	T	I	K	P	M	S	H

NOTES: [a] I = Indonesia, H = Hong Kong, K = South Korea, M = Malaysia, P = Philippines, S = Singapore, T = Thailand. Ordinal ranking in descending order of "bad" fundamentals;
[b] In SDRs, June 1997;
[c] 1996;
[d] 1997;
[e] Change (%) in 1996 less the average change (%) over previous three years;
[f] June 1997;
[g] Unclear from source, but probably average of 1996 and 1997;
[h] 1997 estimates;
[i] May 1996;
[j] Growth of credit to private sector relative to nominal GDP, 1996;
[k] June 1997;
[l] June 1997;
[m] Equal weights to all fundamentals (including two others included in original sources);
[n] Greater weights given to fundamentals in which Thailand is weakest
SOURCE: Goldstein and Hawkins (1998b).

in the case of the East Asian crisis, where Thailand had the worst fundamentals, followed by Indonesia, which was the most severely impacted by the crisis. Hong Kong and Singapore, which seem to have had the best fundamentals, were the least affected, and Malaysia and the Philippines were somewhat "in between".

An important agenda for empirical research is how relevant the various causes of contagion were in the case of the East Asian crisis. In any case, regardless of the exact transmission mechanisms and definitions (Rajan 2000b), there is an important message that emanates from the above discussion — economic policy slippages in any one economy can and do reverberate rapidly to other economies in the region in the form of contagious currency crises, with consequent detrimental effects on the real economies.[4] This in turn provides the analytical basis for encouraging some sort of "peer pressure", "club spirit" or some broader form of economic co-operation that promotes the pursuit of sustainable and prudent macroeconomic policies in each economy in the region.

Financial and Macroeconomic Co-operation in ASEAN: Existing Policy Initiatives

Since the 1990s, ASEAN has gradually but increasingly been looked upon as a vehicle for deepening regional economic linkages, epitomized by the launch of the ASEAN Free Trade Area (AFTA) in 1992. Given this shifting focus of ASEAN to economic issues, one would have expected the alliance to play a leading role in regional co-operative initiatives to tackle the crisis. Indeed, in the areas of financial and macroeconomic co-operation, ASEAN has been actively promoting schemes such as the intensified use of ASEAN currencies in regional trade through the creation of a network of Bilateral Payments Arrangements (BPA) and the creation of regional bond markets (Setboonsarng 1998). Without minimizing the importance of these and other initiatives, undoubtedly the single most important regional initiative was the endorsement by the ASEAN finance ministers in November 1997 of a regional monitoring system in Manila to complement and supplement the IMF's global surveillance role.

The ASEAN Surveillance Process (ASP)

The ASEAN Surveillance Process (ASP) was initially under the purview of the Asian Development Bank (ADB) before being transferred to the ASEAN Secretariat in Jakarta. The overall objectives of the ASP are broadly to: (a) assist ASEAN members in spotting a potential crisis and responding to it accordingly; (b) assess the vulnerability of ASEAN members to financial disruptions and crises; (c) improve the co-ordination of ASEAN members' economic policies through the dissemination of sound practices that meet international standards; and (d) promote a "peer monitoring" environment among ASEAN members through a review of potentially vulnerable sectors[5] (ADBI 1998). Conceptually, the ASP was envisaged to involve not only conventional macroeconomic indicators, but also to examine the regulatory and supervisory functions in the financial sector, corporate governance issues, and various measures of external indebtedness. While the IMF's Article IV arrangements with member countries involve bilateral discussions, the ASP has taken a regional approach, somewhat akin to the Organization for Economic Co-operation and Development (OECD). The ASP is supervised by a Select Committee of ASEAN central banker governors and finance ministers.

An ASEAN Surveillance Quality (ASQ) Unit has been established in the ASEAN Secretariat in Jakarta, Indonesia.[6] The ASQ is responsible for the construction of indicators to monitor the regional economies (focusing on macrospecific areas) and the preparation of surveillance reports for the ASEAN Select Committee. The ADB is to provide the ASP with various regional technical assistance (RETA) projects. The ADB has recently established an in-house Regional Economic Monitoring Unit (REMU) to assist in its regional operations. The REMU co-ordinates and implements the ADB's RETA projects for the ASP. This project assistance involves providing inputs to the ASP reports (the first report of the ASP was submitted to the Select Committee in October 1999) and generally strengthening the research and technical capacities of ASEAN officials on surveillance-related matters. The REMU has been fortified by assistance from AUSAID and has set up an Asian Recovery Information Centre (ARIC) (launched in November 1999). The ARIC consolidates all information (data and research) on the ASEAN and East Asian economies most directly impacted by the regional crisis.[7]

Potential Constraints on the Effectiveness of the ASP

While the ASP has gotten off the ground, one has to be concerned about how effective it can and will really be for a number of reasons.

The first potential impediment to a well-functioning monitoring mechanism has to do with the lack of transparency in economic data and general public documentation of economic and financial activities in the region. To be sure, the authorities in the region have tended to be less than forthcoming about their economic and financial situations, and have used economic data as a strategic tool rather than a public good. The need to establish benchmarks for timely and accurate data is essential if foreign investors and lenders are to be able to make rational and economically viable decisions with reasonably accurate perceptions of risks and benefits.[8]

The second constraint has to do with the *real-politik* of ASEAN. Substantial asymmetries in the sizes, levels and stages of economic development of member nations, on the one hand, and the ASEAN policy of strict non-intervention in one another's affairs (economic and particularly political), on the other, may make it extremely difficult to operate a regional surveillance mechanism effectively. This is so, as criticisms of an economy's misguided and unsustainable economic policies may be perceived as being incompatible with the "ASEAN spirit". Lastly, notwithstanding assistance from the ADB, there is a question of whether ASEAN has the institutional capacity to develop an effective surveillance mechanism on a regular basis, given its small and poorly financed Secretariat in Jakarta and loose and highly decentralized organizational structure.

The above obstacles are not insignificant. For instance, the ASEAN Secretary-General, Rudolfo Severino, reportedly stated in late 1998 that the ASEAN Secretariat's inability to manage and supervise the mechanism and the reluctance by some member economies to reveal "too much" information and data, have been the primary reasons for the initial slow progress (Nath 1998). It remains doubtful whether these issues have been adequately sorted out since then.

Manila Framework

In the light of these constraints, the effectiveness of the regional surveillance process might be enhanced if this were extended to

include the APEC economies. This would provide greater
opportunities (and resources) for developing the Asia-Pacific
economies to benefit from the expertise of the more advanced
members of APEC. As noted previously, from the perspective of
contagion, during the East Asian crisis, the eventual currency crisis
in South Korea was in part caused by contagion from ASEAN, the
Korean crisis in turn reverberating back to Southeast Asia. Similarly,
withdrawals of bank loans by Japan and South Korean banks played
an important role in intensifying the crisis in ASEAN (Kaminsky
and Reinhart 2000).

Presumably in recognition of this, ASEAN finance ministers and
central bankers have significantly intensified intraregional
consultations as well as those with other key economies in the larger
East Asian region (such as China, Japan and Korea) since 1997. In
fact, ASEAN has been among the drivers of APEC's Manila
Framework for Enhanced Asian Regional Cooperation to Promote
Financial Stability, which was agreed to at the Fifth APEC Summit
in Vancouver in November 1997. The Framework included the
following initiatives[9]: (a) a co-operative financing arrangement that
would supplement IMF resources; (b) enhanced economic and
technical co-operation, particularly in strengthening domestic
financial systems and regulatory capacities; and (c) a mechanism
for regional surveillance to complement the IMF's global
surveillance.

Little public information is available for an objective evaluation
of the progress and accomplishments to date of the Manila
Framework. Apparently, the recent push towards maximum
transparency by the IMF and the World Bank and the availability of
timely information on their activities for public consumption has
not rubbed off onto the regional bodies in Asia![10] At the very least,
the discussion of surveillance results at the ASEAN/APEC levels
ought to be made readily available along the lines of the IMF's Public
Informational Notices (PINs) after the Executive Board's discussions
of policy papers and Article IV consultations. Indeed, the IMF
Executive Board recently agreed to release the Letters of Intent,
Memoranda of Economic and Financial Policies, and Policy
Framework Papers that underlie IMF-supported country programmes
(*IMF Survey*, 27 September 1999). ASEAN, APEC and the regional
organizations in East Asia should follow suit, taking the attitude that
the greater the transparency and timely availability of information
(not just data), the better.

All this being said, one does recognize the need to balance this push towards transparency, on the one hand, and the need for the regional economies to want to preserve some degree of confidentiality, on the other. However, as a rule, the bias in the case of ASEAN/APEC at present is clearly towards confidentiality, which is at odds with that of greater disclosure by the international community.

Towards Enhanced Regional Financial and Macroeconomic Co-operation in East Asia.

Having highlighted the major regional initiatives that have been undertaken in the financial and macroeconomic spheres in ASEAN (and APEC), the next question that arises is what further types of co-operative arrangements ought to be undertaken in light of the regional dimension of contagion. For reasons noted above, in the areas of financial and macroeconomic co-operation, it makes more sense to think in terms of larger Asia-wide co-operative initiatives, with ASEAN playing a key influencing role in the larger region.[11]

The Executives' Meeting of East Asia-Pacific (EMEAP) Central Banks

In this regard, the East Asian and Pacific region does, in fact, already have an existing co-operative scheme in place in the form of the EMEAP, or the Executives' Meeting of East Asia-Pacific Central Banks. The EMEAP is a co-operative organization comprising central banks and monetary authorities of eleven economies: Australia, China, Hong Kong, Indonesia, Japan, South Korea, Malaysia, New Zealand, the Philippines, Singapore and Thailand. Its primary objective is to strengthen the co-operative relationship among its members. The EMEAP's activities broadly encompass three levels: (a) annual meetings of the EMEAP governors; (b) semi-annual ones involving the deputy governor; and (c) three Working Groups on Banking Supervision, Financial Markets and Payments and Settlement Systems. Specifically, while the deputy governors have been meeting regularly since 1991, the governors have started doing so only since 1996, with four meetings since then: the first and third in Tokyo (19 July 1996 and 14 July 1998), the second in Shanghai

(25 July 1997), and the fourth in Hong Kong (9 July 1999). Each
of these meetings have had a broad theme: the first was on the
"means of strengthening central bank cooperation to enhance
financial stability and market development in the region"; the second
was on "asset prices and (their) impact on monetary policy"; the
third on the "relationship between international investment and
financial stability"; and the fourth on the "international financial
architecture".[12] It was only after the governors started their regular
meetings from 1996 that the EMEAP became fairly active (and
certainly took on a higher profile), with the establishment of the
various Working Groups noted above.

In addition to the Working Groups, following — indeed, spurred
on by — the Tequila crisis of 1994–95, substantive steps towards
monetary co-operation have been taken by the EMEAP. For instance,
a number of member economies signed a series of bilateral
repurchase (repo) agreements in 1995 and 1996. Hong Kong and
Singapore also reached an agreement to intervene in foreign
exchange markets on behalf of the Bank of Japan (Moreno 1997).
These creditor regional economies also attempted to help defend
the Thai baht for a period before the Bank of Thailand succumbed
to the speculative pressures.

A useful starting point might simply be to expand the scope of
the EMEAP itself rather than to establish an entirely new framework/
organization. This is so not only because of the well-documented
fact that the economies in the East Asian region are generally averse
towards building new institutions, but also because of the EMEAP's
close linkages with the regional Bank for International Settlements
(BIS) and the IMF (since the EMEAP is, after all, a body of central
bankers). An appropriate and realistic charter for the EMEAP might
be to focus primarily on its original goals of enhancing regional
monetary and financial co-operation; exchanging and pooling of
information; and coming to the aid of regional currencies that are
susceptible to speculative pressures (Rajan 2000b).

However, in order to be a more effective deterrent against such
attacks (that is, monetary defence mechanisms), a monetary facility
could be established, with "appropriate" contributions from member
economies of the EMEAP, thus ensuring the availability of a large
pool of reserves. The ability to access this pool of funds and reduce
moral hazard concerns (that is, the ready availability of "easy/cheap
money") ought to be conditional on/tied to the member economies

maintaining some predetermined standards of macroeconomic and financial stability, and, if and when necessary, be willing to subject themselves to peer pressure to undertake necessary policy adjustments.[13] Obviously, such macro-cum-prudential oversight needs to be complemented by both peer review (as defined in note 5) and an effective regional surveillance process-cum-early warnings system that tracks national, regional, and international macroeconomic developments, and facilitates necessary policy corrections in a timely manner. Seen in this light, one could easily envisage the ASP being expanded to include the other non-ASEAN members of the EMEAP and possibly even being housed in the latter.[14]

Regional Bank for International Settlements (BIS) and Lender of Last Resort (RLLR)

While more contentious, a "beefed up" EMEAP could be seen as a step towards the creation of an Asian Regional Bank for International Settlements (BIS). Such a body would ensure the development of region-wide banking and financial sector standards and codes (consistent with international best practices) and monitoring their implementation in addition to taking on the role of a *de facto* regional lender of last resort (RLLR) prior to a crisis (Sasaki 1996; and Grenville 1998).[15] With a regional body playing a major role in setting and ensuring implementation of such standards, this may engender a greater sense of "ownership" of the standards and norms by the regional member economies. This stands in sharp contrast to the current situation, where there seems to be a "top-down" approach towards such issues, with decisions being made largely by the G-7 (group of seven) industrialized economies with little input from the smaller, developing ones.[16]

The suggestion of a RLLR warrants some discussion. There are, of course, a number of well-known difficulties with the lender of last resort (LLR) function, particularly at the international level (that is, ILLR). These range from the usual moral hazard problem, which may lead to overborrowing and overlending, to the costs of international institution-building. In addition, there is the perennial question of whether an ILLR would have sufficient resources to create confidence that its operations will be successful.[17] Uncertainties over the liquidity of an ILLR would undoubtedly undermine its credibility and its powers of stabilization. Unlike the ILLR, an Asian RLLR has the capacity to raise funds when needed, and is not exposed to the same type of resource constraints. To be sure, Japan alone holds about US$200 billion in foreign reserves (excluding gold), China, Hong Kong, Singapore, Taiwan, and Korea together hold about US$400 billion, while India, Thailand, and Malaysia hold another US$70 billion in aggregate. By comparison, the United States holds US$70 billion and the European Union US$350 billion.[18] The moral hazard problem of an LLR function ought to be reduced at the regional level, where the other member economies can exercise peer pressure.[19]

The resources of the regional body could be further consolidated if it negotiates guaranteed lines of credit with private banks on behalf of its member economies in times of distress. This is not unlike the Argentine arrangement, in which the country entered into an agreement in December 1996 with a group of thirteen foreign banks to lend Argentina up to US$6.1 billion, against collateral at a premium over the London Interbank Offer Rate (LIBOR) for a certain "commitment fee". In the case of East Asia, a large part of the pre-crisis lending was by regional — mainly Japanese — banks (Table 6.4).[20] Thus, a regional body may have greater "leverage" over the private banking community and be able to play a more effective co-ordinating role between them and its regional members.

TABLE 6.4
Nationality of Banks Providing Loans ($ billions) to Southeast Asia as at June 1997 and Mexico as at June 1994

From / *To*	*Japan* (1)	*Germany* (2)	*France* (3)	*USA* (4)	*UK* (5)	*Hong Kong* (6)	*Total*[1] (7)	*1/7* (%)	*(2+3+5)/7* (%)	*4/7* (%)
Indonesia	23	6	5	5	4	6	61	37.7	24.5	6.6
Thailand	38	8	5	4	3	18	99	38.3	16.1	4.0
Malaysia	10	6	2	2	2	3	33	30.3	33.3	8.5
Philippines	2	2	3	3	1	4	17	11.8	35.2	6.1
Mexico (June 1994)	4	4	20	20	16	0	71	5.6	32.4	28.2

NOTE: [1] Includes economies not listed in this table.
SOURCE: Goldstein and Hawkins (1998a).

Common Basket Peg

A number of economists have proposed the creation of a common currency basket for the East Asian economies (Kusukawa 1999; and Williamson 1999a, b).[21] Invariably, such a common currency basket would require greater co-ordination among participating monetary authorities. Kusukawa (1999) actually goes on to recommend the establishment of a regional body to support the common basket system — possibly some kind of regional monetary facility. The argument in favour of a currency basket is far from settled. For instance, Rajan (2000a) finds that the computed weights of the yen in the optimal baskets of individual economies (using data for 1996–97) seem quite dissimilar, and suggests that individual basket pegs may be preferable for the time being. However, if all the regional economies do pursue such a currency basket regime, it may be the case that, over time, the optimal basket pegs for the regional economies may see a convergence. A common basket may then be economically justifiable and politically tenable. In such a case, the "beefed up" and expanded EMEAP (in terms of functions, membership, and resources) might be the "natural" co-ordinating monetary authority to deal with such a currency basket regime.

Concluding Observations

The first part of this chapter provided the analytical basis for enhanced regional co-operation in the spheres of financial and monetary co-operation. The emphasis was on detailing the various transmission channels leading to regional contagion or negative spillovers, with a speculative attack, and resulting devaluation-induced recession in one economy possibly infecting the neighbouring economies. Broadly, a distinction was made between "pure contagion" (that is, regional spillovers that cannot be accounted for by trade and finance linkages), on the one hand, and "interdependencies" (which can be accounted for by trade and finance linkages), on the other. It was noted that existing currency crises models of contagion — which require the existence of multiple equilibra — suggest that the regional economies must have some existing weakness in "fundamentals" to be negatively impacted by a currency crisis in a regional economy.

Available theory and evidence suggest that *pure contagion* is not random or arbitrary. This underscores the need for the primary focus to be placed squarely on the domestic policy arena. In the ASEAN context, this broadly involves strengthening the financial systems and corporate and industrial structures. However, given the fact that regional *interdependencies* (whether real or financial) are fairly high in ASEAN, even relatively "strong" regional economies can be and have been affected by crises in the "weaker" neighbouring economies. These geographically concentrated policy externalities suggest the need for some form of regional co-operation in the financial and macroeconomic spheres.

Some might argue that *pure contagion* may be less important in the future, as investors seem to have differentiated between the regional economies following the crisis (Van Rijckeghem and Weder 1999). This view is clearly debatable. In any case, indications are that at least regional *interdependencies* will probably rise significantly in the future, as the stronger economies, such as Singapore, have sharply escalated their investments in economies such as Thailand.[22]

It was noted that the major initiative to date in ASEAN has been the ASEAN Surveillance Process. It has been suggested that there may be a strong case for shifting the focus from the surveillance of only ASEAN economies to the larger East Asian region. In fact, the Manila Framework, which ASEAN members played an important role in shaping, explicitly set out regional surveillance as one of the goals. However, the failure of both ASEAN and APEC to provide more timely and up-to-date information on the progress and achievements (or lack thereof) of the initiatives, has precluded a detailed evaluation of either of them. The most promising regional surveillance effort (or at least the one on which most information is currently available) seems to be the recently established Regional Economic Monitoring Unit within the ADB.

The chapter then shifted focus to the issue of concrete policy proposals for future co-operation. There are no doubt a number of "soft" regional co-operative initiatives of importance that could be taken up by the regional economies, in the form of human resource development and training, information gathering and dissemination, experience sharing/policy dialogue, and such.[23] These are fairly uncontroversial and are not dealt with here. Rather, the focus of this chapter was on one substantive/major proposal — namely, the expansion of the role of the EMEAP, so as to act as the central co-ordinating body for regional financial and macroeconomic co-operation. It was suggested that the EMEAP might be the appropriate body within which a regional monetary facility could be established. The primary responsibility would be to assist member economies in times of financial market turbulence and weakness, as opposed to acting as a "substitute" to the functions of international organizations like the IMF. If anything, just the opposite is true, as such a "fortified" and expanded EMEAP-cum-regional facility could play a highly complementary role to the IMF in aiding distressed economies during the crisis management and resolution periods.

The reason for suggesting the expansion and "beefing up" of a credible existing regional body, rather than proposing an entirely new standing institution in East Asia, is the recognition of the region's concerns about developing layers of institutions. Drawing an analogy to international institutional arrangements, what has been proposed here is one organization effectively taking on some functions of the BIS, IMF, and various sector-specific international groupings or regulators, supervisors and central bank experts, as summarized by Teitmeyer (1999). If this is found infeasible (for whatever reason[24]), a distinct organization to deal with some of the above issues could be established, though the lines of functional responsibilities with the EMEAP and other regional alliances would need to be clearly worked out.

No doubt, there will be a number of sceptics to such a proposal. It is, however, insufficient to merely find fault with the proposed scheme. Rodrik (1999, p. 3) has argued that:

> (a)s long as capital flows remain large relative to the liquid assets held by national governments and are easily reversible, the international economy will be hostage to spectacular boom and bust cycles.

Insofar as this is true, and given the absence of substantive steps towards the reform of the monetary and financial architecture at an international level,[25] alternative policies and initiatives for regional financial and macroeconomic co-operation need to be put forward as "self-help" mechanisms for the small open economies in ASEAN in this era of globalization of capital flows.

NOTES

1   See Corsetti et al. (1998); Radelet and Sachs (1998a, b); and Rajan (1999a)
    for detailed, data-intensive discussions of the East Asian crisis.
2   This section draws on Rajan (2000b).
3   There is no firm consensus yet as to what is meant by "fundamentals".
    However, empirical analyses have found that the strength of the domestic
    financial/banking sector, the extent of lending booms, the degree of currency
    overvaluation and the size and maturity structure of external debt, are
    among the most important variables to be concerned about (see, for instance,
    Krueger et al. 1998; and Tornell 1999). De Gregario and Valdes (1999) find
    that the likelihood of a contagion attack is inversely related to the average
    debt maturity structure.
4   It is easy to show how an initial devaluation could actually prove to be
    contradictory in the short and medium terms, with the domestic financial
    and corporate sectors caught in a downward spiral, leading to a sharp
    discrete decline in the domestic currency following the initial breakdown
    of the exchange rate peg. This point is developed within a simple "bank-
    centred" Mundell-Fleming framework (Rajan and Sugema 1999).
5   While the terms "peer review" or "peer monitoring" have come into vogue
    in ASEAN and the international financial community as a whole, they have
    usually been left undefined. Former Bundesbank president, Hans Tietmeyer
    (1998), provided the most succinct and effective definition, when he
    referred to:

>   the importance of assessing domestic vulnerabilities in the light of evolving
>   global conditions, as well as of relaying such assessments to interested parties
>   to forestall delays in correcting inadequate structures and destabilising trends.

6   See "ADB Supports ASEAN Surveillance Process", *ASEAN Press Release*,
    25 March 1998.
7   The website of the ARIC project is *http:// www.aric.adb.org.*
8   The theoretical basis for the need to provide accurate and timely economic
    data and related information is seen in the new capital-crisis models (Calvo
    1998).
9   See the *APEC Economic Leaders' Declaration*, "Strengthening the
    Foundations for Growth", 18 November 1998.
10 In search of details of both the ASP and substantive progress on an
    APEC-wide basis, I undertook a detailed search of recent articles,
    statements, etc. on the ASP and Manila Framework on the websites of APEC
    (*http://www.apecsec.org.sg/*); ASEAN (*http://www.aseansec.org/*); and the
    ADB (*http://www.adb.org/*). The search proved almost totally unfruitful!
    The most informative source of regional surveillance arrangements was that
    available on the new ARIC website (see note 7).
11 This is broadly consistent with Plummer's (1998) analysis of the nexus
    between ASEAN and APEC. Specifically, he noted that:

>   APEC will continue to be "nested" in ASEAN in that the subregional
>   organisation is playing a central role in moulding the direction of APEC to
>   be consistent with the goals of ASEAN economic cooperation.

The remainder of this section focuses on a single key proposal for regional co-operation.

12   Information on EMEAP is available on their website: *http://www.emeap.org:8084/*

13   There are a number of other channels and mechanisms through which regional or international support may create moral hazard concerns and the accompanying perverse incentive structures (though many do tend to be exaggerated). No attempt is made in this chapter to tackle this subject systematically.

14   We have not directly tackled issues arising from Australia's and New Zealand's membership, that is, is the facility purely East Asia-focused (and if so, which ones), or should it be expanded beyond the EMEAP members to include others in APEC or even non-APEC Asian countries of significance, such as India, for that matter (which has been included in the new G-20 forum noted in the next subsection)? The Japanese Government, for instance, hosted a "Tokyo Dialogue" in December 1997 among finance ministry officials and central bankers of ASEAN, China, South Korea, and India. Would this be an appropriate grouping? The chairman of the Pacific Economic Cooperation Council's Financial Market Development Group (PECC-FMD), Jesus Estanislao (1999a, p. 10) has noted:

> (o)n a functional basis..(PECC-FMD)..(has) followed the financial markets in their judgements that in East Asia — as the financial and economic crisis has shown — ten economies have to consult more freely with each other. Indonesia, Malaysia, the Philippines, Singapore and Thailand are the original ASEAN 5. Japan, China, Hong Kong, Chinese Taipei and South Korea are APEC economies in North East Asia. These economies are the East Asian 10. They are the very core of crisis Asia.

Comparing Estanislao's suggestion to existing membership of EMEAP, the non-East Asian economies of Australia and New Zealand are excluded (though both have been actively involved in the PECC-FMD activities), but Chinese Taipei is included.

15   The Asian BIS concept was initially put forward in 1995 by the former governor of the Reserve Bank of Australia, Bernard Fraser.

16   Admittedly, there have been some improvements in representation following the East Asian crisis, with the establishment of the G-20 and other international financial groupings that have included representatives from developing economies in the consultation process (Rajan 2000b).

17   As noted by the deputy governor of the Bank of England, Mervyn King (1999):

> (t)he current resources of the IMF — between US$125 billion and US$150 billion depending on how they are measured — are wholly inadequate for an ILOLR. Nor are resources on the appropriate scale likely to be forthcoming.

Indeed, with the new Supplemental Reserve Facility (SRF) introduced at the end of 1997, which enables economies to far exceed the conventional quota-based limits on borrowing from the IMF, the increased lending activity has created liquidity problems for the institution. For recent discussions of the IMF and the ILLR function, see Fischer (1999) and Giannini (1999).

18 Figures are as of mid-1998 from the *Economist* magazine, and Tateishi (1998). Data for the EU excludes Finland, Greece, Ireland, Luxembourg, and Portugal.

19 Following the U.S.-assisted bail-out of Mexico, the argument has sometimes been made that the United States has been the *de facto* LLR for Mexico.

20 See Peek and Rosengren (1998) for a detailed discussion of Japanese bank lending to ASEAN during the crisis period. See also Kaminsky and Reinhart (2000), who rightly emphasize that the sharp escalation in bank lending to East Asia just prior to the crisis was largely due to the European banks.

21 Note that the focus is on a *currency basket* and not on a *common currency*. In the light of the turbulence faced by the East Asian economies following the regional crisis, on the one hand, and the seemingly successful introduction of the euro by the European Union (EU), on the other, leaders of ASEAN agreed to study the feasibility of a common ASEAN currency system (announced as part of the latest ASEAN summit meeting in Hanoi and included in the Hanoi Plan of Action; *Business Times*, Singapore, 15 December 1998). From an economic standpoint, Bayoumi and Mauro (1999) and Eichengreen and Bayoumi (1999) have suggested that East Asia may be as close to — or, rather, as far away from — being an optimum currency area (OCA) as Western Europe. However, the European experience has emphasized the need for strong political will and consensus towards such a policy goal. As they go on to note, such leadership and single-mindedness does not seem to be present in ASEAN or the larger East Asian region at the current time.

22 Thus, figures from the Thai Central Bank show Singapore's direct investment in Thailand to have jumped to 31.7 billion baht in 1998, an increase from 9.9 billion baht in 1997, making Singapore the third largest investor in the country after the United States and Japan (*Far Eastern Economic Review*, 21 October 1999, p. 68).

23 For instance, while sharing the view of this chapter that the initial emphasis must be on domestic reforms, Estanislao (1999b) has proposed the setting up of a "Regional Stability Forum" to allow for more systematic co-operation in the areas of human resources development and training, information and experience sharing, and other "soft" forms of co-operation on a sustained and regular basis. He envisages that such a forum would be a first step towards a "long-term, ambitious program (of) coordination and joint actions", including considerations of an eventual monetary union.

24 For instance, there may be some who support an Asian-type BIS but may not necessarily support a regional monetary facility (though one has to wonder about the rationale for the objections in the light of the discussion here).

25 While this is an overused term, Eichengreen (1999) notes that initiatives under way under the banner of "reform of the international financial architecture" are (ought to be) organized under four pillars: international

standards, Chilean-type taxes on short-term foreign borrowing; greater exchange rate flexibility; and collective action clauses in loan contracts as an alternative to IMF bail-outs. As he further notes (pp. 3–4) of such initiatives:

> (t)he danger is that the process losing steam … (A)s time passes, the sense of urgency recedes and second thoughts inevitably develop.

REFERENCES

Asian Development Bank Institute (ADBI). "Executive Summary of Workshop on Economic Monitoring of Financial Systems in East and Southeast Asia". Mimeographed. ADB, 1998.

Bayoumi, T., and P. Mauro. "The Suitability of ASEAN for a Regional Currency Arrangement". Working Paper 99/162. IMF, 1999.

Calvo, G. "Varieties of Capital Market Crises". *The Debt Burden and its Consequences for Monetary Policy,* edited M. King. New York: St. Martin's Press, 1998.

Corsetti, G., P. Pesenti and N. Roubini. "What Caused the Asian Currency and Financial Crisis?" Mimeographed. March 1998.

De Gregario, J., and R. Valdes. "Crisis Transmission: Evidence from the Debt, Tequila, and Asian Flu Crises". Mimeographed. October 1999.

Eichengreen, B. "Strengthening the International Financial Architecture: Where Do We Stand?" Mimeographed. October 1999b.

Eichengreen, B. and T. Bayoumi. "Is Asia an Optimum Currency Area? Can It Become One? Regional, Global and Historical Perspectives on Asian Monetary Relations". In *Exchange Rate Policies in Asian Emerging Countries,* edited by S. Collignon and J. Pisani-Ferri. London: Routledge, 1999.

Estanislao, J. "New Cooperation in East Asia: Peer Assistance and Review". In *Working with Peers for Financial Reforms in East Asia.* Manila, Philippines: Foundation for Community-Building in the Asia-Pacific, 1999a.

————. "Toward a Regional Stability Forum". In *Working with Peers for Financial Reforms in East Asia.* Manila, Philippines: Foundation for Community-Building in the Asia-Pacific, 1999b.

Fischer, S. "On the Need for an International Lender of Last Resort". Paper presented at the American Economic Association, New York, 3 January 1999.

Giannini, C. "The IMF and the Lender-of-Last-Resort Function: An External View". *Finance and Development* 36 (1999).

Goldstein, M. and J. Hawkins. "The Origin of the Asian Financial Turmoil". Research Discussion Paper RDP9805. Reserve Bank of Australia, May 1998a.

————. "The Role of Contagion in the Asian Financial Crisis". Mimeographed. Reserve Bank of Australia, 1998b.

Grenville, D. "The Asian Crisis and Regional Co-operation". Paper presented at the International Seminar on East Asian Financial Crisis, Beijing, 21 April 1998.

Institute of International Finance (IIF). "Capital Flows to Emerging Market Economies". April 1999.

Kaminsky, G., and C. Reinhart. "Bank Lending and Contagion: Evidence from the Asian Crisis". In *Regional and Global Capital Flows: Macroeconomic Causes and Consequences,* edited by T. Ito and A. Krueger. Chicago: University of Chicago Press, 2000.

Katada, S. "The Japanese Government in Two Mexican Financial Crises: An Emerging International Lender-of-Last Resort?" *Pacific Affairs* 7 (1998): 61–79.

King, M. "Reforming the International Financial System: The Middle Way". Speech delivered at the Federal Reserve Bank of New York, 9 September 1999.

Krueger, M., P. Osakwe and J. Page. "Fundamentals, Contagion and Currency Crises: An Empirical Analysis". Working Paper 98–10. Bank of Canada, 1998.

Kusukawa, T. *Asian Currency Reform: The Options of a Common Basket Peg.* Tokyo: Fuji Research Institute Corporation, 1999.

Lane, T. and Associates. *IMF-Supported Programs in Indonesia, Korea, and Thailand: A Preliminary Assessment.* Washington, D.C.: IMF, 1999.

Masson, P. "Contagion: Monsoonal Effects, Spillovers, and Jumps between Multiple Equilibria". Working Paper 98/142. IMF, 1998.

Masson, P. and M. Mussa. "The Role of the IMF: Financing and Its Interactions with Adjustment and Surveillance". Pamphlet Series No. 50. International Monetary Fund, 1997.

Moreno, R. "Dealing with Currency Speculation in the Asian Pacific Basin". Economic Letter No. 97-10. Federal Reserve Board of San Francisco, 1997.

Nath, A. "The Financial Crisis". *Asia 21* (November 1998): 56–60.

Obstfeld, M. "The Logic of Currency Crises". *Cahiers Economiques Et Monetaries 43.* Banque De France, 1994.

Peek, J., and E. Rosengren. "Japanese Banking Problems: Implications for Southeast Asia". Mimeographed. October 1998.

Plummer, M. "ASEAN and Institutional Nesting in the Asia-Pacific". In *Asia-Pacific Crossroads: Regime Creation and the Future of APEC,* edited by V. Aggarwal and C. Morrison. New York: St Martin's Press, 1988.

Radelet, S., and J. Sachs. "The Onset of the East Asian Financial Crisis". In *Currency Crises,* edited by P. Krugman. Chicago: University of Chicago Press, 1998a.

————. "The East Asian Financial Crisis: Diagnosis, Remedies, Prospects". *Brookings Papers on Economic Activity* 1 (1998b): 1–74.

Rajan, R. "Economic Collapse in Southeast Asia". *Policy Study.* Claremont, California: The Lowe Institute of Political Economy, July 1999a.

_____ . "Selected Policy Issues for Financial Stability". In *Working with Peers for Financial Reforms in East Asia.* Manila, Philippines: Foundation for Community-Building in the Asia-Pacific, 1999b.

_____ . "Examining the Case for Currency Basket Regimes for Southeast Asia?". Visiting Researchers Series No.1. Singapore: Institute of Southeast Asian Studies, 2000a.

_____ . "Examining the Case for an Asian Monetary Fund". Visiting Researchers Series No.3. Singapore: Institute of Southeast Asian Studies, 2000b.

Rajan, R. and I. Sugema. "Capital Flows and the Credit Transmission Channel in Southeast Asia". Discussion Paper 99/25. Centre for International Economic Studies, University of Adelaide, 1999.

Rodrik, D. "Governing the Global Economy: Does One Architectural Style Fit All?" Mimeographed. July 1999.

Sasaki, F. "Significance and Feasibility of the Asian BIS Concept". *Nomura Asia Focus Quarterly* (Winter 1996/97), pp. 34–39.

Setboonsarng, S. "ASEAN Economic Co-operation: Adjusting to the Crisis". *Southeast Asian Affairs 1998.* Singapore: Institute of Southeast Asian Studies, 1998.

Tateishi, T. "The Plaza Accord Saved America from Fiscal Downfall". *Asia 21* (November 1998): 24–25.

Tietmeyer, Hans. "Evolving Cooperation and Coordination in Financial Market Surveillance". *Finance and Development* 36 (1999).

Tornell, A. "Common Fundamentals in the Tequila and Asian Crises". Working Paper 7139. NBER, 1999.

Van Rijckeghem, C., and B. Weder. "Financial Contagion: Spillovers Through Banking Centres". Mimeographed. September 1999.

Williamson, J. "The Case for a Common Basket Peg for East Asian Currencies". In *Exchange Rate Policies in Asian Emerging Countries,* edited by S. Collignon and J. Pisani-Ferri. London: Routledge, 1999a.

_____ . "Future Exchange Rate Regimes for Developing East Asia: Exploring the Policy Options". Paper presented at a conference on "Asia in Economic Recovery: Policy Options for Growth and Stability", organized by the Institute of Policy Studies, Singapore, 21–22 June 1999b.

7

Food Security in ASEAN

MYA THAN

Introduction

The ASEAN Eminent Persons Group (EPG), in June 1999, decided
to draft the following proposals for the ASEAN Summit in 2000.
They included the ASEAN Vision 2020, and proposals related to
Post-Asian Crisis Economic Scenarios, Food Security, ASEAN
Monetary Fund, and Civil Societies. Among these, the food security
issue has been a top priority subject in ASEAN for some time. The
ASEAN Ministers of Agriculture and Forestry (AMAF) oversee the
co-operative efforts in the area of food, agriculture, and forestry in
the region. It has established several priority areas: to promote the
food, agriculture, and forestry sectors. Among them, strengthening
food security in the region has been given top priority. This is
because the incidence of malnutrition in Asia, according to the Food
and Agriculture Organization (FAO) estimates, accounts for nearly
two-thirds of the chronically undernourished in the world. It further
indicates that by the year 2010, Asia will account for one-half of
the world's malnourished population (FAO 1998, p. 1).

   This suggests that food security is an issue that needs to be
addressed urgently, and it will continue to be an important issue in
the future. For the purpose of this study, the definition of "food

security" will be borrowed from the FAO. According to the FAO, "food security is generally understood as access to adequate food to all households at all times to enable them to lead a healthy and active life" (FAO 1998, p. 79).

Hence, the objective of this chapter is to review the food security situation in the region in the framework of the economic and social environment and to explore ways and means to ensure food security in the region in the short-term and long-term perspectives. The first section will analyse the economic and social performance of the region in general and the salient features of Southeast Asian agriculture in particular. The second section will address the status of food security in the region in terms of adequacy, stability, and the quality of food. The third section will discuss the software issues, such as macro policy reforms, agricultural development policies, and programmes related to food security. The impact of the regional crisis on food security will be discussed next. The conclusion will sum up the findings of the study and discuss the problems and challenges of the region with regard to food security.

Macroeconomic and Social Performance, and Agricultural Situation in ASEAN

Despite rapid urbanization and industrialization in the region, nearly three-quarters of the population continue to live in the rural areas where most of them depend on agriculture for meagre employment and income. Hence, agricultural and rural development is closely related to food security and a key component of poverty alleviation in the region. This is the reason why this section will explore and analyse the agricultural situation in the ASEAN member countries.

Southeast Asia is a large geographical region composed of ten countries all of which are members of ASEAN, as of April 1999. The region has diverse historical, geographical, cultural, ethnical, and language characteristics, with varied natural endowments and different levels of development. It can be divided into two subgroups based on income and development level (Table 7.1). The first subgroup includes countries with middle-level income, such as Indonesia, Malaysia, Philippines and Thailand (ASEAN-4). Singapore and Brunei are excluded from this group as the agricultural sector does not play an important role in their

TABLE 7.1
Socio-economic Indicators (1995)

	Population (mil.)*	Area ('000 km²)	GNP($) (per/cap)	Literacy (%)	Life Expectancy	CPI (%)#
Cambodia	10.2	181	270	65	53	7.5
Indonesia	203.5	1,905	980	84	64	8.8
Laos	4.7	237	350	57	52	22.6
Malaysia	21.0	330	3,980	83	71	3.3
Myanmar	46.8	677	280**	83	59	26.4
Philippines	70.7	300	1050	95	66	9.8
Thailand	59.2	513	2,740	94	69	5.0
Vietnam	76.6	332	240	94	68	12.7

NOTE: *   for 1997, from UN/ESCAP (1998)
         #   for 1985–95, from FAO (1998)
         ** estimate
SOURCE: World Bank, *World Development Report*, 1997 and 1998.

economies. The other subgroup includes Cambodia, Laos, Myanmar, and Vietnam, which are low-income countries and known as newly emerging transitional economies of mainland Southeast Asia (TEMSEA). Cambodia and Laos have been excluded in the later part of this study because of the lack of relevant data.

Compared with other Southeast Asian countries, TEMSEA are more dependent on agriculture, which is the dominant sector in terms of output, employment, and exports (see Table 7.2 and 7.3). Before the reform, agriculture accounted for more than 40 per cent of gross domestic product (GDP), employed more than 70 per cent of the total population, and accounted for about 30 to 80 per cent of exports in most of these countries. Moreover, rice is by far the most important crop in these countries, accounting for more than 70 per cent of cultivated land in Vietnam (Green and Vokes 1997, p. 262), and 46 per cent of total cultivated area in Myanmar.

The levels of development (see Table 7.1) among the ten Southeast Asian countries differ because of differences in their natural endowment, and political and economic systems. The newer members of ASEAN, that is, Cambodia, the Lao PDR, Myanmar, and Vietnam (CLMV), have been transforming their centrally planned economies into a market-oriented system since

TABLE 7.2
Shares of Major Sectors in GDP

	Agriculture			Industry			Services		
	1970	1980	1998	1970	1980	1998	1970	1980	1990
Myanmar	49.5	47.9	43.5	12.0	12.3	16.6	38.5	39.8	39.9
Thailand	30.2	20.2	12.0	25.7	30.1	40.4	44.1	49.7	47.6
Vietnam	—	42.7	23.9	—	26.3	34.0	—	31.0	42.1
Malaysia	—	22.9	11.3	—	35.8	45.8	—	41.3	42.9
Indonesia	35.0	24.4	17.2	28.0	41.3	42.3	37.0	34.3	40.5
Philippines	28.2	23.5	19.4	33.7	40.5	35.5	38.1	36.0	45.1
Laos	—	63.0*	52.6	—	13.1*	22.0	—	23.9*	25.4
Cambodia	—	51.4#	43.4	—	15.3#	20.8	—	33.4#	35.8

NOTE: *for 1985, UNIDO (1994),
#for 1987, World Bank, June 1994.
SOURCE: ADB, *Key Indicators*, 1996; and ADB, *Asian Development Outlook*, 1997 and 1999.

TABLE 7.3
Share of Agriculture in the Labour Force and Exports

	Share of Agricultural					
	Labour in Total Employed			Exports in Total Exports		
	1976	1986	1995	1976	1986	1995
Myanmar	67.9	64.6	72.1	68.2	64.6	47.4
Thailand	75.8	64.6	72.1	68.2	44.2	16.0
Vietnam	68.6@	72.3	69.3	—	46.4	28.0
Laos	90.0	90.0	77.3	—	31.1	24.3*
Cambodia	85.0	85.0	72.8	—	—	11.4
Indonesia	61.6	55.1	53.2	15.1	16.4	12.1
Malaysia	43.6	31.7	22.9	49.4	29.4	11.1
Philippines	53.8	50.0	42.2	42.1	25.8	10.8

NOTE: @ For 1978
* for 1992.
SOURCE: ADB, *Key Indicators*, 1996; FAO, *Trade Yearbook* (1995); and FAO, *Production Yearbook* (1995).

the late 1980s. Compared to the ASEAN-4, their level of development is much lower. Per capita GDP of the CLMV in 1995 ranged from US$240 (Vietnam) to US$350 (Laos), whereas among the ASEAN-4, they ranged from US$980 (Indonesia) to US$3890 (Malaysia).

However, in terms of social indicators such as life expectancy, literacy rate, infant mortality rate, per capita calorie consumption level, and so forth, the two groups do not differ much since the formerly socialist countries have relatively impressive records in their social sectors (see Table 7.1).

Although there exists a development gap between the two groups, as far as agriculture is concerned, there are some common features (for details, see Mya Than 1998). Firstly, agriculture is at the mercy of the monsoon rains which last from June to October. Climatic conditions in the region allow the production of crops throughout the year provided there is adequate water and water management. However, the intensity of land use is not more than 1.5 crops per year although up to four crops can be harvested with proper methods of cultivation (for example, crop rotation), fertilization and good water management (ibid., p. 3).

Secondly, most of the crops, especially rice, are rain-fed and hence labour-intensive, mainly in the planting and harvesting stages in the cultivation cycle. There are two types of crops: traditional crops and commercial plantation crops. Shifting cultivation is practised in many countries in ASEAN, but it is losing its importance. The most common crops found in this region are rice, maize, and rubber (Table 7.4.).

Thirdly, the average farm size is very small because of the high density of the rural population, and farm size is gradually shrinking. The average per capita cropped land (areas covered by food crops) in the region, which is gradually decreasing, is less than one-fifth

TABLE 7.4
Major Crops of Southeast Asia

Country	Crops
Indonesia	rice, maize, rubber, oil palm, and tobacco
Cambodia	rice, rubber, and maize
Laos	rice and maize
Malaysia	rice, rubber, coconut, oil palm, and pineapple
Myanmar	rice, maize, beans and pulses, rubber, and sugar-cane
Philippines	rice, maize, coconut, sugar-cane, abaca, and tobacco
Thailand	rice, rubber, maize, cassava, and kenaf
Vietnam	rice, sugar-cane, cassava, and sweet potatoes

of a hectare, with the exception of Thailand where per capita cropped land is about 0.49 hectare. However, the region's average farm size is still larger than that of South Asia, China, and Japan. Large commercial farms are usually for plantation crops such as rubber, coconut, and palm oil, whereas small farms prevail in the areas of traditional crops. More importantly, as a result of the growing population, the per capita farm size is declining in all countries of the region and there is scarcity of additional land for conversion to agricultural use.

Fourthly, agriculture plays a very important role in the economies of these countries. For one group of countries, mostly latecomers in terms of economic reforms and classical development, such as Cambodia, Laos, Myanmar and Vietnam, agriculture's contribution to their GDP is about 40 to 50 per cent whereas for the ASEAN-4, it is between 10 and 21 per cent (Table 7.2). More importantly, however, the role of agriculture has shrunk significantly from 1970 to 1994 to the benefit of the industrial sector in all the ASEAN nations.

For example, agriculture's contribution to GDP in Thailand declined from 30 per cent in 1970 to only about 12 per cent in 1998, while the industrial sector increased from 26 per cent to 40 per cent at the same time. This is regarded as an indicator of economic health in terms of industrialization. In the case of the transitional economies of mainland Southeast Asia, there has been a decline but not as sharp as in the case of the ASEAN-4 (Table 7.2). In terms of labour as a percentage of total employed persons, the Indochinese states and Myanmar accounted for about 69-77 per cent in 1996, while that of the ASEAN-4 was between 23 per cent in the case of Malaysia and 60 per cent in the case of Thailand in 1995 (Table 7.3). It is important to note that this declined more markedly in the ASEAN-4 (with the exception of Thailand) between 1976 and 1995, but in Myanmar and Vietnam, it increased. "This trend seems to go against the grain of conventional wisdom which generally portends a reduction in agricultural labour as a result of economic progress" (Que 1998, Chapter 2).

With regard to agricultural exports as a percentage of total exports, its contribution in Myanmar and Indochina was between 25 and 47 per cent and that of the ASEAN-4 was only about 10–20 per cent. Here again, the role of agricultural exports in total exports decreased more markedly in the ASEAN-4 between 1976 and 1992, but less in the case of the TEMSEA (see Table 7.3). In other words, the role of the agricultural sector is more pronounced in TEMSEA than in the ASEAN-4 although it is still a significant sector for both groups.

Last but not the least, technological factors (with government support, especially in the TEMSEA), such as extension services, rural infrastructure, the introduction of high yielding varieties (HYVs), and institutional factors such as the availability of rural credit also play very important roles in this development process in the region. (The positive relation between food production and inputs like fertilizers and irrigation is indicated in Table 7.5)

In other words, the active role played by the government in promoting agricultural development, in terms of price and non-price interventions, is one of the major reasons for improved agricultural production in Southeast Asia. However, as James (1987) has mentioned, these interventions to promote agricultural development work better under stable and favourable macro-economic conditions. In other words, sector-specific policies and projects have been successful when macroeconomic conditions are conducive to agricultural development.

On the other hand, it could be argued that the market in the form of traders and middlemen played such an important role in

TABLE 7.5
Food Production and Inputs

	Food Production per cap ann. gr. rate (1979–93)	Fertilizer Consumption (100 gm/ha) (1979–93)	Irrigation Ratio*	
			1978	1993
Cambodia	n.a	n.a	4.7	3.9
Indonesia	2.2	5.1	22.4	24.3
Laos	−0.2	−0.3	11.8	16.0
Malaysia	4.3	5.9	32.1	32.7
Myanmar	−1.3	−2.9	10.3	11.3
Philippines	−1.3	2.7	22.1	28.6
Thailand	0.0	10.4	16.1	25.0
Vietnam	2.2	14.3	23.5	33.8

NOTE: Irrigated area/arable land, see FAO, *Production Yearbook*, 1994.
SOURCE: World Bank, *World Development Report, 1994*.

TABLE 7.6
GDP Growth Rate

Country	Overall				Agriculture			
	1996	*1998*	*1999*	*2000*	*1996*	*1998*	*1999*	*2000*
Cambodia	7.0	0.0	4.0	5.0	2.4	1.4	4.8	—
Indonesia	7.8	−13.7	0.0	4.0	3.1	0.2	—	—
Laos	6.9	4.0	—	—	2.8	3.7	—	—
Malaysia	8.6	−6.2	0.7	3.9	2.2	−5.9	3.9	4.2
Myanmar	6.4	4.0	3.0	4.0	5.0	3.0	3.0	3.0
Philippines	5.8	−0.5	2.4	4.5	3.8	−6.6	2.5	3.0
Thailand	5.5	−8.0	0.0	5.0	3.8	2.1	1.6	2.5
Vietnam	9.3	4.0	3.7	4.5	4.4	2.7	—	—

SOURCE: ADB, *Asian Development Outlook, 1999.*

informing farmers of the new technology and providing credit and marketing services that farmers often preferred them to the government, especially in the ASEAN-4. Nevertheless, it can be concluded that technological factors play a very important role in agricultural growth in the region.

As far as overall economic growth is concerned, the performance of all the ASEAN countries, with the exception of the Philippines, was impressive during the period 1990–97. However, during the same period, the agricultural sectors in Myanmar, Vietnam, and Laos performed best among the ASEAN countries. During the crisis from 1997 to 1998, overall economic growth as well as the growth of the agricultural sector in all the Southeast Asian countries stagnated, but in 1999 and 2000, the Asian Development Bank saw the recovery of the whole economy as well as the agricultural sector (Table 7.6).

As Indonesia's case indicates, unless agricultural productivity and food production grow significantly in these countries, there is a possibility that political and social crises could occur. Hence, more economic reforms are needed to sustain the present momentum of growth and productivity in order to meet food demands so that undesirable crises could be avoided in the future.

Status of Food Security in the ASEAN Nations[1]

The Food and Agriculture Organization defines food security as follows: "The concept of food security implies adequate availability and stability in the supply of food and, more importantly, access to food" (FAO 1998, p. 85). There are three factors determining food security: adequacy of food availability, stability of food supply, and access to food. In line with this concept, the food security situation in the ASEAN nations will be assessed from the macro (country level) and micro (household level) perspectives. At the macro level, agricultural and food production will be analysed, while at the micro level, per capita availability and the requirement of energy intake (in terms of calories) will be assessed. This section will also look at the issue of stability in food availability in view of the production instability in this region.

Food Availability: Domestic Production

Table 7.7 illustrates the growth rates of agriculture and food production between 1987 and 1997 in the ASEAN countries. The growth rates of both agriculture and food production during the period were impressive. The highest growth rates were achieved by Vietnam, with 9.5 per cent in agricultural production and 9.2 per cent in food production, while the rates for Thailand were 5.1 per cent and 4.3 per cent respectively during the same period. On average, ASEAN achieved 6.7 per cent growth in agricultural production and 7.2 per cent in food production. If the ASEAN nations' growth rates of domestic agriculture and food production are compared with their respective average annual growth rates of population, they are quite impressive; the former is far ahead of the latter. In other words, for countries in the region which are food-exporting or food self-sufficient, there is security in terms of food.

When the growth rates of cereal production in the ASEAN countries are compared with their respective population growth rates, however, only Malaysia, Thailand, and the Philippines showed weaknesses (Table 7.7). The growth rates of cereal production of the remaining countries surpassed their respective population growth rates during the period 1987–97. It seems that, compared to other ASEAN nations, Malaysia and the Philippines were more vulnerable to food insecurity.

On the other hand, almost all the ASEAN countries imported cereal and, with the exception of Vietnam, cereal imports increased

TABLE 7.7
Growth Rates of Agricultural/Food Production, by Item, 1987–97

Item	INS	MAL	MY	PHI	THA	VIE
Cereal, total	2.6	1.7	3.9	1.7	1.3	5.7
Maize	4.9	4.4	2.5	−0.5	2.0	9.5
Rice	2.2	1.6	4.0	2.7	1.3	5.5
Pulses	4.8	—	12.5	1.5	−3.2	2.4
Oil crops, total	9.0	6.2	2.3	3.0	4.6	4.8
Vegetables	4.3	5.6	1.9	2.7	1.0	3.9
Sugar-cane	1.8	3.9	1.0	3.1	8.1	9.6
Meat, total	7.0	8.2	1.9	0.9	3.9	4.5
Cow's milk	6.4	3.1	−1.3	3.2	12.7	2.2
Hen's eggs	7.8	6.1	1.4	4.9	7.1	5.1
Agricultural production @	7.1	7.4	6.1	5.4	5.1	9.5
Food production @	7.3	10.8	6.0	5.8	4.3	9.2
Popul. Growth Rate (1970–95)	2.0	2.5	2.1	2.4	2.0	2.2
Popul. Growth Rate (95–2015)	1.2	1.7	1.5	1.7	0.7	1.8

NOTE: Statistically insignificant at the 10 per cent level.
        @ Computed from the Index of Food/Agricultural Production.
SOURCE: FAO; and UNDP, *Human Development Report 1998*.

in these countries between 1980 and 1996 (Table 7.8). However, in terms of commercial food imports as a percentage of total merchandized imports, cereal imports were not significant and it declined in most countries of the region during the period 1980–93. With growing urbanization and rising incomes, demand for wheat and wheat products increased, hence wheat imports increased although domestic production of wheat also rose. There was a change in cropping patterns in the region; for example, in Thailand, soybean production increased in response to the increased demand for cattle feed. According to an FAO study, changes in cropping patterns have an important bearing on food security (FAO December 1998).

At the same time, except for Indonesia, the table suggests that none of the countries in the region received any food aid in cereals as of 1995. This was probably because food production had increased significantly in these countries. However, during times of natural calamity or armed conflicts or economic crisis, there might be a need for food aid. For example, during the regional crisis, especially in 1998, Indonesia received more food aid in cereals.

TABLE 7.8
Per Capita Energy Supply

Economies	Daily per cap supply of calories		Per cap supply of cereals (kg)		Daily per cap supply of fat (gm)		Daily per cap supply of protein (gm)		Food production per cap index (1980 = 100)	Food imports (as % of mech imports)	Food aid in cereals ('000 tons)	Food consumption (as % of total household consumption)
	1970	1995	Total 1994/95	% change 1970–95	Total 1994/95	% change 1970–95	Total 1994/95	% change 1970–95	1996	1993	1994–95	1980–85
Cambodia	2,059	1,996	170	–9	25	32	34	–58	132	—	64	—
Indonesia	1,859	2,699	187	51	55	90	63	62	146	7	15	48
Laos	2,154	2,105	180	–13	5	9	55	–2	99	—	10	—
Malaysia	2,518	2,765	127	–19	86	54	65	27	149	17	0	23
Myanmar	1,997	2,728	220	35	47	42	68	31	125	—	5	—
Philippines	1,670	2,319	139	25	47	42	57	30	94	8	44	51
Singapore	2,743	3,187	116	–19	142	46	106	25	58	6	—	—
Thailand	2,148	2,247	129	–18	45	55	52	2	106	5	3	30
Vietnam	2,122	2,438	178	2	33	50	56	10	149	—	64	—
All developing countries	2,131	2,572	165	14	58	77	65	25	139	—	5,935	—
World	2,337	2,702	157	11	71	48	73	20	132	—	—	—

SOURCE: UNDP, *Human Development Report 1998.*

TABLE 7.9
Daily per Caput Energy Availability from 1989–91 to 1994,
Compared with Energy Requirements in 1995

Country	Availability (1989–91)	(in Kcal) (1994–96)	Requirement (in Kcal) (1995)	Availability as % of requirement*
Cambodia	1871	1981	2136	−0.92
Indonesia	2561	2880	2194	31.3
Laos	2134	2103	2034	0.03
Malaysia	2710	2849	2147	32.7
Myanmar	2543	2711	2153	25.9
Philippines	2351	2366	2108	12.2
Thailand	2247	2351	2256	4.2
Vietnam	2226	2449	2097	16.8

NOTE: * Calculated based on Table 149 in FAO (1998).
SOURCE: FAO (1998), Table 149.

Table 7.7 suggests that as far as the rates of growth of food production for all items in comparison with the respective population growth rates are concerned, Vietnam and Indonesia seems to be in a better position than other neighbouring countries. In this sense, Malaysia is weak in cereals and rice; Myanmar in sugarcane, milk and eggs; Philippines in maize, pulses, and meat; and Thailand in cereals, pulses and vegetables.

In general, in the near-term perspective, by looking at the extent of domestic production of agriculture and food, absolute and relative size of food imports, and food aid in cereals, unlike in the African continent, food security in ASEAN is not in an alarming state, if not encouraging.

Food Availability: Calorie Intake

This section will look at the food availability in terms of per capita supply of calorie or daily per caput energy availability presented in the UNDP's *Human Development Report 1998* (Table 7.8). In terms of daily per caput supply of calorie between 1970 and 1995, with the exception of Cambodia and Laos, all ASEAN nations showed improvement.

As in Table 7.7, there was negative growth in per capita supply of cereals in Cambodia, Laos, Malaysia, and Thailand during the period of study. On the other hand, daily per capita supply of fat increased significantly in all the ASEAN countries. However, in terms of daily per capita supply of protein, there was an increase in all ASEAN countries except Cambodia and Laos, which was mainly due to the decline in the supply of cereals during the same period.

Changes in the Sources of Calories

The composition of the sources of calories, or dietary composition, is an important indicator as it shows the change in the quality of food. In other words, changes in the composition of sources of calorie are more important than the improvement in calorie intake. The Appendix illustrates the changing quality of food in selected ASEAN countries. It suggests the general tendency that calories from animal sources have a progressively larger share compared to those from vegetable sources. And, within the vegetable sources there has been a shift from cereal to non-cereal sources, and from roots and tubers to better cereals such as rice and wheat. These qualitative changes are most likely due to an improvement in income and standard of living of the ASEAN countries between the late 1980s and the mid-1990s.

Stability in Food Availability

Another approach to measuring food security is to look at the stability in food availability which can be measured in terms of inter-year variations in food availability (Table 7.10)[2]. An FAO study (ibid, pp. 89–90) suggests that, in terms of year to year stability, the overall availability of food became more stable, and supplies of both major components of food (vegetable food and livestock products) exhibited more stability in Southeast Asia. By country, the study indicated that there was a decline in the instability of the availability of cereals in general, and rice in particular, and so with milk.

However, the same study noted that domestic food production cannot be faulted for year to year fluctuations, as instability was more the result of trade. This suggests that trade policy failed to lead to stability in the availability of food.

TABLE 7.10
Trends in the Instability of Food Availability (Calories), Southeast Asia
(10 years moving standard deviations preceding the reference point
of annual growth rates)
(In percentage points)

Year	Indonesia	Malaysia	Philippines	Thailand	Vietmam
1981	2.82	0.78	2.31	1.51	5.90
1982	2.79	0.80	2.41	1.42	5.99
1983	2.60	0.79	3.08	1.19	6.03
1984	2.61	0.78	2.85	1.34	6.01
1985	2.57	0.80	2.86	1.29	4.23
1986	2.34	0.95	2.76	1.29	3.60
1987	2.36	0.80	2.65	1.97	3.69
1988	2.66	0.72	2.58	1.98	4.09
1989	2.57	1.11	3.04	2.37	3.55
1990	1.27	1.32	3.14	2.67	3.40
1991	1.26	1.32	4.21	2.72	3.71
1992	1.22	1.64	4.26	2.72	3.60

SOURCE: FAO, *Poverty Alleviation and Food Security in Asia* (1998),
Table 7.9.

In sum, as far as the general availability of food is concerned, it has improved in all the countries in ASEAN, and the supply of food has become more stable over the years. This suggests that the food security of the people in the ASEAN nations can be enhanced.

Accessibility to Food

Even if the availability of food is improving and the supply is stable, there is no guarantee that households have access to the required quantity and quality of food. At the national level, it can be quantitatively and qualitatively estimated whether all citizens have food security by looking at agriculture and food production and per caput consumption of energy in terms of calorie intake per day, or in terms of calorie intake as a percentage of requirement over a reference period. Or it can be measured indirectly by the level of purchasing power to enable access to stipulated food intake. In fact, these indicators represent the poverty level of a country. Therefore,

poverty figures are used as indicators of household access to food
(FAO 1998). However, it is important to note that even though the
non-poor are assumed to be food secure, the quality of food intake
is in question.

Table 7.11 shows the percentage of the population below the
poverty line. The table suggests that the proportion of poor
households, and presumably food insecure households, in total
households, has declined in selected Southeast Asian nations.
According to the FAO study, "in some of the ASEAN countries, for
example, Indonesia and Malaysia, the decline was very rapid, in
Thailand moderate, and in the Philippines and Vietnam, slow" (ibid,

TABLE 7.11
Percentage of the Population Below the Poverty Line

Country/Year	Rural	Urban	Total
Indonesia			
1976	40.4	38.8	40.1
1990	14.1	16.8	15.2
Malaysia			
1973	—	—	37.0
1987	—	—	15.0
1995	—	—	10.0
Myanmar			
1990	—	—	40
Philippines			
1971	57.7	40.6	52.2
1991	50.7	36.7	44.6
Thailand			
1975/76	35.6	17.6	31.7
1990	21.4	10.1	18.2
1995*	—	—	13.0
Vietnam			
1992/93	57.0	25.0	51.0

NOTE: * Estimates
SOURCE: FAO (1998), Table 7.10.

p. 91). In general, it could be interpreted that most households in the region had improved in terms of food security and quality during the early 1990s.

However, these poverty indicators may be misleading. Since the indicators divide the population into two groups — poor and the non-poor — the decline of poor households does not necessarily reflect the intensity of poverty. And even though the non-poor are assumed to have food accessibility, the quality of their food intake is in question. Nevertheless, it is not totally wrong if we accept the assumption that, as the poverty level declines, the food security situation should improve in the region.

Another way to assess the quality dimension of food intake is to look at the output aspect in terms of infant mortality rate, life expectancy, and percentage of children suffering from malnutrition, which is reflected by underweight, wasting, and stunting, since inputs (nutrients intake) are not available nor reliable. Table 7.12 illustrates the nutritional status.

The table shows that there could be three groups: better performing group, moderate group, and less performing group. The first group includes Malaysia and Thailand; the second, Indonesia and the Philippines; and the third, Vietnam and Myanmar. However, according to an FAO report, "a welcome feature has been a reduction in the proportion of underweight children in recent years in all these countries" (ibid., p. 92). It is also important to note that, even within

TABLE 7.12
Indicators of Nutritional Status

Life Expectency 1995	Country	Underweight Moderate and severe	Severe	Wasting	Stunting	Under 5 mortality (per thousand births) 1995
64	Indonesia	39.9	—	—	—	50
71	Malaysia	24.0	1	—	—	11
59	Myanmar	38.0	—	11	50	78
67	Philippines	32.9	5	5	39	40
69	Thailand	25.8	—	6	22	27
66	Vietnam	45	11	9.4	57	34

SOURCE: FAO (1998), Table 7.11.

TABLE 7.13
Asia: Food Demand–Supply Projection
(In thousand tons)

Crop	1982-88	2000	2005
Wheat	−36,376	−41,931	−44,433
Paddy	4,361	−7,451	−3,512
Corn	−16,811	−40,254	−56,353
Other cereals	−3,957	−5,874	−6,831
Root	22,964	20,554	17,222
Pulse	−403	−2,581	−3,787
Total	−30,219	−70,831	−97,683

SOURCE: *Japan's New Strategy on Asian Agriculture and Rural Development* (Tokyo: IDCJ, 1995).

these countries, there exist strong differences among different regions.

Furthermore, food security also means ensuring of the supply of food across the country, particularly to the poorer sections of the population. However, owing to a lack of information on distribution channels, it is difficult to assess the situation in the Southeast Asian countries in this aspect.

In general, it can be said that the food security situation in the ASEAN countries is so far not bad if not satisfactory, at least in the near-term. On the other hand, one Japanese study, based on demand-supply projections, suggests that in the longer-term perspective demand for food crops may surpass the supply (Table 7.13).

Software Issues

Food security does not only depend on the production of food, the quality of food, and the accessibility of food but also on the country's software, such as macroeconomic, social, and agricultural and rural development policies. For example, the poor can benefit from a fast growing economy, which has a "trickle down" effect, provided that the growth rate of GDP is higher than the population growth, the growth in GDEP is sustained over a period of time, the infrastructure is well developed to allow the "spread effect", and the poor have assets or skills to respond to market stimuli (FAO 1998, p. 92).

With the exception of some of the new ASEAN member countries and before the regional crisis of 1997–98, most of the above conditions were satisfied for the region. However, history has shown that bad development strategies (such as an inward-looking development strategy, an urban biased strategy, and so on), poor macroeconomic policies (such as over-expansion of money supply, over-exposure to foreign indebtedness, and growing budgetary deficits), and wrong sectoral policies (for example, internal intervention) have hurt the rural sector (Mya Than 1998, p. 8). This, in turn, has affected the food security situation in some of the countries in the region. Moreover, the handling of poverty issues is important in addressing food security issues.

For example, in Indonesia, after passing through several crises, such as high inflation in the 1960s, payment crisis in the midst of an oil boom in 1975, "Dutch Disease" and devaluation of the currency in 1978, and recession in the oil market in 1980, a sort of stability was reached in the mid-1980s. Since then, several reform measures have been introduced and as a result, there was sustained growth in GDP for more than a decade. Although a concrete conclusion cannot be drawn because of the involvement of several factors, it seems that the pace of development and the pattern of public expenditure helped the poor. Generally, the containment of inflation and diversification of industries created jobs for the urban areas and lightened the heavy burden of poverty of the poor. Between 1976 and 1990, the proportion of the population below the poverty line decreased from 40 per cent to 15 per cent (Table 7.11). This was the biggest achievement in Indonesia's economic history, which, in turn, created food security to some extent in Indonesia. However, one of the negative impacts during this phase of growth was the rise of landlessness.

Agricultural and rural development policy measures also helped the poor in the rural areas with respect to food security. Since the late 1960s, Indonesia had instituted input subsidies on fertilizers, high variety seeds, and pesticides and insecticides, particularly for paddy farmers. Since 1970, the National Logistic Agency (BULOG), has been pursuing an active policy of guaranteeing a minimum support price. The programme is executed through village-level co-operatives, and BULOG stores the stocks acquired through these co-operatives. The stocks are used by BULOG as a buffer to meet shortages as well as for open market operations to regulate prices.

In addition, the protection of rice prices during the 1980s and the 1990s through the mechanism of price support, was able to raise rural incomes and achieve a reasonable rate of growth in agricultural production and to shift the focus to international competitiveness. Monetary instruments, such as money supply and exchange rate, and the growth of the economy had positive effects on the agricultural sector's share in GDP. According to Anderson and Pangestu (1995), the positive relationship between cost reduction policies (improvement in yields, input subsidies, etc.) and a fall in the relative prices of paddy helped to ensure better access to food.

Like other Southeast Asian countries, the government encouraged the establishment of cottage industries in the rural areas, which created more job opportunities for the rural population. This alleviated poverty effectively as most of the poverty was concentrated in the rural areas.

These experiences in Indonesia suggest that development strategies, macroeconomic policies, and agricultural and rural development policies could help the country's poor to ensure food security. Similarly, the experiences of the other countries in the region also indicate the same conclusion. (For details, see FAO 1998, pp. 92–102).

Chao et al. (1997) have given more comprehensive suggestions. They have suggested that Asia's food security can be maintained only if international and domestic policies, institutional frameworks, and public expenditure patterns are conducive to cost-effective and sustainable agricultural development.

Food Security and the Impact of the Regional Crisis

Food security is closely related to human security as well as political and economic security. If food security is threatened, all the other aspects will also be affected. To preserve food security, therefore, human security, political security as well as economic security are required.

It is obvious that the regional crisis has affected the lives of millions of people in the Southeast Asian countries. This has impacted on political stability, and affected the social, economic, and financial sectors. "It has had several negative impacts, among them falling incomes, rising poverty and malnutrition, declining public services, reduced access to education, deteriorating health-care status, heightened pressure on women, and increased crimes and violence" (Chia and Bhanu 1998, p. 53). As far as food security is concerned, the effects of the crisis are acute in Indonesia and to some extent in Thailand, Malaysia, and the Philippines.

The food security situation in Indonesia, the hardest hit in the region, has been affected not only by the regional crisis but also by the El Nino effect. A shortfall in the rice harvest in late 1997 was the worst in half a century. It should be noted that rice, like most other Southeast Asian countries, is the staple food in Indonesia and many poor households spend up to 50 per cent or more of their income on rice alone. Extra food imports were necessary to offset the food shortage because of the sharp devaluation of the local currency — the rupiah — and the fivefold escalation in the price of rice from Rp1000 to Rp5000, making the food security issue even more acute (ibid., p. 68). As a result, the government has introduced large subsidies to stabilize prices, and the total cost of emergency subsidies in the 1998/99 fiscal year was expected to cause a budget deficit of about 8.5 per cent of GDP.

Ensuring the distribution of rice across the nation, particularly to the poorer groups, is considered to be an important aspect of food security. The ethnic violence that occurred in May 1998 disrupted the rice distribution channels, especially because these channels were mostly generated by ethnic Chinese traders. There were reports that the poor people did not have enough money to buy rice. Meanwhile, the Ministry of Agriculture and Horticulture estimated that more than 17 million families nation-wide, or about 80 million (about 40 per cent of the total population) individuals, faced food shortages in 1998. According to one report, more than 30 million people in Central and East Java could only afford one meal per day. Eastern Indonesia has been the hardest hit and there have been reports of widespread famine and deaths in the thousands owing to the El Nino droughts and related crop delays or failures. In 1998, Indonesia had to import four million tonnes of rice to avert famine (*Straits Times*, 21 August 1999).

Furthermore, as a result of the regional economic crisis, malnutrition has spread among the poorer segments of Indonesian society. The *Straits Times* (16 October 1998), quoting a UNICEF source, reported that the crisis may produce a "lost generation" as malnutrition drives the country's Intelligence Quotient (IQ) down by some 7 percentage points below the average IQ of 100, with

65 per cent of children under three years of age being anaemic and 50 per cent of those under two suffering from a lack of micronutrients, such as vitamin A, iron, and iodine. The UNICEF report noted that such a "lost generation" would be a "very long-term negative impact" of the crisis over the space of ten years, which would hurt Indonesia's competitiveness (Chia and Bhanu 1998).

The same source mentioned that in Malaysia the rise in the cost of food items such as sugar, fruits and vegetables, meat, coffee and tea, and oils and fats, is difficult to contain because of the high import content of the country's food supply. In 1997 alone, Malaysia had to import M$9 million worth of food. The government is taking measures to cut imports by introducing large-scale production of food and at the same time to reduce the number of poor farmers by becoming shareholders in estates with high incomes.

As the crisis has bottomed out, there is confidence among the Southeast Asian countries that the food security situation will improve as the agricultural sector is expected to grow, and most governments, after taking lessons from the crisis, are introducing safety nets in various forms.

ASEAN Co-operation in Food Security

One of the fundamental goals of ASEAN is food security. The Declaration of ASEAN Accord, signed in Bali in 1976, established the basic framework for regional co-operation and accorded high priority to co-operation in the field of basic commodities, particularly food and energy. Following the Bali Declaration, the ASEAN Committee on Food, Agriculture and Forestry (COFAF) was established in 1977, which could be considered as a landmark and a starting point towards greater regional co-operation in food security issues. In the following year, COFAF's Working Group on Food Security Reserve recommended a system of regionally co-ordinated national reserves for rice and a system for the exchange of information on national rice reserves. This recommendation of the Working Group was subsequently endorsed by COFAF and the Meeting of Economic Ministers (MEM).

In November 1978 in Bangkok, the Meeting of the Inter-Governmental Group on ASEAN Food Security Reserve (AFSR) proposed the establishment of an ASEAN Food Security Reserve Board (AFSRB). Its terms of reference included co-ordination of periodic exchanges of information on food, evaluation of the food situation and prospects, examination of short and long-term policy actions for minimum food security, assessment of the ASEAN Emergency Rice Reserves (AERR), and evaluation of the regional supply and demand situation for rice, among other things.

In addition, the Agreement on ASEAN Food Security Reserves was signed by the ASEAN Foreign Ministers in New York in October 1979. It provides for the co-ordination of national food reserves, establishment of the AERR, the release and replenishment of the AERR for emergency requirements, arrangements for mutual support, the establishment of a food information early warning system, and the establishment of the ASEAN Food Security Reserve Board. According to its general provisions, it emphasizes the promotion of stability in food prices, strengthening of the food production base in the member countries, and possibilities for long-term trade arrangements, among others. The AFSRB came into force in 1980 and the Secretariat Office was instituted in Thailand. However, currently, the stockpile volume of rice managed by the AFSRB is very low and will not be able to cope with any serious catastrophe in the region.

Apart from rice, there is also an initiative to include more staple food items, such as sugar, soybean and corn, as well as add more items like cooking oils and others.

Another effort of the ASEAN Secretariat with regard to the food security issue in the light of the ASEAN Free Trade Area (AFTA) was the development of an Action Programme for Strengthening Food Security in the Region, which was reflected in the Medium-Term Programme of Action for ASEAN Cooperation in Food, Agriculture, and Forestry (1995–99). This Action Programme focuses strongly on food security management, co-ordination of research, technical application, and training network, and improvement of information exchange on technologies and data, and was signed by the AMAF in 1994.

In 1990, ASEAN requested the FAO to prepare a technical proposal to present to donor countries, and in 1996 it made another request to the FAO to provide technical assistance to develop a regional food data and information system. In response, the FAO organized a meeting for the establishment of a Regional Food Security Information System for ASEAN in 1997, which provided baseline approaches focusing on the identification of information needs, determination of an institutional framework and operational procedures, and a tentative action plan. However, much work will be needed to establish comprehensive statistical information on ASEAN food security.

These activities suggest that various efforts have been made to strengthen regional co-operation in food security in Southeast Asia. However, despite these efforts, it seems that there is little regional impact so far. One of the reasons may be that there has not been strong and solid effort towards the establishment of a common food production (agricultural) policy in ASEAN. "For food security reasons, it is understandable that each of the countries will strive to achieve self sufficiency in food crops but it must be emphasized that extra effort must be directed at achieving excellence in the areas ... where they have strong comparative advantage over the others. This way, the region's resources will be more efficiently utilized" (Cabanilla 1992).

Conclusion

Table 7.7 indicates that agricultural and food production in the last decade (1987–97) was quite impressive in almost all the countries in Southeast Asia, with the exception of Cambodia because of political instability and bad weather. During the period of the regional crisis, setback was witnessed in the region as a result of both the financial crisis and the El Nino effect. However, according to ADB estimates, it seems that growth in the agricultural sector has been recovering along with the economy in 1999 and 2000. The good news is that Cambodia is planning to export staple food products such as rice, beans, and fruits for the first time since civil war broke out in 1970 (*Straits Times*, 28 October 1999). In short, growth in agriculture and the food production sector in the short term is likely to be favourable for most of the countries in the region. However, for the longer-term perspective, the situation would depend on technological factors, price factors, and climatic conditions. Table 7.7 reinforces this statement.

Again in Table 7.7, the growth rates of agriculture and food production are compared with the population growth rates for the respective periods, and it was found that growth rates of production surpassed those of the population. Since there is a declining trend in population growth, if the countries in the region could maintain the present food production growth rates, there is little to worry about food insecurity even for the longer term.

As far as food availability in terms of per capita supply of calorie is concerned, with the exception of Cambodia and Laos, there was an increase during the period between 1970 and 1995. In Laos and Cambodia, 1995 was climatically not a good year and hence, there was a reduction in agricultural food production. In 1998 and 1999, however, there was an increase in daily per capita supply of calories for all the nations. (Singapore, as always, remains a food-importing country.)

If daily availability of calorie supply is compared with the daily requirement of calories, with the exception of Cambodia, all countries in the region have impressive records. Cambodia's situation has improved recently, and it is even planning to export some agricultural products.

Availability of food alone is not enough to say that there is food security in the region because of the unpredictable nature of the agricultural sector. However, as mentioned before, the overall availability of food has become more stable, except during the regional crisis.

Again, even if food is available and the food supply is stable, it is of no use if there is no accessibility to the food. In other words, if a household is poor, because of a lack of income, it has no accessibility to food even though food is available. However, data regarding household income are lacking in many countries in the region. In such cases, poverty indicators are used to measure the accessibility to food. Poverty indicators suggest that the poverty level in the region has been reduced significantly as a result of achievements in economic development which, in turn, has given more households better accessibility to food than previously. Moreover, the FAO reported an improvement in nutrition level in most of the countries in terms of underweight children in recent years.

There is more good news. "Fortunately, the establishment of the World Trade Organization (WTO) would give, at least in the long run, favourable effects to many developing countries by discouraging perpetuating cheap food imports, which is causing an increasing import and heavy drains of foreign currency" (Takase and Saito 1996).

In sum, the food security situation in Southeast Asia is satisfactory, at least in the near-term perspective. For the longer term, to ensure food security, the region needs to improve its technology in agricultural and food production, introduce correct development strategies, appropriate macroeconomic policies (such as domestic market reforms), and agricultural and rural development policies, as well as credible measures for poverty alleviation and population control.

APPENDIX
Availability of Major Food Groups as Percentage of Total Dietary Energy Supply

Country	Cereals & Prod.	Roots & Prod.	Pulses & Prod.	Treenuts & Prod.	Oilcrops (excl. Prod.)	Fruits & Prod.	Veg. & Prod.	Sweeteners	Alc. Bev.	Veg. Oils & Prod.	Ani. Fats & Prod.	Total Veg. Prod.	Total Ani. Prod.
1989–91 Averages (%)													
1. Cambodia	84	2	1	0	1	2	2	1	0.2	1	0.6	94	6.3
2. Indonesia	65	6	1	0	8	2	1	5	0	8	0.3	96	4.1
3. Laos	76	6	4	0	1	2	0.4	1	2	1	0.3	94	5.9
4. Malaysia	42	3	1	0	3	3	1	13	0.4	16	1.2	83	16.8
5. Myanmar	80	0.	2	0	2	1	1	2	0	7	0.4	96	3.9
6. Philippines	55	4.5	0.4	0	1	5	2	11	4	5	0.8	88	12.2
7. Thailand	57	1	2	0	5	5	1	8	4	5	0.7	90	10.1
8. Vietnam	73	7	1	0	1	3	1	3	0.4	2	1	92	8.0
1994–96 Averages (%)													
1. Cambodia	78	2	1	N/S	4	2	1	2	N/S	5	1	92	8
2. Indonesia	63	6	1	N/S	13	2	1	5	N/S	7	0	96	4
3. Laos	78	4	1	N/A	1	2	1	2	3	1	1	95	5
4. Malaysia	40	2	1	N/S	8	3	1	18	N/S	11	1	80	20
5. Myanmar	79	0	3	N/S	3	1	1	2	N/S	7	N/S	96	4
6. Philippines	49	4	0	N/S	2	6	2	12	4	6	1	86	14
7. Thailand	52	1	2	N/S	6	5	1	12	5	5	1	89	11
8. Vietnam	73	5	1	N/S	1	2	1	4	1	2	1	91	9

NOTE: N/A – not available; N/S – not significant
SOURCE: FAO (1998), Tables 156 and 157.

NOTES

1 This section draws in part from a FAO study, *Poverty Alleviation and Food Security in Asia: Lessons and Challenges* (Bangkok, December 1998).
2 The same study mentioned that from the perspective of poor households, inter-seasonal stability is more important than inter-year stability. Fragmentary evidence suggests that in most of the countries, food availability declines during the period before the harvest of the principal food grain, that is, rice, and improves after the rice harvest. It is reflected in the bi-monthly trends in the prevalence of underweight children, which suggest strong seasonality effect (FAO 1998, p. 89).

REFERENCES

Abdul Aziz Abdul Rahman. "Food Agriculture and Food Security: Developments in ASEAN — Prospects and Challenges". Unpublished paper, Universiti Putra Malaysia, Selangor, 1999.

ADB. *Asian Development Outlook*. Manila: Asian Development Bank, various issues.

————. *Key Indicators*. Manila: Asian Development Bank, various issues.

Cabanilla, L. S. "ASEAN Cooperation in Food, Agriculture, and Forestry". In *The ASEAN Reader*, edited by K. S. Sandhu et al. Singapore: ISEAS, 1992.

Chao, Y. P. et al. "Food Security in Asia". *Asian-Pacific Economic Literature* 11, no. 1. Oxford: Blackwell Publishers, May 1997.

Chia, S. Y. and S. Bhanu. "Human Security Dimensions of the Asian Financial Crisis: A Compendium of Research Materials". In *The Asian Crisis and Human Security: An Intellectual Dialogue on Building Asia's Tomorrow*. Tokyo: JCIE, and Singapore: ISEAS, 1998.

FAO. *Poverty Alleviation and Food Security in Asia: Lessons and Challenges*. Bangkok: FAO Regional Office for Asia and the Pacific, December 1998.

————. *Production Yearbook*. Rome, various issues.

————. *Selected Indicators of Food and Agriculture Development in the Asia-Pacific Region, 1987–1997*. Bangkok: FAO Regional Office for Asia and the Pacific, 1998

————. *State of Food and Agriculture, 1998*. Rome, 1998.

Green, D. J , and R. Vokes. "Agriculture and the Transition to the Market in Asia". *Journal of Comparative Economics* 25 (1997): 256–80.

James, W., et al. *Asian Development: Economic Success and Political Lessons*. ICEG, San Francisco, University of Wisconsin Press, 1987.

Khan, Adil M. *Economic Development, Poverty Alleviation and Governance: The Asia Experience*. Sydney: Avebury, 1996.

Mya Than, "Development Strategies, Agricultural Policies and Agricultural Development in Southeast Asia". *ASEAN Economic Bulletin* 15, no. 1 (April 1998).

Que, T. T. "Economic Reforms and their Impact on Agricultural Development in Vietnam". In *Development Strategies, Agricultural Policies and Agricultural Development in Southeast Asia*, edited by Mya Than. Special focus issue of *ASEAN Economic Bulletin* 15, no. 1 (Singapore: ISEAS, April 1998).

Takase, K., and F. A. Saito. *Triad Agricultural Revolution Saves Sub-Saharan Africa*. IDCJ Summary Series No. 7. IDCJ, June 1996.

UNDP. *Human Development Report 1998*. Oxford: Oxford University Press, 1998.

UNIDO. *Lao People's Democratic Republic: Industrial Transition*. Industrial Development Review Series. Geneva, April 1994.

World Bank. *World Development Report, 1994*. Washington, D.C., 1994.

8

ASEAN Co-operation and the Environment

SIMON S. C. TAY*

The Dubious Importance of Institutions and Regionalism

Much writing on environmental issues tends to be confined to the environment as an exclusive subject. We may hear about endangered species, the loss of rainforests and wetlands, global climate change as well as the problems of cities, such as over-population, and dwindling fish stocks. Less often do we hear about the institutions and processes (or regimes) that are supposed to address these environmental issues. Yet, institutions and processes — at the local, national, regional, and international levels — are fundamental to the making and implementation of environmental policies and laws. Without them, the hopes of environmentalists remain merely hopes. They may not even come to be penned in a formal document, let alone be implemented and complied with.

When there is consideration of institutions and processes in the field of the environment, there is usually condemnation. Writers stress the weaknesses of international regimes in providing environmental governance and protection. In this, there is sometimes an assumption that environmental institutions and regimes are weaker than their counterparts in other areas of concern, such as in trade and in security. There seems, in this regard, to be an aspiration for the holy grail of world government or a binding and authoritative global regime, comparable to the World Trade Organization (WTO). Only a minority of more recent work have suggested the significant role that environmental institutions, without equalling the WTO or approximating world government, can and do play.[1]

There is also, in a number of writings, an assumption in favour of regional frameworks for the environment. Some academics have suggested that the region is the optimal level for environmental rule-making and compliance. They argue that this is because most environmental problems are too large for a single state to solve, while international environmental agreements are often watered down to the lowest common denominator.[2] In comparison, they believe that the region provides sufficient physical space to match the ecological boundaries to the political boundaries. They also suggest that regionalism allows for neigbouring countries to reach agreement more readily on good environmental standards, as they are more immediately affected by a failure to meet such standards.

The faith in environmental regionalism is largely built on examples drawn from the European context. The European Community has witnessed a number of successes, such as efforts to address long distance transboundary air pollution. The European Community has also had some successes in harmonizing its environmental standards in connection with economic activity in trade and manufacturing. Efforts to address pollution of the Mediterranean has also seen considerable success, with the European countries working with other states that share the sea.

How do these ideas apply to Southeast Asia? Typically, studies of the environment in Southeast Asia point to deleterious and harmful effects on the bio-physical level.[3] The international concern with rainforests and biodiversity — for which Southeast Asia is one of the world's last frontiers — is a case in point. There are a large number of accounts detailing and condemning the destruction of the forests in the region.[4] There are fewer studies that seek to understand and explain the institutional gaps and failures and the policies behind this degradation.

Those that do seem to demand too little or too much of institutions in the region. There are some that suggest that ASEAN has already done or can easily do all that needs to be done. Many of these describe the action plans and declarations of ASEAN and the Asia-Pacific region as if these were sufficient to make environmental policies work.[5] There are others that barely mention ASEAN, preferring to focus their analysis on the local and national level, or at the global level. Such analysis suggests that the problem is how to get local and national levels to comply with international norms and practices.[6] Most environmental studies of the Southeast Asian region, as such, either neglect ASEAN or look directly and simply at its environmental record.

This chapter differs from the approaches described. It seeks to describe efforts by ASEAN as an institution, with its own processes and norms, as they apply to the field of the environment, and not the environment *per se*. In so doing, it draws from and makes suggestions about ASEAN in other fields of activity and concern. As such, it does not compartmentalize ASEAN's environmental activity, but seeks to understand it as part of a larger picture of the regional institution.

There are, of course, limits to what can be done in a chapter of this length. But within those limits, it seeks to discuss as much about ASEAN as about the environment. Its analysis therefore tries to address both institutional and environmental questions, rather than only the latter.

First is a survey of ASEAN's development across different fields of activity and concern. This situates environmental co-operation in the broader institutional context. Secondly, the chapter reviews ASEAN's environmental heritage and its efforts in co-operation to protect that heritage. This review gives particular attention to the ASEAN agreement on Nature and Natural Resources, the only attempt to date to conclude a binding environmental treaty. Thirdly, it reviews ASEAN's efforts to deal with the greatest environmental challenge it has faced: the Indonesian fires and resulting regional haze pollution. In so doing, it goes beyond a description of efforts made thus far, to suggest why these measures have been insufficient.

Fourthly, the chapter suggests ways in which this issue can be effectively addressed by ASEAN. In this connection, it also reviews the broader institutional questions that arise; how environmental co-operation is contributing and can further contribute to the evolution of ASEAN processes and institutions.

It is also suggested that the mode of ASEAN co-operation, known as the "ASEAN way", does not serve well in dealing with environmental challenges. Yet, efforts to foist international approaches and principles onto ASEAN have so far failed because they have tried to substitute themselves for the ASEAN way. As such, suggestions are made on how the ASEAN way, without either being ossified or abandoned, can be evolved and changed. Such evolution and change has implications not only for the environment, but also for the future shape of ASEAN.

In so doing, the chapter rejects the assumption that regionalism is always or normally the best focal point for environmental protection. It suggests instead that regionalism must be understood to be both open to international influences and yet resilient to the special needs and norms of the region. Only then does it make sense to speak of a regional approach and co-operation for the environment.

ASEAN's Development in Brief

Before its current problems, ASEAN enjoyed a reputation as one of the most productive regional or sub-regional organizations outside the European Community. This reputation developed for both political and economic reasons.

In the 1980s, ASEAN drew international attention to the Cambodian situation, leading the way to the intervention of the larger powers and the conclusion of the Paris Peace Accords.[7] In the 1990s, the economies of the ASEAN member states grew at rates that led many to cite them as evidence of the East Asian "miracle".[8] Singapore led the region as one of the newly industrialized economies, and the ASEAN-4, comprising Malaysia, Thailand, Indonesia, and the Philippines, followed in emphasizing export-led industrialization.[9]

During this period, ASEAN expanded to include oil-rich Brunei, Vietnam and, at its thirtieth anniversary in July 1997, Myanmar and Laos.[10] In April 1999, Cambodia was formally admitted to the grouping, completing the ASEAN-10 vision. ASEAN was noted for its success in transforming an area of political tensions and economic backwardness into one of the most dynamic regional groupings.[11]

Many commentators attributed this success to the pursuit of an "ASEAN way". This "ASEAN way" emphasized, among other things, the norm of non-interference in other states' affairs, preferring consensus and non-binding plans to treaties and legalistic rules, and relied on national institutions and actions, rather than creating a strong central bureaucracy.[12]

Building on its economic and political achievements, ASEAN had considerable success in engaging the major powers through such sub-groupings as the Asia-Pacific Economic Cooperation (APEC), the ASEAN Regional Forum (ARF), and the Asia-Europe Meeting (ASEM).[13] The "ASEAN way" was also applied to these new initiatives, although the new groupings spanned areas and included members from outside Southeast Asia.[14]

Even during this period of success, ASEAN had its detractors and its limitations. In security and peace, it was notable that while ASEAN kept the Cambodian issue alive, its role in the processes leading to the Paris Peace Accords, and in UNTAC thereafter, was somewhat in the shadow of the great and medium-sized powers, such as France and Australia. It was also notable that, in this period, ASEAN self-help and resilience did not extend to a concerted regional effort to deal with the outflow of boat people and refugees from Indochina. There was instead heavy reliance on the United Nations and the developed countries.

In economic matters too, even before the crisis, people pointed to the shortcomings in ASEAN. The early efforts at cross-border industrial co-operation did not amount to much. When foreign investment did flow within the region, it was most often bilateral or sub-regional, in the form of a number of growth triangles, quadrangles, and special zones. Many, moreover, were declared as approved, rather than actually implemented. Economic agreements across ASEAN as a whole came late, with the free trade agreement first mooted in 1992 and still undergoing further negotiation and implementation.

Institutional questions about ASEAN have also been raised. The norms of the ASEAN way, especially the norm of non-interference and the aversion to a strong central bureaucracy, meant that ASEAN was more an association than an institution. This was particularly so in the first phase of ASEAN development, from 1967 to 1976. In this period, ASEAN was characterized by a loose and highly decentralized structure with functions and programmes driven by national governments. ASEAN itself was labelled a "letter box". In the next phase, from 1976 to 1992, ASEAN was much like a "travelling circus" with increasing activity in different fields but with only minimal and largely administrative support from the ASEAN Secretariat. Only from 1992 onwards, with the Singapore declaration and the first economic undertakings did ASEAN require greater co-ordination and institutionalization.[15]

Since the crisis, these doubts about ASEAN, and newer ones, have returned. A number of critics have suggested that ASEAN is out of its depth.[16] The criticisms range from ASEAN efforts (or the lack of them) to deal with the economic crisis, the East Timor question and Indonesia's transition, the admission of Cambodia and Myanmar to the grouping, and (most relevant to this essay) the Indonesian fires and haze.

In the context of this mix of admiration and anguish at ASEAN's record, what has been its record on the environment?

ASEAN's Environmental Record

The Southeast Asian region is the seat of a rich environmental heritage, with some of the largest tracts of tropical rainforest and coral reefs, both known for their biological diversity. Of the ASEAN members, no less than three — Indonesia, Malaysia, and the Philippines — have been named among the world's top ten "mega-diversity" countries. In Laos and other parts of Indochina, areas that are newly opening up to the outside world have revealed species that were thought extinct.

ASEAN's record in appreciating and protecting this rich environmental heritage has been mixed. The ASEAN countries have often come under criticism from environmentalists and non-governmental organizations (NGOs), especially concerning tropical deforestation and the member states' lack of conservation efforts.[17] To date, many countries in the region have experienced the trials of industrialization on one hand and the continuing problems of poverty and the lack of infrastructure on the other.[18] Some contend that, whatever attention politicians gave to the rhetoric of sustainable development, the *de facto* policy of development was "pollute first, clean up later."[19]

ASEAN took its first step towards environmental protection in 1978, when the grouping convened its first meeting of ASEAN experts on the environment.[20] Its first ministerial level declaration on co-operation on environmental issues followed in 1981.[21] It has, however, become better known for taking a pro-developing country stand, as at the 1992 Earth Summit in Rio de Janeiro.[22] This stance emphasizes the rights of developing states to permanent sovereignty over their natural and other resources[23] and over development[24] and de-emphasized the concepts of the environment as a global commons and heritage for all humankind. This position was most pronounced with regard to the conservation of rain forests and biodiversity.[25] Malaysian Prime Minister Dr Mahathir Mohamad spoke for many ASEAN members when he said "[n]ow the developed countries have sacrificed their own forests in the race for higher standards of living, they want to preserve other countries' rain forests — citing a global heritage — which could indirectly keep countries like Malaysia from achieving the same levels of development."[26]

The ASEAN countries also rallied to lobby successfully against Austrian eco-labels on tropical timber.[27] Most recently, they have played a central role in the World Trade Organization's (WTO's) challenge of U.S. laws prohibiting shrimp imports from nations that do not mandate the use of production methods that safeguard against the killing of sea turtles.[28]

More positively, the ASEAN members have taken some steps towards improving environmental co-operation among themselves and with the non-ASEAN states. Such steps include environmental programmes that evolved through three phases to form an ASEAN Strategic Plan of Action (1994–98).[29] The strategies cover a broad range of environmental concerns and adopt many of the approaches recommended in Agenda 21. Broadly, the ASEAN strategy seeks to integrate environment and developmental concerns in the decision-making process of governments through such mechanisms.[30] The Strategy Plan also recognizes the need to foster government and private sector interactions;[31] strengthen institutional and legal capacities;[32] establish a regional framework on biological diversity conservation and sustainable use;[33] promote the protection of coastal zones and marine resources;[34] and promote environmentally sound management of toxic chemicals and hazardous wastes[35] and a system for promoting environmentally sound technologies.[36]

The effectiveness of such measures, however, suffers from weaknesses in monitoring, assisting, and ensuring state compliance. These weaknesses are endemic to the ASEAN way and its preference for non-interference in the domestic affairs of member states; for non-binding plans, instead of treaties;[37] and for central institutions with relatively little independent initiative or resources. As such, the ASEAN environmental undertakings may be characterized as plans for co-operation between national institutions, rather than the creation or strengthening of any regional institutions as a central hub for policy-making or implementation.[38]

This limits the stability and certainty of ASEAN co-operation. Environmental undertakings, whether in Action Plans or elsewhere, no matter how solemn and well-meant, are left to the individual states to implement or to delay, as they decide for themselves.

The nature and limit of ASEAN co-operation on environmental matters can be seen in the fate of the ASEAN Agreement on the Conservation of Nature and Natural Resources. The Agreement was drafted for ASEAN by a group of experts from the IUCN (World Conservation Union), a blue-chip international organization, with expertise and influence.[39] The 1985 Agreement was notable for a number of innovative principles and forward-looking approaches. Many of these have found their way into subsequent international treaties, such as the Convention on Biodiversity, concluded at the 1992 Rio Summit.[40] Despite this, while the Agreement was initially signed by the ASEAN members, it has failed to achieve the required number of ratifications to come into force. Academics have bemoaned the fact and praised its drafting.[41] But after fifteen years in limbo, the Agreement may well be still-born.

Why? The ASEAN countries that have yet to ratify the Agreement — Brunei, Malaysia and Singapore — have not publicly stated their reasons.[42] Nor, tellingly, have the other ASEAN members pressed them for their reasons. The reasons are therefore subject to speculation.

But the preliminary assessment of this chapter is that the Agreement has not come into effect in ASEAN not despite its forward-looking principles and approaches, but because of them. In crafting the Agreement, the international experts on the environment seem to have given insufficient attention to either the ASEAN way, or the ASEAN response to international and Western approaches to environmental protection, as seen later in their joint position on the Rio (Earth) Summit.

Other reasons can also be suggested. In drafting the Agreement, there seems to have been little attention given to the fact that ASEAN had then (and still has) very few binding agreements among its members. Furthermore, the principles of the Agreement suggest that one ASEAN country might be under an obligation to consider funding other ASEAN members to help in the conservation of the region's natural heritage. Such a principle of substantial transfers from one ASEAN member to another has no precedent in the grouping.

As such, it is suggested here that the Agreement succumbed to over-ambition, idealism and perhaps ignorance of the norms and institutional practices of ASEAN.

Yet it is too easy to suggest that environmental co-operation within ASEAN can and must only follow the ASEAN way as it is. To do so would beg the question whether the ASEAN way and institutions in their present form can in fact effectively protect the environment. If not, then any environmental agreement that is acceptable will prove ineffective. The answer to this important question may be found in an examination of the ASEAN response to the Indonesian fires and resulting haze pollution in the region.

ASEAN and the Indonesian Fires

In 1997 and early 1998, Southeast Asia suffered outbreaks of fires and smoke haze of great human and environmental consequence. Centred in the Indonesian provinces of Kalimantan and Sumatra, the fires spread as smoke haze across borders to affect the region, especially Malaysia, Brunei, and Singapore, and forcing some 20 million people to breathe potentially harmful air for prolonged periods.[43] The chief of the United Nations Environment Programme (UNEP), Dr Klaus Toepfer, declared the fires "a global disaster".[44] The fires and regional haze pollution are the most important and prominent challenge to ASEAN co-operation on the environment. What has been done?

ASEAN environment ministers agreed to a Co-operation Plan on Transboundary Pollution in June 1995.[45] This was followed by a Regional Haze Action Plan in 1997. These will be briefly described and assessed for their effectiveness.

The Co-operation Plan set out broad policies and strategies to deal with atmospheric and other forms of transboundary pollution and outlined efforts to be made at both national and regional levels to deal with the 1994 haze. Each country agreed to establish focal points and enhance its national capability to deal with forest fires. Countries also agreed to share knowledge and technology on the prevention and mitigation of forest fires and to establish a mechanism for co-operation in combating forest fires.[46]

In the Co-operation Plan, ASEAN ministers also agreed to develop a common air quality index and a fire danger rating system for the region. ASEAN institutions like the Specialized

Meteorological Centre were asked to develop ways of predicting the tracts and spread of smoke haze. The Co-operation Plan also envisaged support from countries outside the region with expertise in fire management systems, such as New Zealand and the United States, as well as from institutions like the Japan-based International Tropical Timber Organization (ITTO).

The Co-operation Plan is less formal than comparable treaties in other regions, such as Europe, that deal with long-distance transboundary harm.[47] Its principles and approach, however, might seem workable and even commendable. First, the Co-operation Plan recognizes that the region is a single eco-system. Additionally, it emphasizes the need to build on both national and regional efforts so that one complements the other and incorporates principles of prevention, mutual assistance, and co-operation. It also recognizes that, although all states have a common interest in reducing or avoiding a recurrence of the haze, they have different abilities and responsibilities in working towards a solution. In this respect, the Co-operation Plan expresses the principle of common and differentiated responsibility, recognized in the Rio Declaration,[48] at a regional level.

However, implementation of the Co-operation Plan has, in large part, failed. Very few of the steps envisaged were actually taken. The outbreak of fires in 1997 demonstrated the lack of follow-up to the Co-operation Plan in almost all areas. Singapore's assistance to Indonesia — providing satellite imaging of fires and "hot spots" — was the lone exception. Instead of working within an agreed system of co-operation, countries were left to bilateral arrangements and emergency discussions, especially between Indonesia and Malaysia, and between Indonesia and Singapore.

Following the 1997 fires, the ASEAN environment ministers agreed in December 1997 to the Regional Haze Action Plan to provide further commitments and detail.[49] Again, the Action Plan set commendable objectives: prevent land and forest fires; establish operational mechanisms to monitor fires; and strengthen regional fire-fighting capabilities. The Action Plan reiterated the need for regional monitoring and for identification of sources of technical assistance from within ASEAN, from non-ASEAN countries, and from international organizations, such as the Asian Development Bank and United Nations Environmental Program. The Action Plan continued primarily to emphasize national plans and capabilities.

However, the Action Plan called for the establishment of a procedure for pooling fire-fighting resources for regional fire-fighting operations.

Upon review in April 1998, the Action Plan agreed to create two sub-regional Firefighting Arrangements for Kalimantan and for the Sumatra/ Riau provinces in Indonesia.[50] Indonesia also announced that it would lay the framework for an ASEAN Research and Training Centre for Land and Forest Fire Management in Central Kalimantan.[51] Discussion of joint funding within the region has so far yielded no agreement.

Many critics blame Indonesia for its handling of the haze as too little and too late. In fact, there are those in Indonesia itself who feel that stronger actions and change are needed.

Clearly, the Action Plan is a welcome attempt to kick-start the stalled work of the earlier and more general Co-operation Plan. Doubt remains, however, as to the ability of ASEAN to fill in the omissions of the Indonesian national system, primarily because of the ASEAN norm for non-intervention in the domestic affairs of member states and the dominant role that Indonesia plays in the grouping. The ineffectiveness of the Plan can also be traced to the lack of sufficient institutional support to prioritize environmental law and policy-making in ASEAN. This relates to the ASEAN aversion to stronger regional institutions.

In the face of these obstacles, ASEAN has to date failed to supplement failures by Indonesia to address the Southeast Asian fires. While efforts continue, the recurrence of the fires in 1998 and 1999 suggest that they have yet to be effective. The lack of regional haze in 1999 has not been because of any ASEAN actions to prevent fires, but because unusually wet weather has dampened the fires that have been started and stopped them from spreading.

What More Can and Should Be Done? Institutions and Co-operation

Various means and methods have been suggested for an effective response to the Indonesian fires and regional haze pollution. These are too many and detailed to canvass fully here.[52] ASEAN has, in fact, agreed to a suggestion by UNEP that studies be undertaken on a possible treaty on the fires.

For the purposes of this chapter, it is sufficient that some suggestions be outlined insofar as they relate to the broader questions of ASEAN co-operation and institutions.

Perhaps the easiest and (to some) ideal solution would be to design ASEAN efforts to deal with the fires in strict accordance with international environmental principles. Some environmentalists might indeed be tempted to go beyond this, to suggest forward-looking principles and innovative approaches, much like the ASEAN Agreement on the Conservation of Nature and Natural Resources. In so doing, the ASEAN way would be put to one side and ignored.[53]

While such an approach has its attractions, others may consider that it would likely fail to find acceptance, again like the ASEAN Agreement.

At the opposite end of the spectrum, the approach to ASEAN co-operation on this important environmental issue might be wholly cast in the existing norms of the ASEAN way. Such an approach might be accepted more easily. However, like the existing ASEAN Co-operation Plan and the Regional Haze Action Plan, this might prove ineffective because of the ASEAN way it embraces.

In the broad space between these two extremes, we can point to an approach to ASEAN co-operation on the fires that recognizes the ASEAN way and yet still endeavours to stretch its limits within what is both politically possible, and possibly effective. This "golden mean" is of course easier to state in broad approach than it is to describe in detail. Details of what is possible and what might be effective are matters of judgment, but judgments might differ. They might also change over time, especially given the installation of a new government in Indonesia, itself mixed between reformers and more established figures, and drawn from across a wide political spectrum.

One possible starting point in this exercise is to begin by understanding how even the existing efforts to address the issue have stretched and changed past ASEAN practices. For while the efforts on the fires have yet to achieve their ambition, ASEAN's institutional approaches have, in the process, thickened and adapted. Three developments stand out in this regard.

The first is the fact of having regular and frequent meetings to review progress. The meetings of senior environment officials have taken place as often as once a month, with some exceptions because of disruptions caused by Indonesia's political transition.

The second is that these meetings have gone beyond the exchange of formalities to a more open and frank discussion of the problems underlying the fires and the lack of sufficient action to address them. It is notable in this regard that ASEAN officials on the environment have officially referred to Indonesia's forestry and land use policies; such issues are literally a matter of sovereign territorial rights. Attempts by the international community to address similar issues on the conservation of tropical rainforests have been repeatedly rebuffed, and no internationally binding treaty on forests and land use has been agreed. Despite this, the ASEAN norm of non-intervention has not thus far intruded or been used as a shield to this increasingly candid review of Indonesia's policies on this sensitive issue.

The third development that is notable in the current practices in addressing the issue of the fires is that ASEAN has increasingly opened its proceedings to international institutions and even to non-governmental organizations. The Asian Development Bank and UNEP have been regularly included in ASEAN discussions on the issue. Their offers of assistance and advice to the ASEAN Secretariat on the issue have also largely been accepted by Indonesia and the other member states.

As for NGOs, ASEAN environment ministers have taken the step — unusual in state-centric ASEAN — of inviting them to support efforts to deal with the fires. In June 1998, the Singapore Environment Council made a presentation to the ASEAN senior officials for the environment on the fires, after an international dialogue on the issue issued a statement on the means to address the issue.[54] This was perhaps the first occasion at which an NGO formally met and made representations to ASEAN environmental officials. Other NGOs have since made similar interventions.

These three developments have not, as admitted, solved the problem of the fires. Nor are they by any means revolutionary. In toto, however, they point to an increasing institutionalization of ASEAN in dealing with this environmental challenge. They may also be significant when we review how environmental institutions in the international sphere and in other regions foster compliance.

For in the international community and in other regions, including Europe, environmental laws and policies are not enforced by world government or (largely) by sanctions and courts that legalistically hold one state responsible and accountable to another.

Instead, studies show that environmental institutions foster compliance through softer and more co-operative means, such as regular and close review of country reports on their progress; providing technical and other assistance; and offering financial assistance from pooled resources.

The reviews in a number of cases are sharpened by having sufficient and independent expertise in the secretariat to assess and query country reports and/or by opening the proceedings or their outcomes to NGOs and to the public.

Compliance with environmental law and policy in this respect depends more on the "sunshine" methods of transparency and "carrots" of assistance, rather than the hard sticks of sanctions and penalties.[55] Those environmentalists who demand world government and treaties with "teeth" have rarely gotten their wish, whether in ASEAN or elsewhere. ASEAN, as such, must be adjudged as having come some way towards the international approaches in dealing with the fires. In the process, the ASEAN way has changed incrementally, but has not been abandoned.

From this recognition, further incremental steps can be suggested briefly, as follows[56]:

1. *Widening the Review Process.* The regular review of action plans and undertakings can be further widened to include relevant inter-governmental organizations, such as the secretariats for the United Nations Convention on Biological Diversity and for the Climate Change Convention. Similarly, the review could be opened to scientists or technical experts for comment.[57] A further step would be to allow recognized NGOs with expertise and interest to participate.[58]

   Additionally, or alternatively, the ASEAN Secretariat itself might serve a role in commenting at such reviews, from a more impartial point of view. Such a role for the ASEAN Secretariat would, however, require that the organization be strengthened in knowledge and capacity, and have the legitimized role of providing such a review.

2. *Strengthening ASEAN Secretariat Capacity.* ASEAN's general capacity for environmental policy-making and assisting compliance will need to be strengthened. As noted, ASEAN's institutional capacity has been limited because the ASEAN way doubts the effectiveness of supranational institutions.

Within ASEAN too, the environment has not been emphasized. Such shortcomings in ASEAN may have to be addressed in dealing with transboundary pollution, as much as national capacities.[59]

ASEAN should have sufficient resources and knowledgeable personnel to add value to national efforts to deal with the transboundary pollution. This might assist and help smooth matters if and when bilateral discussions become ruffled. The use of good offices and of preventive diplomacy by the ASEAN Secretary-General might also be strengthened; this could go beyond environmental issues to cover other transboundary and regional concerns, either within ASEAN or in a broader framework, such as the ASEAN Regional Forum.[60] Only then can ASEAN play an adequate role in monitoring and ensuring the compliance of states with the Plans and any other agreements that concern efforts to prevent or control the fires.

3. *Official Recognition of Cost.* There should be a recognition of the human, economic, and other costs of the fires and haze that is acknowledged by all states involved. This follows from the precept that the seriousness of the harm increases the prospects of finding co-operation and, conversely, the relative insignificance of the problem lowers those prospects.

At present, many of the cost estimates have come from NGOs and think-tanks. The ASEAN governments will need to take these estimates into their official consideration or to generate figures of their account. This may assist the Indonesian political system in recognizing the real costs to their own people and the economic system. It would also be a basis for affected states to make the economic commitment to fund the necessary steps for the prevention and control of future fires. This has not been done to date.

Perhaps for this reason, despite NGO estimates of losses running into hundreds of millions of dollars, neither Malaysia nor Singapore have been forthcoming on the suggestion for a multilateral revolving fund or, to some degree, to assist in UNEP's request for US$10 million for interim fire-fighting measures.[61]

It is common sense that co-operation will only succeed if, for all parties, the benefits are greater than the costs.[62] Part of the response to this reality must then be to fully recognize the benefits to be gained by controlling transboundary pollution.

4. *Linking Environment and Economic Policy.* The possibility of linking environmental and economic concerns within ASEAN should be considered. It is clear that initiatives such as the SIJORI Growth Triangle, between Singapore, Johor, and the Riau Islands and Sumatra provinces of Indonesia, enhance economic interdependence, as do ASEAN-wide programmes.[63] So do the ASEAN Free Trade Area (AFTA) and the ASEAN Investment Area (AIA).[64] It is also discernible that environmental standards have an economic impact on traders and, especially, investors. Higher standards might exact higher costs for businesses and, therefore, to attract investment, countries may lower or be loathe to increase environmental protections.[65] There is, therefore, economic sense to connect ASEAN's economic agenda to its environmental concerns.[66]

Conversely, a link to economics would help prioritize the environment. On the whole, such connections would help the ASEAN countries to take steps towards sustainable development, reconciling the environment with economics. ASEAN has rejected the idea of sanctions and environmental conditionality for trade and aid, as noted earlier. However, the links between the environment and economics among the ASEAN members could be positive and co-operative — "carrots" rather than "sticks".

None of the above suggestions would require a binding treaty to be concluded on the fires. This may be best as such treaties still remain the exception in ASEAN. If a treaty on the fires is desired, however, there are a number of ways in which it can be made more amenable to the ASEAN way, while still borrowing from international practices and standards that have proved effective.

The following are (briefly) two suggestions for such a treaty:[67]

5. *Specific Targets: National Standards and the Golden Rule.* The ASEAN Plan or treaty can evolve towards setting specific targets for atmospheric pollution fires and haze. This might well be difficult, given different environmental priorities, stage of industrial development and administrative, and technical capacities between countries. There are even different measurement systems in ASEAN for airborne pollutants. Harmonizing limits, such as seen in the European Community experience,[68] in such a situation might not be achievable.

If a common system cannot be achieved, an alternative would be to require states to set their own national laws and limits and then to hold them to it, through an intergovernmental panel. This approach is seen in a number of agreements on transboundary pollution.[69] It is less difficult than reaching common agreement. It also avoids the imposition by any one country of its own unilateral standards. Instead, like the Golden Rule, each country is held to do to others what it would do domestically for itself.[70]

6. *Privatizing Conflict.* The idea of one member suing another or seeking to hold them legally responsible may be seen by some as contrary to the ASEAN way and to ASEAN solidarity. This is notwithstanding that such a judicial approach would be in keeping with ASEAN's emphasis on the peaceful settlement of disputes.

If this concern is keenly felt by the ASEAN countries, there are ways of accommodating it within a treaty, while still allowing the possibility of holding wrong-doers responsible for the fires. This is found in the concept of privatizing environmental conflicts. Such a concept would aim to devolve disputes and suits from the inter-state level to legal proceedings at the level of municipal laws.

Such proceedings could be instituted against the polluter as a private claim, such as in the law of tort, or as a public interest suit. There would be advantages in allowing such suits, as opposed to emphasizing inter-state mechanisms. A government would not take a suit against another government. Rather, they would only create the framework for private suits.[71]

Suits outside Indonesia have been considered by Indonesian officials, at least with regard to foreign investors who might be implicated in the fires. Suits against Indonesian corporations have also been publicly suggested in Singapore.[72] This could be done either with a special framework, created at the consent of the different countries, or without such a framework, depending solely on each country's jurisdictional rules.

The countries could provide a treaty framework to allow for access to their national courts. One example of such a framework is the 1974 Nordic Convention between Denmark, Finland, Norway, and Sweden. This provides citizens in each of these countries the right to bring a suit in the court of another country for compensation for transboundary pollution.[73] As applied to the Southeast Asian fires, such a treaty approach could, for example, provide Singaporeans automatic access to the courts of Indonesia.[74]

The six suggestions above might be considered too much by some. In their judgment, ASEAN may not be ready to take on such measures. To others, they may seem too little. They do not believe such measures will prove effective to the challenge of the fires.

Details of what is possible and what might be effective are matters of judgment and, as previously stated, judgments might differ. As such, it bears repetition that what we hope to achieve in setting out these possibilities is to describe an approach to ASEAN co-operation on the fires that recognizes the ASEAN way and yet still endeavours to stretch its limits within what is both politically possible, and possibly effective.

These possibilities, as such, point to ways to evolve ASEAN co-operation on the environment and to develop the necessary institutions for such co-operation.

Conclusion: Evolving ASEAN Co-operation

Amidst the regional economic crisis, discussion of ASEAN and the ASEAN way has become polarized and perhaps simplified. Some suggest that ASEAN will always be what it is today, and nothing needs changing. Others advocate radical change and a sharp abandonment of the ASEAN norms of the past.

This chapter argues that in the field of environmental co-operation, there is the view that ASEAN is not static. ASEAN is changing and the pace of change is accelerating in response to the crisis of the fires and haze. But the changes are far from radical. They are neither widely recognized, nor do they have a predetermined and agreed end goal and road map. Nor is it certain that the existing changes are sufficient to be effective in addressing the immediate problems of the fires and haze.

Are these changes true to the ASEAN way, or are they increasingly taking on board influences, principles and approaches from the international community and other regions? Much depends on how we describe the ASEAN way and the norms of the environmental community, both internationally and in other regions.

Some hold that other regions and the international community should prescribe sanctions and strict state accountability for environmental pollution. If so, then what we see in ASEAN today and for the foreseeable future is indeed different. There are few who think that ASEAN's co-operation will take on such ideas at the risk of damaging inter-state relations; this is especially as (to many) the environment continues to be considered a peripheral issue, notwithstanding the fires.

Yet, when we look more closely at the norms of other regions and the international environmental regimes, we see little evidence of such approaches. Instead, we see an increasing emphasis on co-operative measures, "carrots" instead of "sticks". We also see environmental institutions that foster compliance with assistance and reporting mechanisms, rather than penalities and sanctions.

From this perspective, the international norms and those of other regions are not so far removed from the ASEAN way. The distance that remains is, however, still significant. An attempt has therefore been made here to suggest some steps for ASEAN to adapt (not adopt) international approaches and evolve the ASEAN way towards greater effectiveness in environmental co-operation.

Such co-operation would be expected to evolve first to meet the crisis of the fires, and then, further down the road, to address the fundamental issues of fostering co-operation for environmental protection and sustainable development in the region.

The international regime for environmental law and policy is still relatively young and evolving. Its modern development can be traced back only to the 1972 Stockholm Declaration, and it gained international prominence only at the 1992 Rio Summit. In its development to date, environmental law and policy has given hope to many in the principles and approaches it has initiated and often pioneered. The environmental cause has also known considerable frustration, particularly at the slow pace of progress and gaps in implementation.

ASEAN and the ASEAN way are also not so old or so fixed. While the Association is thirty-three years old, many of its members and initiatives are very recent. There is, therefore, a real prospect and a need for ASEAN, its norms and institutions to change to be relevant to the times and needs.

The modes of ASEAN co-operation, known as the "ASEAN way", do not serve well in dealing with environmental challenges such as the fires. Yet, efforts to foist international approaches and principles onto ASEAN have so far failed because they have tried to substitute themselves for that ASEAN way. As such, perhaps the best hope is that the ASEAN way, without either being ossified or abandoned, can be allowed to evolve and change. Such evolution and change would have implications not only for the environment, but also for the future shape of ASEAN.

NOTES

*   I am grateful to Dr Mubariq Ahmad and other colleagues at the ASEAN Roundtable 1999 for their valuable comments.

1   See Peter M. Haas et al., eds., *Institutions for the Earth: Sources of Effective International Environmental Protection* (MIT Press, 1993); and Oran Young, ed., *Global Governance* (MIT Press, 1997).

2   Birnie and Boyle, *International Environmental Law* (Oxford University Press, 1993).

3   For example, see Harold Brookfield and Yvonne Byron, eds., *Southeast Asia's Environmental Future: The Search for Sustainability* (United Nations University Press, 1993); Robin Broad and John Cavanagh, *Plundering Paradise* (University of California Press, 1993); and Victor T. King, ed., *Environmental Challenges in Southeast Asia* (Curzon Press, 1998).

4   There is considerable literature written on the subject. For a recent overview of world trends, see Janet N. Abramovitz, *Taking a Stand: Cultivating a New Relationship to the World's Forests* (Washington D.C.: Worldwatch Institute, 1998); Nigel Dudley et al., *Bad Harvest?: The Timber Trade and the Degradation of the World's Forests* (London: Earthscan, 1995). For critical studies of deforestation in Asia, see, for example, James Rush, *The Last Tree: Reclaiming the Environment in Tropical Asia* (New York: Asia Society, 1991); David Lee, *The Sinking Ark: Environmental Problems in Malaysia and Southeast Asia* (1980); Philip Hurst, *Rainforest Politics: Ecological Destruction in Southeast Asia* (London: Zed Books, 1990); Christine Padoch and Nancy Lee Peluso, eds., *Borneo in Transition: People, Forests, Conservation, and Development* (New York: Oxford University Press, 1996); *The Battle for Sarawak's Forests* (1989); Nancy Lee Peluso, *The Endangered Rainforests and the Fight for Survival* (1992); *Rich Forests, Poor People: Resource Control and Resistance in Java* (Berkeley: University of California Press, 1992); *Malaysia: Sustainability and the Trade in Tropical Timbers* (1991); William W. Bevis, *Borneo Log: The Struggle for Sarawak's Forests* (Seattle: University of Washington Press, 1995); Peter Dauvergne, *Shadows in the Forest: Japan and the Politics of Timber in Southeast Asia* (Cambridge, Mass: MIT Press, 1997); and Noeleen Heyzer, *Gender, Population, and Environment in the Context of Deforestation: A Malaysian Case Study* (Kuala Lumpur: Asian and Pacific Development Centre, 1996).

5   See, for example, Sompong Sucharitkul, "ASEAN Activities with Respect to the Environment", *Asian Yearbook of International Law* 3 (1994): 317–38; and Gregory Rose, "Regional Environmental Law in Southeast Asia, *RECIEL* 4, no. 1 (1995): 40. For a more balanced view of the region, see Boer, Ramsey and Rothwell, *Environmental Law in the Asia-Pacific* (Kluwer, 1998).

6   A number of recent works focus on the local "environmental politics" in Southeast Asia. These include Philip Hirsch and Carol Warren, eds., *The Politics of Environment in Southeast Asia: Resources and Resistance* (Routledge, 1998); and Michael Parnwell and Raymond Bryant, eds., *Environmental Change in South-East Asia: People, Politics and Sustainable Development* (Routledge, 1996).

7   On ASEAN and Cambodia, see Kim Hourn Kao and Jeffrey A. Kaplan, eds., *Dynamo or Dynamite?: Cambodia's Future in ASEAN* (London: ASEAN Academic Press, 1999). See also Frederick Z. Brown and David G. Timberman, eds., *Cambodia and the International Community: The Quest for Peace, Development, and Democracy* (Singapore: Institute of Southeast Asian Studies, 1998); Tim Huxley, *ASEAN and Indochina: A Study of Political Responses, 1975–81* (Canberra: Australian National University, 1985); Donald E. Weatherbee, *ASEAN After Cambodia: Reordering Southeast Asia* (New York: Asia Society, 1989).

8   See the World Bank, *The East Asian Miracle* (1993); see also Asian Development Bank, *Emerging Asia: Changes and Challenges* (1997). For a revisionist view after the crisis, see Bernard Arogyaswamy, *The Asian Miracle, Myth and Mirage: The Economic Slowdown is Here to Stay* (Westport, Conn: Quorum Books, 1998).

9   For a discussion and projection of trade-led growth in the region, see UN ESCAP, *Trade Prospects for the Year 2000 and Beyond for the Asian and Pacific Region*, Studies in Trade and Investment No. 12 (New York: 1995). Table 1, p.16, singles out the trade performance of the ASEAN-4.

10 The admission of Cambodia was postponed, pending elections to resolve the leadership dispute between rival factions. On recent developments in ASEAN, see Hadi Soesastro, ed., *ASEAN in a Changed Regional and International Political Economy* (Jakarta: Centre for Strategic and International Studies, 1995); and Amitav Acharya and Richard Stubbs, eds., *New Challenges for ASEAN: Emerging Policy Issues* (Vancouver, BC: UBC Press, 1995). For an overview of ASEAN, see Kernial Singh Sandhu et al., eds., *The ASEAN Reader* (Singapore: Institute of Southeast Asian Studies, 1992).

11 The classic exposition of the region as a basket case is Gunnar Myrdal, *Asian Drama: An Inquiry into the Poverty of Nations* (Twentieth Century Fund, 1968).

12 For an analysis of the ASEAN way, see, generally, Michael Antolik, *ASEAN and the Diplomacy of Accommodation* (Armonk, N.Y.: M. E. Sharpe, 1990); Michael Haas, *The Asian Way to Peace* (New York: Praeger, 1989).

13 On the ARF, see Desmond Ball, ed., *The Transformation of Security in the Asia/Pacific Region* (Frank Cass, 1996); and Derek da Cunha, ed., *The Evolving Pacific Power Structure* (Singapore: Institute of Southeast Asian Studies, 1996). On ASEM, see Hanns Maull et al., eds., *Europe and the Asia Pacific* (London: Routledge, 1998). On APEC, see Bijit Bora and Christopher Findlay, *Regional Integration and the Asia-Pacific* (Melbourne: Oxford University Press, 1996); Chia Siow Yue, ed., *APEC: Challenges and Opportunities* (Singapore: Institute of Southeast Asian Studies, 1994).

14 For an examination of the ASEAN way in its application to the ARF, see Simon S. C. Tay with Obood Talib, "The ASEAN Regional Forum: Preparing for Preventive Diplomacy", *Contemporary Southeast Asia* 19, no. 3 (1997): 252.

15 For a study of the different periods in ASEAN, see Chin Kin Wah, "ASEAN Institution Building", in *ASEAN Towards 2020*, edited by Stephen Leong (ISIS, 1998). See also Simon Tay and Yeo Lay Hwee, "Institutionalizing ASEAN and the Asia-Pacific" (Paper presented at the ASEAN-ISIS ASEAN 2020 conference, July 1999). For a more conceptual discussion of the meaning and significance of institutions and institutionalization in the Asia-Pacific, see Amitav Acharaya, "Realism, Institutionalism and the Asian Economic Crisis", *Contemporary Southeast Asia* 21, no.1 (April 1999).

16 For example, John Funston, "Is ASEAN Out of Its Depth?" *Contemporary Southeast Asia* 20, no. 1 (April 1998).

17 For an examination of the role of international NGOs in relation to deforestation in Sarawak, see Margaret E. Keck and Kathryn Sikkink, *Activists Beyond Borders* (Ithaca and London: Cornell University Press, 1998), pp. 150–63.

18 UN ESCAP, *Report on the State of the Environment in the Asia-Pacific*, (1990); UN ESCAP, *Report on the State of the Environment in the Asia-Pacific* (1995).

19 See Bryant and Parnwell, op. cit., note 5, introduction, pp. 1–12, conclusion, pp. 330–38. For an analysis of the over-exploitation of natural resources, see Eduardo Tadem, "Conflict over Land-Based Natural Resources in the ASEAN Countries", in *Conflict over Natural Resources in Southeast Asia and the Pacific*, edited by Lim Teck Ghee and Mark Valencia (New York: Oxford University Press, 1990).

20 For a compilation of ASEAN documents, see K. L. Koh, ed., *Selected ASEAN Documents on the Environment* (Singapore: Asia Pacific Centre for Environmental Law, 1996). There has not been to date a definitive study of ASEAN's environmental record. Shorter studies of interest include: Ben Boer et al., *International Environmental Law in the Asia Pacific* (London: Kluwer Law International, 1998), which discusses the ASEAN region in Chp. 12, from p. 225; and Somphong Sucharitkul, "ASEAN Activities with Respect to the Environment", edited by Ko Swan Sik et al., *Asian Yearbook of International Law 3* (Kluwer Academic Press, 1994), p. 317.

21 See K. L. Koh, ed., op. cit.

22 Ibid., p. 69.

23 Resolution on Permanent Sovereignty Over Natural Resources, G.A. Res. 1803, U.N. GAOR, 17th Sess., Supp. No. 17, p. 15, U.N. Doc.A/5215 (1963).

24 Declaration on the Right to Development, G.A. Res. 41/128, U.N. GAOR, 41st Sess., Supp. No. 53, p. 187, U.N. Doc. A/41/53 (1986). This right is controversial and the Declaration was not widely supported among developed donor countries, with the United States among those who voted against the resolution. Principle 3 of the Rio Declaration is notable for being the first document containing this right to which both developed and developing countries have agreed.

25 For a discussion of developing country views, as well as alternative paradigms for justifying conservation in a developing country context, see R. Jayakumar Nayar and David Mohan Ong, "Developing Countries, 'Development' and the Conservation of Biological Diversity", in *International Law and the Conservation of Biological Diversity*, edited by Michael Bowman and Catherine Redgwell (London: Kluwer Law International, 1996).

26 See *Asian Yearbook of International Law 1*, Chronicle Section, p. 295, edited by Ko Swan Sik et al. (1991) (citing *Far Eastern Economic Review*, 1 August 1991, p. 20). For a discussion of the issue of sovereignty and global environmental concerns, see S. H. Bragdon, "National Sovereignty and Global Environmental Responsibility: Can the Tension Be Reconciled for the Conservation of Biological Diversity?", *Harvard International Law Journal* 33 (1992): 381, 387. On Malaysia's influence on UNCED and international environmental policy, see Fauziah Mohd Taib, "Malaysia and UNCED: An Analysis of a Diplomatic Process 1989–1992" (Ph.D. dissertation, 1997).

27 For a description and analysis of the Austrian trade measures on tropical timber, the ASEAN reaction, and the likely outcome in the light of GATT rules, see Brian Chase, "Tropical Forests and Trade Policy: The Legality of Unilateral Attempts to Promote Sustainable Development under the GATT", *Hastings International and Comparative Law Review* 17 (1994): 349, 374–79. On the attitudes of ASEAN and the Asia-Pacific countries towards trade and environment issues, see Simon S. C. Tay, "Trade and Environment: Perspectives from the Asia-Pacific", *World Bulletin* 13 (1997): 1. See also Alexander Gillespie, "The Malaysian Agenda and Influence on the International Tropical Deforestation Debate", *Asia Pacific Journal on Environmental Law* 25 (1996): 40–44.

28 See World Trade Organization Panel Report: United States Import Prohibition of Certain Shrimp and Shrimp Products, *International Legal Materials* 37 (Washington D.C.: The American Society of International Law, July 1988): 832.

29 See K. L. Koh, op. cit., p. 181, note 80. See also Ben Boer et al., *International Environmental Law in the Asia Pacific* 225 (1998), for an outline on the ASEAN region.

30 See K. L. Koh, op. cit., p. 183, note 80.
31 Ibid., p. 184.
32 Ibid., p. 185.
33 Ibid.
34 Ibid., p. 186.
35 Ibid., p. 187.
36 Ibid., p. 188.
37 The one treaty that was negotiated among the ASEAN members, the Agreement on the Conservation of Nature and Natural Resources, has not been ratified by a sufficient number of members and, as such, is not in force. The Agreement was signed by all six of the then ASEAN members in Kuala Lumpur, Malaysia, on 9 July 1985. Only three countries have ratified the agreement, one less than is required to bring it into force. See K. L. Koh, op. cit., p. 27, note 80. For a comparison of the ASEAN Agreement and other biodiversity treaties, see Robin Churchill, "The Contribution of Existing Agreements for the Conservation of Terrestrial Species and Habitats to the Maintenance of Biodiversity", in *International Law and the Conservation of Biological Diversity*, edited by Bowman and Redgwell (Kluwer, 1995).
38 An example of this institutional weakness is that the first ASEAN State of the Environment Report was produced largely by the UN Environment Programme, with minimal input from ASEAN.
39 Founded soon after World War II, the IUCN has state members as well as individual members. It is therefore a mix between a non-governmental organization and an inter-governmental institution. The IUCN has advised many governments on conservation issues and has pushed forward initiatives such as the Convention against International Trade in Endangered Species (CITES), one of the most successful international environmental agreements.
40 *International Legal Materials 188* (1992).
41 For academic praise of the ASEAN Agreement, see Ben Boer, Ross Ramsay, and Donald R. Rothwell, *International Environmental Law in the Asia Pacific* (Kluwer Law International, 1998), pp. 227–29; Robin Churchill, "The Contribution of Existing Agreements for the Conservation of Terrestrial Species and Habitats to the Maintenance of Biodiversity", in *International Law and the Conservation of Biodiversity*, edited by Bowman and Redgewell (Kluwer, 1995); and Koh Kheng Lian, "ASEAN Agreement on the Conservation of Nature and Natural Resources, 1985: A Question of Ratification and Implementation" (Paper presented at the conference on "Environmental Treaties: The Asia Pacific Dimension", Darwin, Australia, 21–22 July 1995).
42 The Agreement was negotiated in 1985 and therefore was limited to the then six members of ASEAN. The newer members have neither negotiated nor signed the Agreement.
43 Nigel Dudley, "The Year the World Caught Fire" (Gland, Switzerland: World Wide Fund for Nature, December 1997).

44 See, "The Fires are Back", *Asiaweek*, 18 March 1998, p. 46.

45 The ASEAN Co-operation Plan traces its development to ASEAN resolutions, meetings and strategic plans on transboundary pollution starting from 1990. ASEAN Cooperation Plan on Transboundary Pollution *http://www.aseansec.org/function/env/plan.htm>* (accessed on 30 January 1999). Notably, immediately prior to the adoption of the Co-operation Plan, the Informal Ministerial Meeting on the Environment held in Kuching, Malaysia, on 21 October 1994, recognized the need to control transboundary pollution within the region by treating it as "one eco-system".

46 Initiated by the 1997 fires, Malaysia and Indonesia concluded a bilateral memorandum of understanding for joint operations to deal with disasters of mutual concern, including fires. In 1997, significant numbers of Malaysian fire-fighters were deployed on Indonesian territory. It was, however, reported that they were often under-utilized. No similar deployment was arranged in response to the 1998 fires.

47 For a comparison of European and other documents concerning transboundary pollution, see Damien Gerardin, "Lessons from the European Community", in *Asian Dragons and Green Trade*, edited by Simon S. C. Tay and Daniel C. Esty (Singapore: Times Academic Press and Asia-Pacific Centre for Environmental Law, 1996).

48 See Rio Declaration, note 82, Principle 7.

49 Regional Haze Action Plan, ASEAN, December 1997.

50 Joint Press Statement, Third ASEAN Ministerial Meeting on Haze, Brunei, 4 April 1998 para. 8, *http://www.aseansec.org/function/env/plan.htm.*

51 Ibid.

52 For a discussion of the possible means, see Simon Tay, "The Southeast Asian Fires: The Challenge to International Law and Development", *Georgetown International Environmental Law Review* (Winter 1999).

53 While it is too early to prejudge, there is a danger that UNEP's offer to outline a treaty on the fires might fall prey to this danger. The study has largely been given over to environmental academics in the region with no strong record of understanding other areas of ASEAN activity and co-operation.

54 For a reprint of the NGO statement, see Simon Tay, "The Southeast Asian Fires". The author chaired the international dialogue for NGOs and made the presentation to the ASOEN.

55 On environmental institutions and means of fostering compliance, see *International Compliance with Non-binding Accords*, edited by Edith Brown Weiss (American Society of International Law, 1997); and *Engaging Countries: Strengthening Compliance with International Accords*, edited by Edith Brown Weiss and Harold K. Jacobson (MIT Press, 1998).

56 These suggestions are discussed more fully in Simon Tay, "The Southeast Asian Fires".

57 The Climate Change Convention sets an example by including scientists and technical experts in its panel of scientific experts.

58 Following the SEC Policy Dialogue, the chairman of the dialogue made an official presentation of its recommendations to the ASEAN Senior Officials for the Environment and Regional Haze Task Force. The *Straits Times*, 25 July 1998, in "Boycott of Haze Fire Firms Next?" reported that: "The NGOs' concerns were presented to the ASEAN environment ministers who met here last week to discuss the smoke haze problem. It was the first time NGOs were allowed to participate in an ASEAN meeting". The SEC Policy dialogue had earlier recommended that ASEAN "institutionalize review of actions taken on the fires by all concerned government officials and, further, to invite expert and concerned international organizations, scientists and academics, and non-government organizations for dialogue and review." See Annex.

59 The SEC Policy Dialogue called on ASEAN "to strengthen the capacity of the ASEAN Secretariat, especially in matters concerning the environment and sustainable development." See Annex.

60 Simon Tay with Obood Talib, "The ASEAN Regional Forum: Preparing for Preventive Diplomacy".

61 The concern of the states involved might legitimately be on the effectiveness of the proposed actions.

62 See Thomas W. Merrill, "Golden Rules for Transboundary Pollution", *Duke Law Journal* 46 (March 1997): 931–1019.

63 See Toh Mun Heng and Linda Low, *Regional Cooperation and Growth Triangles in ASEAN* (Singapore: Times Academic Press, 1993); and Edward K. Y. Chen and C. H. Kwan, eds., *Asia's Borderless Economy: The Emergence of Subregional Economic Zones* (St. Leonards, N.S.W.: Allen and Unwin, 1997). See also Linda Low and Simon S. C. Tay, "Growth Triangles and Labour in Southeast Asia", in *Liberalization and Labour*, edited by Rajah Rasiah and Norbert von Hofmann (Singapore: Friedrich Ebert Stiftung, 1996), pp. 86–145.

64 See Pearl Imada and Seiji Naya, eds., *AFTA: The Way Ahead* (Singapore: ASEAN Economic Research Unit, Institute of Southeast Asian Studies, 1992).

65 The literature on environmental effects on economic investment and industry migration is mixed. Many theorize that there is a race to the bottom in standards to attract foreign investment and trade. Others argue that the actual cost increase from environmental standards is small and does not determine investment decisions, which are based on a much wider consideration of competitiveness. See Richard L. Revesz, "Rehabilitating Interstate Competition: Rethinking the 'Race-to-the-Bottom' Rationale for Federal Environmental Regulation", *New York University Law Review* 67 (December 1992): 1210–54.

66 Both the EC and NAFTA have taken environmental factors into consideration, in different ways, in undertaking greater economic integration.

67 For more details, see Simon Tay, "The Southeast Asian Fires".

68 See Graham Bennet, ed., *Air Pollution Control in the European Community: Implementation of the EC Directives in the Twelve Member States* (London: Graham & Trotman, 1991). For an overview of the harmonization techniques within the EC, see Damien Gerardin, "The European Experience", in *Asian Dragons and Green Trade*, edited by Simon Tay and Daniel Esty (Singapore: Times Academic Press, 1996).

69 The North American Free Trade Agreement (NAFTA) between Canada, Mexico, and the USA takes a similar approach, thereby avoiding the need to harmonize limits. The OECD Council Recommendations on Principles Concerning Transfrontier Pollution uses a "principle of non-discrimination" by which states control their transboundary pollution to the same standards as applicable to similar pollution within their borders, and allow private plaintiffs access to their courts for redress, no matter where the damage is suffered.

70 See Merrill, "Golden Rules", p. 997.

71 The normal recourse would be to bring the suit where the damage was done; that is, in the case of the fires, in Indonesia. However, given the difficulties of effective prosecution or civil suits in Indonesia against polluting companies, there is some temptation to bring the suit before the courts of other jurisdictions.

72 "Boycott of haze fire firms next?", *Straits Times*, 25 July 1998, reporting a talk by Prof Tommy Koh, Singapore's ambassador-at-large, which suggested that companies involved should be exposed and boycotted by consumers.

73 See Bengt Broms, "The Nordic Convention on the Protection of the Environment", in *Transboundary Air Pollution*, edited by Cees Flinterman et al. (Dordrecht, Boston: M. Nijhoff, 1986).

74 A different approach would be to allow a suit by Singaporeans in Singaporean courts, notwithstanding the *forum conveniens* rules. This, however, would be adventurous litigation. Such cases would face considerable problems in terms of the jurisdiction of the courts over the defendants, the civil or penal laws invoked, and the proof of illegal acts and causation. Even if successful, there might well be difficulty in effectively enforcing the judgment. At best, bringing a suit in Singapore would provide an avenue to focus public attention against the defendants. For a fuller discussion, see Simon Tay, "Southeast Asian Fires".

9

ASEAN and the International Trading System: Regional Trade Arrangement vs. the WTO

H. S. KARTADJOEMENA *

Introduction

This chapter examines ASEAN regional economic arrangements in the light of the emerging global trading system operating within the multilateral framework of the World Trade Organization (WTO). It focuses on the issues to keep in mind when a government of an ASEAN country considers the relation between regional integration and the multilateral system. In so doing, it looks at the prevailing reality in ASEAN and the WTO. It assumes that it is the intention of the ASEAN states to continue the economic co-operation that has been undertaken since its creation but also to enjoy the benefits of WTO membership.

In this study, the question of regionalism versus multilateralism is posed in the context of internal ASEAN processes. However, the debate on regionalism has been pulled by two external factors which are influencing ASEAN in distinct but somewhat related ways. The two factors are the European model, which has been used as a reference point (not appropriately), and an example for achieving growth and prosperity, and, on the other hand, the pull of the global system, in which ASEAN has a strong long-term interest and from which it has profited. Against that background, this study argues for a specific approach to deal with regionalism and the multilateral system which is more appropriate for ASEAN. That approach requires regional integration be viewed from the specific context of ASEAN realities.

In view of the extensive experience in European economic and political integration, which has made it a reference point for other integration endeavours, we shall first briefly look at the European experience. The creation of the European Economic Community had an impact on the thinking about economic integration in other regions and also the development of the multilateral system under the General Agreement on Tariffs and Trade (GATT). We shall therefore look at the GATT/WTO system and examine regional economic integration in the light of the multilateral rules and study the way that regional arrangement has been treated in the GATT/ WTO system over time.

We shall then look at ASEAN both in the light of the European example and in the light of the implications of the GATT/WTO system on economic integration. Looking beyond the present context, we shall also briefly examine what possible scenario can be drawn about the future shape of the ASEAN regional integration process and the options available. What are the realistic options for ASEAN as a collective unit in a more complex global economic and trading system which is in the making? We shall deal with these points later in this chapter.

In looking at the prospects ahead, given current trends, it seeks to reconcile possible contradictory policy implications between various options while highlighting the areas of possible policy compatibility. Stated in a simplified way, the controversy centres on the choice between: (a) developing a trading system based primarily on a regional grouping, or, (b) developing a system which operates globally, based on the principle of non-discrimination and openness to markets in all countries. Are the two goals inherently incompatible, or will a more flexible approach taken by ASEAN be able to bridge the two opposing options?

ASEAN Regionalism, European Precedence, and the WTO

In the following, this study attempts to formulate an approach to the debate on regionalism versus multilateralism of trade which is more appropriate in the context of ASEAN. In so doing, it seeks to deal with the strategic choice available to ASEAN in approaching its regional arrangement and to place it within the broader global context and the development objectives of the region. The question can be posed in a manner which is currently fashionable: is regional arrangement a building block or a stumbling block to the open world trading system? What does this debate mean in the ASEAN context?

The debate involves both economic and political considerations which cannot be easily separated except for analytical purposes. On the economic side, there is the classic debate on whether regional integration is "trade creating" or "trade diverting". The answer is that it depends on how the system is put in place. But politically, even if a regional arrangement is shown to be trade diverting, and less efficient than global trade, if there are other motives which are deemed to be strategically and politically attractive to the regional members, there is sufficient reason to do so. We shall deal with this point later.

Economic Case for Multilateralism

Economically, given the prevailing realities and the growth objectives of the region, ASEAN's focus should be centred on strengthening the open global trading system.[1] This open system has been largely responsible for providing the market access needed and kept exports high. Globally, the open world trading system in the post-war period has been helpful in providing the environment for high growth in both the developed and developing countries. World trade and economic growth in the period 1947–73 was the highest in history, and the developing countries benefited equally from it.[2]

In the period 1970–80 ASEAN enjoyed high growth because of this open world trading system and sound macroeconomic discipline as well as appropriate exchange rate policies. High exports also led to high growth in the region, which in turn attracted foreign investment. In short, the global system enabled the region to grow rapidly, interrupted only by the Asian economic crisis, which was a crisis largely of our own making.[3] Similarly, during the period 1980–93 the founding members of ASEAN (ASEAN-5) enjoyed high growth rates of gross domestic product (GDP), with increasing exports to the rest of the world, indicating the importance of the world market for the region's good performance.[4] This system must be kept open.

In pursuit of that goal, ASEAN should continue to join hands with those who have the same interest in the expansion and maintenance of the global system. APEC's open regionalism, however puzzling it may be in some of its details, provides the broader alliance of countries with a similar interest in the maintenance of an open world trading system. It can be a strong voice in the WTO to maintain the momentum of openness. As a footnote to the above, future APEC initiatives should contain more elements of interest to ASEAN than they have been so far.

Nevertheless, the same debate on regionalism versus multi-lateralism that other regional arrangements had to face is also confronting ASEAN. For Europe, the temptation to opt for an inward-looking regionalism is not insignificant among the electorate. This European context needs a brief elaboration. Although we may regard it as undesirable, it should be noted that an inward-looking Europe is politically viable, if growth is not an objective. If low growth is an acceptable condition for the European electorate, then an introverted, fully-integrated and protectionist Europe should not be ruled out. It would be costly for the European consumers as well as for other countries seeking entry into the European market. Growth would be constrained, but it might be sustainable for some time. However, such a luxury is clearly not available to ASEAN.

Political Case for Strengthening ASEAN

Despite the strong *economic* case for anchoring ASEAN trade policy on the *multilateral system*, there is also a strong *political* case for continuing to strengthen the growth of *regional interdependence*. Why should ASEAN still pursue its objective of intensifying this process of regional integration? Politically, ASEAN has been instrumental in maintaining regional peace, without which the region would have faced great uncertainties. Political uncertainties would have led to diminishing domestic and international confidence and probably lower investment flows and hence, probably also lower growth rates. The process of strengthening ASEAN's political stability, under changing conditions of post-Cold-War and post-Asian-crisis, requires serious attention as this will be the basis necessary for regional growth.

Choice of Emphasis

For ASEAN, the policy issue at stake is not the question of whether ASEAN takes an open attitude or a closed attitude. For ASEAN, the choice is clear. ASEAN cannot afford to look inwards the way Europe might be tempted to do. Rather, at stake is the choice of emphasis on whether:

1. the ASEAN states should concentrate *primarily on the global system* while regional integration would be adjusted to the requirements of the global system;
or, alternatively,
2. the engagement with the global system would be *modulated* in such a way that it would ensure that *regional economic integration would be the primary focus.* This is basically closer to the European approach, although without the "fortress" illusion.

These are political issues. However, should regional integration as the primary focus be the choice, there is the technical question of whether such a choice would have an operational meaning. Thus, in ASEAN, regionalism may not be an adequate *economic* substitute to multilateralism, but it is arguably quite necessary to achieve the *political* objective of regional stability.

Dual Focus

The above point leads to the need for ASEAN to maintain a dual focus. The focus would centre ASEAN's attention on: (a) strengthening the open trading system as a basis for recovery from the crisis, and continued future growth — that is, for *economic* purposes, and (b) strengthening regional economic co-operation, for the *political* purpose of maintaining regional peace and stability. This leads to two questions: are the two objectives contradictory? Does strengthening ASEAN necessarily mean the process of economic integration as that notion is conventionally understood, that is, the European model?

The above questions can be posed in another way: given that the economic basis of growth for ASEAN is the global system, and given that the political basis of sustained activity is regional peace and stability, is the debate on regionalism versus multilateralism a relevant one? Yes, but only up to a point. In the ASEAN context, is the dichotomy necessary? The answer is no. Having said that, a more appropriate approach is needed. These questions will be addressed below.

Towards a "Constructive Ambiguity"

The above discussion on the strategy for ASEAN regional arrangement is full of nuances. As Hindley and Messerlin has alluded, regional arrangements sometimes become an option because there is a fear of being left behind by others who have moved towards regional arrangements. Therefore, regional arrangements sometimes emerge even if the economic fundamentals are not fully in place to justify the initiative.[5] Ambiguity, therefore, will be a permanent feature of ASEAN regional economic co-operation for quite some time. This is not necessarily undesirable, provided that ASEAN does not take an excessively ambitious regional goal in the short-term.

In evaluating ASEAN economic integration, it is inappropriate to measure the "success" or "failure" of ASEAN integration in terms of the criteria applied to the European Union, which contain extensive, structured, ambitious, and treaty-based commitments. ASEAN's economic integration process must be allowed to be more flexible, reflecting the level of development of most of the ASEAN countries as developing countries, with more incomplete modernization in the practices in the economy. However, it should be a "constructive ambiguity", pragmatically moving towards maximizing what is possible in the regional context.[6]

Some steps can be taken towards greater integration in order to modulate the dependence on the international system should fragmentation take place. These steps need not be dramatic, but they should be designed to expand the horizon of compatible practices and norms, leading to the development of common economic and business practices which are increasingly widespread and, over time, would cover virtually all sectors. In this respect, the example of how GATT, through evolution, has moved from its humble beginning as an *interim agreement* to become surreptitiously a permanent fixture in the global system, and a full-fledged international organization, with effective rules, is instructive. We shall deal with this further when we discuss the option for "soft" integration.

Regional Integration Movements: The Broader Picture and the European Precedence

Because the European experience has been a reference point in discussions on regional integration, this section examines its relevance to ASEAN. Although there are economic arguments for regional integration, the determining factor in the *decision* to proceed with integration is more often based on strategic and political considerations. This is particularly true when the process moves beyond the level of a free trade area.[7] In this connection, whatever our views may be on its impact on the global system (positive or negative), regional integration cannot be meaningfully discussed without looking at the European experience as the longest sustained, most extensive, and successful endeavour of voluntary economic integration, with binding and scheduled commitments. And European integration is a political act.

The literature on economic integration expanded beyond the analysis of free trade areas and customs union when six Western European countries signed the Treaty of Rome in 1957 and proceeded to undertake a process of economic integration which has evolved since then. The European Economic Community (EEC) was launched to establish the European Common Market. The Treaty had traced the long-term trajectory for Europe to move along the path from a free trade area, to a customs union, a common market, and economic integration.[8] Since the European integration movement in the 1950s, the process has moved much further, both in terms of the breadth of substantive coverage and the depth of integration. Moreover, numerous institutional innovations have been developed in Europe some of which may be useful institutional examples in the ASEAN context.

Economic Arguments for Integration

In summarizing the economic arguments for regional integration, taking the political motivation as given, Hoekman and Kostecki have enumerated the following points:

1. a subset of like-minded countries can go much further in liberalizing trade flows among themselves than can the full set of WTO members;

2. a way for countries to enhance their market power and circumvent the GATT/WTO rules for non-discrimination;
3. to lock in certain agreed-upon regulatory reforms and liberalization; and
4. seek access to an existing free trade area (FTA) in order to gain access to its market.[9]

These motivations have their own dynamics reflecting the specific context of the region undertaking the process of economic integration.

Based on the motivations above between 1948 and the end of the Uruguay Round in 1994, more than 100 preferential trading arrangements had been notified to the GATT Secretariat.[10] Judging from the number of notifications to the GATT/WTO, there appears to be growing political attractiveness of this approach for quite a number of countries. The multilateral system must therefore deal with the question in a systematic way. This aspect will be discussed further below.

The Political Motivation: Europe

The original motivation for the creation of the European Union (EU), which has become the reference point among regional arrangements, and the one which has achieved a major influence in the global economy, was primarily based on political considerations. The situation at the time of the creation of the EEC dictated that the path to force European countries to co-operate more closely with each other was by making them economically interdependent. The early effort to put in place the European Coal and Steel Community, and subsequently the EEC, was political and strategic.[11]

The Cold War further reinforced the political motivation to proceed with economic integration and the strengthening of Western Europe in facing the rival Eastern bloc. In the process, with strategic considerations in mind, many GATT rules have been waived to enable Western Europe to proceed with economic integration. Thus, many GATT rules were left aside because the EEC was a major political commitment on the part of the member countries. In the field of agriculture, notwithstanding the "chicken war" between the EEC and the United States in the 1960s, the process of European integration was in some aspects undertaken at the cost of sacrificing non-enforcement of some of the GATT rules.[12]

The Political Motivation: ASEAN

In ASEAN, the political motivation was largely similar, namely, to foster the foundation for a peaceful and co-operative environment in a region which might otherwise have become explosive. Unlike the EU, however, in ASEAN the political aspect of co-operation had surprisingly progressed faster and more successfully than the process of economic integration.[13] This situation is the inverse of the European experience. With some degree of exaggeration, it can be said that the need for closer economic ties in ASEAN has been motivated by the desire to put some economic "meat" to the bones of a surprisingly successful political co-operation.

By contrast, in Europe the difficult process of political co-operation in the post-war period was achieved through working together on economic issues, leading to mutual dependence, because the political aspect of co-operation was judged to be more difficult.[14] But the tenacity that the EEC maintained on the political importance of integration led to a situation that was not always in full conformity with the GATT. In the event when the GATT "blinked", it permitted the EEC to deviate from its rules by maintaining silence. We shall deal further with these issues as we discuss the relations of the WTO to regional integration.

Post-Cold War Scenario

The point has been reached in Europe where *economic* and *political* integration efforts have been able to move in a mutually reinforcing manner.[15] However, it had taken Europe forty years and the end of the Cold War to make this possible. Expansion of membership has moved beyond the countries of Western Europe and will continue eastwards to embrace countries which were formerly members of the Warsaw Pact. The question is whether expansion of European unification would lead to a more "inward-looking" Europe, or whether Europe would continue to be outward-looking.[16]

Similarly, the ending of the Cold-War has made it logical for the entire community of Southeast Asia to become a part of ASEAN, which has become an open system accessible to all states in the region, that is, to embrace the principle of universal membership of the region. Now with more countries co-operating under the umbrella of ASEAN as an all-inclusive regional association, the technical question is how to make ASEAN an economic zone of market economies becoming further engaged in a process of increasing economic interdependence and integration.

If the model chosen is the European model, then the process of integration would be extremely difficult. But more fundamentally, is it imperative for ASEAN to achieve economic integration along the same path as the European model? Is there another path? Is regional integration of the European model a necessary goal? We shall deal with this question later, but first, let us look at the process from the perspective of the WTO system.

Economic Integration and the WTO

We have touched on the "European reference" to regional integration. There is also the WTO dimension to regional integration. The issue of compatibility between the two must be answered. The GATT/WTO system was created to establish an open non-discriminatory world trading system. One of the pillars of the system is the principle of most-favoured-nation (MFN). However, the GATT agreement of 1947 allows for the creation of a free trade area or a customs union, which are departures from the MFN principle. Article 24 of the GATT permits the creation of such arrangements with specific requirements. After the Uruguay Round, the sectoral coverage was expanded to include trade in services. Article 5 of the General Agreement on Trade in Services (GATS) specified the rules on economic integration consistent with WTO rules.[17]

Evolution of Regional Trading Arrangements Since 1947

Looking back to the early days of the GATT, only a handful of attempts had been made at establishing free trade areas and customs unions, notably the BENELUX. The operating principles in the GATT were found in the GATT agreement, which is still valid today. Article 24 states that free trade areas and customs union would be permissible under the GATT, provided that existing commitments already made to third parties which had been in place at the time of the creation of the free trade area and customs unions remain intact.[18]

The question became more current when the European integration movement took more definite shape and when the European Economic Community's version of regional integration won over the rival version of the European Free Trade Area (EFTA). In formal terms, Article 24 defines it very much along the lines of Jacob Viner's definition.[19]

To the extent that regional arrangements depart from the principle of most-favoured-nation, which is the pillar of the multilateral system, the departure from the principle had to be further specified to make it compatible with the multilateral system. The Article defines how FTAs and customs unions ought to be established to qualify them to be treated as such, and how preferential treatments within the regional arrangements, which are not applied on an MFN basis, could be implemented to conform to the GATT agreement.[20]

Post-Uruguay Round Development

After the Uruguay Round, another dimension was added to the older GATT system. This was the expansion of the sectoral coverage of the GATT/WTO system from only trade in goods to services as well. After the Uruguay Round, services became an integral part of the GATT/WTO system. The General Agreement on Trade in Services has a specific article dealing with integration, namely, Article 5.[21]

With respect to Article 5 of GATS, it is interesting to note that, as a sign of changing times and the evolving nature of regional trade agreements, the word "economic integration", which was absent in the GATT vocabulary before the days of European integration, appeared in the GATS agreement. Since then, economic integration has become a part of the new vocabulary in the WTO lexicon.

We must presume that the intention was to explicitly introduce the concept of economic integration as a continuum, evolving from a simple free trade area to a customs union, to economic integration and possibly, a political union as demonstrated by the EEC, which later became the European Union. It is equally interesting to note that this concept of economic integration has entered into the lexicon of ASEAN and has also appeared in various important documents and declarations about the ASEAN Free Trade Area.

Jurisprudence in the GATT/WTO

In the GATT context, setting aside the subtleties of argumentation that have developed in the GATT/WTO jurisprudence over time, the crux of the issue is whether regional trade arrangements, emphasizing preferential treatment to members, are compatible with the multilateral principle of non-discrimination. The subsequent question is whether an acceptable form of an exception to the rule of non-discrimination could be formulated and still be consistent with the universal and non-discriminatory nature of the multilateral system.

In the GATT/WTO system, preferential, that is, discriminatory treatment between members and non-members of the regional arrangements, is resolved by asking the question whether the arrangements affect a *substantial* part of an economy and not just a cartelization of sectoral arrangements between a number of countries.[22] However, in practice, the application of the notion "substantial" has been flexible, raising a controversy about the discipline of the principle.

Another important issue is that the regional arrangement does not nullify the acquired access of WTO members which do not belong to the regional trade arrangement in question, and that the GATT procedure for negotiating concessions for changes in acquired access be followed. In the GATT/WTO system, this process is governed by GATT Article 28 on the modification of tariff schedules, which must be done by negotiation, and by Article 21 of the GATS for trade in services.

Threat to the Multilateral System

The question of regional arrangements in the context of the WTO becomes more disquieting when important trading countries begin to develop free trade areas, leading to discriminatory arrangements between members and non-members to the arrangements. The EU's preferential treatment of ACP (African, Caribbean and Pacific) members of developing countries and the North American Free Trade Agreement (NAFTA) arrangement between the United States, Canada, and Mexico have led to concern on the part of the developing countries which are not members of those arrangements as they would then be excluded from the markets of the major developed countries, which are significant economic entities, because of the discrimination.[23]

Within the GATT system, if these regional arrangements multiplied along the "North-South axis" — for example, EU arrangements with ACP countries, and NAFTA expanding to the Americas — then the threat of regional blocs would be real. Therefore, what has become of serious concern is the trend towards the emergence of sub-systems consisting of blocs of countries, each composed of major economic entities, together with their own associates of developing countries. The fear is that each bloc would compete with the others and each would become a closed system.[24]

To the extent that these groupings become mutually exclusive, there is a serious threat of the breakdown of the multilateral system. From the outside, both the EU and NAFTA are seen as possible threats to the multilateral system, particularly by developing countries outside those systems.[25]

APEC: An "Open" Regionalism?

The emergence of the Asia-Pacific Economic Co-operation (APEC) was initially seen as a counterweight to the growing fear that Europe would move inwards. It was seen by some as an answer from the Pacific Rim countries to the perceived trend towards a more inward-looking Europe that "two can play the game". But the question was diffused when APEC declared itself as an association of economies with an attitude of "open regionalism".

APEC is a departure from the traditional notion of a regional arrangement through its emphasis on voluntary dismantling of trade barriers in goods and services and developing trade facilitation measures to increase trade. It also allows members the freedom to apply the principle of MFN to non-members, thus building interdependence through better and freer flow of foreign investment. Moreover, the composition is intercontinental and includes major economic entities other than those from Europe, both developed and developing countries.

APEC is therefore a new development that could be interesting if it succeeds, but we should not be surprised if member countries are still not clear about their roles in it. It has also added another dimension to the activities of regional co-operation that the ASEAN states must deal with. As we shall see below, a scale of priorities needs to be drawn up on where the attention should be focused if three economic fora are to be considered, namely, ASEAN, APEC, and WTO.

Economic Integration and ASEAN

Closer economic ties among the ASEAN countries are inevitable over time and necessary in a world of increasing interdependence. But also important are economic ties among countries across regions, and between the ASEAN countries and other regions. At present, the degree of economic interdependence among the ASEAN countries has not reached the point where they are each other's most important economic partners. Moreover, when we look at the issue in a broader perspective, the pull to move towards closer regional economic co-operation is counter-balanced by the equally attractive pull for trade with countries outside the region, and with stronger economic logic.

In ASEAN, the effort to speed up the process of closer economic integration can be said to be somewhat "artificial". The process has been undertaken because it has been regarded as politically desirable and sensible, and therefore must be encouraged to move faster than its "natural" path. This point should not be construed to mean that it is therefore useless to do so but simply to point out that there are political considerations which underlie the effort to enhance economic integration even if economic factors indicate that it would be technically premature to do so.

In regional integration, we can make a case that unless it is completely and hopelessly irrational, it should be undertaken, however sub-optimal it may be, if there is strong political motivation to proceed with the endeavour. In this connection, we need to consider the economic cost of deviating from the open global system. If the cost is considered affordable and the political inclination is strong, then the process would likely be continued.

Nevertheless, ASEAN efforts have not been negligible although the results have not always been impressive. They have largely been in institution-building.

Early ASEAN Efforts

In the early 1970s, there was an emerging desire to intensify economic interdependence among the ASEAN countries roughly along the European model. Indeed, dialogue with the European Community was the first step by ASEAN to develop relations with external partners in what was to be subsequently a system of dialogues with other economic partners. It is not entirely a coincidence that when ASEAN started its move to consolidate its intra-regional and extra-regional economic co-operation, the first step was to establish a dialogue with the EEC and the European Commission in Brussels. The ASEAN Brussels Committee was established to deal with relations with Europe.[26]

Intra-regional economic co-operation, however, moved more slowly. In the early days of ASEAN, tariffs in many member countries were high. The economic structures of the individual countries were such that they would not have been able to trade with each other since their exports were principally primary products. Their "natural" partners were thus industrial countries in need of primary products, and not each other.[27] While some significant shifts in the structure of the economies of the ASEAN countries began to take place, and new areas of manufactures and cross-border intra-corporate and inter-corporate trade started to emerge, the growth prospects of those sectors lay in the future.[28] In this state of ambiguity, it is logical to ask the question: why push for intra-regional trade if the time has not come?

First Wave in the Creation of an ASEAN Free Trade Area

The emergence of the ASEAN free trade agreement, which has been criticized by some as being somewhat belated and insignificant, has its blessings. Indeed, ASEAN did not address the question of a free trade area in a concrete manner until the early 1990s.[29] However, let us look at an alternative scenario. If the early pressure for a free trade area in ASEAN had been accommodated in the 1970s and early 1980s, and the members had agreed to it before the Uruguay Round, ASEAN might very well have inadvertently turned to a more protectionist regional trade system.[30]

A free trade area with vast differences in tariff levels for third countries would have been difficult to accept for some high-tariff members because it would have deprived them of the benefit of preferential protection against imports coming from non-members. If, because of the differences in tariff, a free trade area was difficult to accept, then one alternative would have been to set a common external tariff, in which case the process would have to be converted to the creation of a *customs union.*

A customs union, with agreed levels of external tariffs, would probably have forced the tariff levels closer to the Indonesian, or Philippine or Thai levels, which were higher, rather than the Singaporean level, which was very low. In such a case, ASEAN would have had a more integrated trading arrangement but it would have been a highly protectionist one. In any case, it is difficult to imagine Singapore being a member of a customs union as this would have required it to raise its tariffs substantially.[31]

Moreover, there is the question of the application of a free trade area and a customs union. It would have required customs authorities to administer a system of rules of origin in which they had little experience.[32] It would have required an elaborate system of controlling and verifying rules of origin to prevent trade diversion, which might be out of proportion to the value of trade generated from the process. Fortunately for the advocates of the open trading system, events moved in a different direction.

In the late 1980s to mid-1990s, the ASEAN states became active in the GATT and the Uruguay Round negotiations instead. As a result, attention was shifted to the multilateral system. Owing to this shift, at the end of the Uruguay Round the ASEAN states cut their tariff levels, bound a substantial range of their tariffs, liberalized their non-tariff regimes, and agreed to the services agreement as well as some binding commitments in services which are applied on an MFN basis. As a result of the exercise in the GATT, the ASEAN economies have become more open and the level of protection much lower than before. Accordingly, ASEAN has become more open to the global system than it would have been had the prematurely initiated free trade area or customs union been applied.

Subsequent Efforts for a Free Trade Area (FTA)

Since the Uruguay Round, there has been a resurgence of initiatives for the creation of a free trade area in ASEAN.[33] In January 1992, the ASEAN Summit agreed, in the Singapore Declaration, to the establishment of the ASEAN Free Trade Area (AFTA) as stipulated in the Framework Agreement on Enhancing ASEAN Economic Co-operation, using a Common Effective Preferential Tariff (CEPT) scheme.[34] It is possible that AFTA could move faster and to a greater depth than anticipated if there is consensus. However, even if agreement materializes with formally "meaningful" and substantial "concessions" from all member countries, there is a need to be reticent about how large actual intra-regional trade could result from the liberalization in the short and intermediate run.[35]

Moreover, if the ASEAN economies are more open, and made on an MFN basis, what would be the incentive to have a differentiated regime where the preference margins are narrower? In the field of services, as WTO liberalization commitments by the ASEAN countries do not cover a broad range of areas, the possibility of preferences is potentially greater. But there remains the irony that the deeper the integration the less margin of preferences would be available, and in that sense it would be less attractive, although it may be attractive for other reasons.

Beyond FTA

Jayant Menon has highlighted the emerging phenomenon of intra-industry trade in ASEAN being a factor for increased intra-regional trade, suggesting that intra-regional trade could escalate as the region becomes more industrialized.[36] This phenomenon will surely be more prevalent when there is a structural shift in the ASEAN economies towards more manufacturing. However, here we enter into an area beyond FTA, the realm of investment.[37]

If we move beyond the endeavour to create a free trade area and develop an approach to encourage intra-industry trade in the region, a more imaginative and flexible policy on investment, with greater harmonization, would then be required.

Successful intra-industry trade in ASEAN would then not necessarily require a free trade area as a prerequisite, if the trading regime in the region is globally more open. However, it does require

greater harmonization on investment policy.[38] The shifting structure
of the ASEAN economies had been signalled in an earlier paper by
Akrasanee on ASEAN trade policy, and will continue to evolve,
changing the landscape of the ASEAN economies into an
increasingly manufacturing region.[39] Harmonization of investment
policy and trade liberalization then becomes essential.

Identifying Steps Towards ASEAN Regional Integration

Political considerations led to the persuasive conclusion that intra-
ASEAN relations must be reinforced. However, because of ASEAN's
great dependence on the international market, its overall orientation
in trade must remain global. As regional efforts are being further
encouraged, the ASEAN countries must also operate in the context
of two other fora, APEC and the WTO. How can a more consolidated
and consistent position be formulated, given these considerations?

In the three decades of its existence, ASEAN has taken some
important steps to intensify regional co-operation, which have been
creditable political achievements in their own right. We have alluded
to these accomplishments in the foregoing pages. However, these
achievements have largely been in the area of dealing with third
parties and in negotiating common positions. They have not
included the process of regional integration, as it is conventionally
defined.

Even the free trade area in ASEAN has not moved far. The
Exception and Exclusion Lists are very long, covering many
important areas. Moreover, even if the ASEAN free trade area is fully
in place, it does not replace trade with the rest of the world in terms
of importance. Given these limited accomplishments, can we
visualize an approach to ASEAN regional integration which accepts
the primordial importance of the WTO for future ASEAN trade and
growth and yet makes use of the advantage of regional integration?
In this section, we shall argue for an approach which is appropriate
for ASEAN.

Economic Integration: The "Hard" Option

There is an ambiguity about the intention of economic integration
in ASEAN when one looks at the declarations and statements of

ASEAN leaders and officials. The word "integration" has been used so often that the time will come when a decision needs to be made on how far the process of integration is intended to go. If we take the concept as described in the mainstream literature, we are really talking about an extensive process and moving towards a degree of intensity of interdependence which is quite far-reaching. This process has taken place in the European Union. Although members of the EU may have different views about the speed of the process, there is less doubt about where they are heading — a politically and economically unified Europe. It is necessary to know how far ASEAN wishes to go on its part.

Widening and Deepening of Substantive Coverage

The mainstream "classical" view of regional integration, as developed by Balassa and Scitovsky, has implications beyond trade. Beyond the stage of a free trade area, wide policy measures are required if the process is to be completed as intended. At the stage of a customs union, ASEAN would have to decide on the appropriate level of common external tariffs. Whose tariff levels would it be: the higher tariff levels of Indonesia, the Philippines, Thailand, and other countries, or the lower tariff levels of Singapore which call for the free movement of goods and services, and factors of production? How far and how fast would this process be pushed?

Institutional Implications

There is also the institutional aspect of economic integration. It calls for a supra-national authority to make major economic decisions. In the prevailing literature, it calls for a common policy on a whole array of major economic areas. The European Union has reached that point and beyond. It is questionable whether this is what has been intended when leaders of ASEAN talk about integration.

Let us take this exercise of stocktaking the policy and institutional issues a step further. Macroeconomic policies in the integrating countries must be compatible, harmonized, and eventually fully unified and attuned to the needs of the region and the realities prevailing in the countries if the objective of integration is to be achieved. Social policies of the individual countries also need to be harmonized. Regional disparities, which have been of concern at the national level, also need to be addressed at the ASEAN level.

"Hard" Option and ASEAN

If ASEAN follows this path of "hard" integration, the process would have wide-ranging implications. Those who wish to measure the success or failure of ASEAN in terms of the criteria above would be engaged in judgements which are not appropriate for ASEAN. There is a limit to which the "hard" integration of the European model can be applied. Relying on the ASEAN domestic market as the main thrust for growth is economically unrealistic. Moreover, the European model is predicated on the implicit (now explicit) goal of complete economic and political unification. That has not been the goal of ASEAN. (For a summary of the "hard" option, see Table 9.1).

Economic Integration: The "Soft" Option

If the "hard" option is not realistic to attain, what is the "soft" option that can be expanded? The fact that "hard" integration cannot be pursued does not mean that "soft" integration cannot take place. The "soft" option centres on institutional questions and trade facilitating measures which are needed in any case, although in themselves they do not lead to the establishment of economic integration as the process is understood by the mainstream literature.

The "soft" option can be examined in further detail as we attempt to formulate a consolidated position of ASEAN on the subject of economic integration, given the economic and political realities prevailing in the region. They could be put in motion by developing the following initiatives

1. *Free Trade Area as the Political Base-line.* At the policy level, an ASEAN free trade area could be encouraged, without necessarily expecting the FTA to produce dramatic economic results. Nevertheless, it would encourage increased interdependence and broader based regional trade than it would otherwise have been the case without FTA. It could be used as the political baseline. This is one element in the "soft" option, which has something in common with the "hard" option.

TABLE 9.1
Economic Integration: The "Hard" Option

Widening and Deepening of Substantive Coverage

Free Trade Area
The mainstream "classical" view of regional integration has implications beyond trade. Beyond the stage of a free trade area, much has to be done if the process is to be completed as intended.

Customs Union
At the stage of a customs union, ASEAN would have to decide the appropriate level of common external tariffs. Whose tariff levels would it adopt — the higher tariff levels of Indonesia, Philippines, Thailand and other countries, or the lower tariff levels of Singapore and Brunei?

Common Market
As the process moves towards further economic integration, it calls for free movement of goods and services, and factors of production. How far and how fast would this process be pushed in ASEAN?

Economic Integration
Beyond the common market, economic integration calls for a common policy applicable to every member country, with policies and rules determined by the centre.

Institutional Implications

Supra-national Authority
There is also the institutional aspect of economic integration — a supra-national authority for major economic decisions. It would call for a common policy on the whole array of major economic areas. The European Union has reached that point and beyond. It is questionable whether this is the intention when leaders of ASEAN speak of integration.

Common Macroeconomy Policy
Macroeconomic policies in the integrating countries are required to be compatible, harmonized, and eventually fully unified and attuned to the needs of the region and the realities prevailing in the countries if the objective of integration is to be achieved.

Social Policy
Social policies of the individual countries need to be harmonized. They are obligations with binding treaties applied throughout the region.

Regional Policy
Regional disparities within each nation, which have been of concern at the national level need to be addressed at the regional level as the integration process advances, if the "hard" integration of the European model is to be adopted.

---

2. *Regional Liberalization through Global Liberalization.* The process of being actively liberalizing and reforming in the context of the global system would lead to much more open economies in individual ASEAN countries. Openness in the region, without much governmental intervention, would be "residual" to the openness maintained at the global level. Continued liberalization of the ASEAN economy with respect to the rest of the world would automatically make the ASEAN economies more open to each other.

3. *Institutional Infrastructure and Facilitation Measures.* The development of institutional "infrastructure" similar to the development in the EU enables ASEAN to undertake harmonization in the way of doing things. Given the experience of the Asian crisis, this institutional development is crucial to enable work on the harmonization of policies and approaches. The "infrastructures" would include the necessary mechanisms and processes of consultation and policy harmonization in the broader area of macroeconomic and monetary management.[40] They would also include specific areas of economic and commercial practices, such as developing best-practices in accounting procedures, the development of the legal system, the development of bank supervision systems and procedures which are more compatible with international standards, developing systems and procedures in customs valuation, and all the "softwares" of a modern trade-oriented economy which would make the ASEAN economies increasingly more competitive globally.[41] These "infrastructural" aspects include:

— *Consultation, Harmonization and Standardization of Policies.* As mentioned, consultations among monetary authorities would make it possible to develop a kind of early warning system about the trends and emergency measures that could be undertaken in the ASEAN economies. They could be useful when there is a run on one of the ASEAN currencies. These facilities for consultation, harmonization of policies, and standardization of important procedures in economic activities would facilitate the co-ordination of economies which are becoming interdependent. On the subject of ASEAN interdependence, we can note that despite the relatively low level of intra-regional trade, the level of interdependence among the ASEAN economies has become greater through the links with the international financial market. This was demonstrated during the regional crisis where events in one ASEAN country had immediate impact on its neighbours.

— *Competition Policy and Nurturing a Competitive Environment.* The subsequent step to be taken by ASEAN to adjust to global competition is to look at the competitive environment of the ASEAN economies at the corporate level. Some may adopt a competition policy. Others may have policies which are competition driven, without finding it necessary to have a competition policy. Harmonization in policy approaches may help to strengthen the corporate base and facilitate the emergence of sound corporate governance and fair competition.[42]

— *Harmonization of Investment Policy.* Harmonization of investment policy may be conducive to making the region more hospitable to foreign investment without engaging in excessive and unnecessary artificial incentives. This process is more formal in the context of "hard" integration, where the process would be specified in a treaty. It would be a necessary component of the principle of freedom of movement of factors of production. In "soft" integration, the process is not necessarily immediately binding, but there is mutual interest to develop a harmonized and compatible policy for the region.

— *Developing a Dispute Settlement System.* Another institutional requirement is the development of a regional dispute settlement mechanism which could be achieved by imitating the EU experience. The system could be encouraged to evolve, thus making business and commercial activities in the region more predictable.

— *Facilitation Measures.* The steps that could be considered have to do with institutional "infrastructure" developments which would facilitate steps towards the integration of the ASEAN economies in less dramatic but crucial ways. These could generically be called *facilitation measures.* The institutional formality of ASEAN, which follows the institutional developments in the EU, has been criticized as being distant from the people, bureaucratic, and elitist, but it is there to be put to use. Its imitation of the European institutions has given ASEAN policy-makers and officials the habit of constant consultations not dissimilar to what the EU has in place.

— *Corporate Governance.* Another crucial but often less obvious requirement, except during a crisis, is the need to strengthen the foundations of good corporate governance. This is critical for the health of the economic system and the competitiveness of the economy in the global economy. The process of encouraging better corporate governance might be more achievable if there is regional pressure to force the adoption of international standards of corporate operation.

There are other important steps in making the economic, business, and legal practices more harmonized and compatible with each other, while focusing on implementing best practices in all fields of endeavour. These "soft" integration efforts are not trivial. They are part and parcel of our modernization efforts and our search for global competitiveness.

Summary of the "Soft" Option

We have argued that most free trade areas and integration initiatives are economic in manifestation but largely political in motivation. However, if there is a strong political desire pushing for ASEAN integration, it should not be necessarily discouraged, even if the economic arguments are not fully persuasive, at least in the short run. Nevertheless, although the impetus is political, it must not be so devoid of supporting economic argument that it would be irrational to proceed.

This study has argued that even if the trade volume produced from an integrated ASEAN is modest, the increasing harmonization of practices, rules, and modern norms of economic and corporate practices as well as the interdependence through the international financial system, would facilitate future regional economic interaction. In the interim, the ASEAN economies would be more efficient internationally by virtue of being more open and by adopting best international practices in every economic endeavour across the board.

If it be the case that trade facilitation, as we have described above, could contribute to increasing efficiency, and deeper regional integration, and that trade facilitation is essential for trade expansion, then trade facilitation should not be treated lightly. It must be a focus of attention even if the conventional view of integration argues that successful integration is only present when the region becomes a common market and integrated under a supranational authority, as is the case in the EU. (For a summary of the "soft" option, see Table 9.2).

TABLE 9.2
Economic Integration: The "Soft" Option

Free Trade Area as the Political Baseline
At a policy level, an ASEAN free trade area could be encouraged, without expecting dramatic economic results. It would promote increased interdependence and a broader based regional trade than otherwise possible. It could be taken as the political baseline. This is one element in the "soft" option which has something in common with the "hard" option.

Regional Liberalization through Global Liberalization
Liberalizing and reforming in the context of the global system would lead to much more open economies in individual ASEAN countries. Regional openness without excessive governmental intervention would be a "residual" to the openness at the global level. Continued liberalization of the ASEAN economies with respect to the rest of the world will automatically make them more open to each other.

Institutional Infrastructure and Facilitation Measures
The development of institutional "infrastructure" which mimics the development in the EU enables ASEAN to undertake harmonization policies and practices. They would include consultations and harmonization on macroeconomic and monetary management, economic and commercial practices by developing best-practices in accounting procedures, establishment of a modern legal system, the development of international standards of bank supervision more compatible with procedures in customs valuation, and all the "softwares" of a modern trade-oriented economy, making the ASEAN economies more competitive globally.

Consultation, Harmonization and Standardization of Policies
Consultations among monetary authorities would make it possible to develop the kind of early warning system about the trends and the emergency measures that could be undertaken in the ASEAN economies. They could be useful when there is a run on one of the ASEAN currencies. These facilities for consultation, harmonization of policies, and standardization of important procedures in economic activities lead to easier co-ordination of economies which are becoming interdependent.

TABLE 9.2 *(cont'd)*

Competition Policy and Nurturing a Competitive Environment
The subsequent steps would be to develop a better competitive environment for the ASEAN economies. Some countries have a competition policy. Other countries have policies which are competition driven without finding it necessary to have legislation on competition policy. Harmonization in policy approaches may help to strengthen the corporate base and promote the emergence of sound corporate governance.

Harmonization of Investment Policy
Harmonization of investment policy may be conducive to making the region more hospitable to foreign investment without excessive and unnecessary artificial incentives. This process is more formal in the context of "hard" integration, where the process would be specified in a treaty. It would be a necessary component of the principle of freedom of movement for factors of production. In "soft" integration, the process is not necessarily immediately binding, but there is mutual interest to do so.

Developing a Dispute Settlement System
As a part of institutional development, a dispute settlement mechanism could be developed in ASEAN. The system could be encouraged to evolve, thus making business and commercial activities in the region more predictable. A regional dispute settlement mechanism could be achieved by mimicking the EU experience.

Facilitation Measures
Facilitation measures have to do with institutional "infrastructure" developments which would facilitate steps towards integration of the ASEAN economies in less dramatic but crucial ways. The institutional formality of ASEAN, which follows the institutional developments in the EU, has been criticized as being distant from the people, bureaucratic, and elitist, but it is there to be put to use. Imitation of the European institution has given ASEAN policy-makers and officials the habit of constant consultations not dissimilar to what the EU has in place.

Corporate Governance
The foundation of good corporate governance needs to be strengthened. This is critical for the health of the economic system and the competitiveness of the economy in the global economy. Better corporate governance might be more achievable if there is regional pressure to force the adoption of international standards of corporate operation.

ASEAN and the Multilateral System: Searching for an "Insurance Policy"

What is the upshot of the arguments above? In the best of all possible worlds, an open and non-discriminatory trading system seems most desirable and, in view of the successful use by the ASEAN economies of the open world trading system, the region has been a beneficiary. The basis of the argument is that an open and non-discriminatory trading system increases welfare and efficiency although sometimes the benefits might be seen to be politically inequitable. On the assumption that growth is necessary for even a semblance of development to take place, the developing countries are on the whole better off with the open trading system. Given the above proposition, how would ASEAN construct a policy which is coherent, taking the global reality above as a starting point, while accommodating the political requirements of regional integration?

Constructing Priorities: Strategic Choices and the Search for an Insurance Policy

Given the situation as described above, the choice of political concentration becomes ambiguous. For the prosperity of the region, a functioning and effective WTO system is a better guarantee of future growth than an inward-looking regionalism.

However, if the multilateral system cannot fully function *the way* it was intended to do and its principles cannot be fully implemented, can a regional system help to overcome this problem? The answer is yes, but only to a limited extent, and under a less efficient condition than it would be under an open world trading system.

The problems of strategic choice would lead to the question concerning which fora would be considered as the "fall back" or the "insurance policy", and which would be the preferred and main focus of concentration. In this connection, given the foregoing arguments, the global system must be the main concentration, and regional economic arrangement, the "insurance policy."[43]

In other words, only if the global system does not work should ASEAN then work on the regional system — that is, ASEAN itself or the broader APEC, as an *alternative* rather than a supplement. The choice between ASEAN and APEC in turn is related to the decision on which of the two groupings would be taken as the focus, and which one the "insurance policy"?[44]

Structuring the Insurance Policy

Given the superiority of the global system, an insurance policy could be structured along the lines described below.

1. *First Option.* Looking at the global system as the focus, participation in the WTO should be maximized in order to ensure continued access to the global market. Should the global system fail to function in the way it was intended, there are two types of "insurance policies" that are available to ASEAN.
2. *First-Level "Insurance Policy".* The first-level insurance policy is APEC, which could act collectively to prevent the global system from moving surreptitiously towards irreversible fragmentation. In general, members of APEC have a predilection to the open system. As an "insurance policy", ASEAN countries' membership in APEC provides the opportunity to participate in making the world trading and investment regime more open.
3. *Second-Level "Insurance Policy".* As a second "insurance policy", if the above is not fully successful, and less-than-open regional arrangements proliferate, the ASEAN free trade area would then provide a less-than-perfect but available cushion against the prospects of being fully shut out of other markets. The more that facilitation and standardization of practices are in place, and the more that mutually compatible individual country policies are also in place, the more workable would an ASEAN alternative as "insurance" become under the bleak scenario of the breakdown of an open global system.[45]

Economic Integration and External Relations: ASEAN, APEC and the WTO

To the extent that ASEAN has a vital interest in maintaining an open global trading system, it also has an interest in being actively present in global commercial diplomacy. The multilateral system is hardly immune from the temptation of the strong to use power in their dealings with other countries. Power can be used to distort a non-discriminatory multilateral system. To the extent that political considerations are important in a less than perfect world, there is always a crucial need to bargain politically in order to ensure that the open trading system is maintained and to prevent the proliferation of unilateral actions by the powerful.

At present, the ASEAN states are actively engaged in three major international economic fora, namely, ASEAN, APEC, and the WTO. It has been argued that simultaneous activity in ASEAN, APEC, and the WTO would not be contradictory. They can be made to be complementary, but a scale of priorities is necessary if a policy is to have focus and a common position, which is needed, is formulated. An ASEAN common position does not require economic integration.

By definition, however, the absence of integration would mean that there would be many more issues in which the ASEAN countries may not necessarily have identical positions. This reality needs to be taken into account. A common ASEAN position on key external issues would strengthen its position to face a stronger economic power in negotiations. However, for this purpose, regional integration is not imperative. There have been some instances when a common position during the Uruguay Round strengthened the position of ASEAN.[46]

A collective stand on important issues could give ASEAN stronger economic and political clout to bargain with major trading partners than would be the case if the ASEAN countries were to do this individually. A collective ASEAN bloc operating within APEC may in turn provide the additional leverage in dealing with large economic entities. However, APEC consists of large economic entities — the United States and Japan — as well as other developed countries, and other developing countries from both sides of the Pacific Rim. It has the attractiveness of economic weight, but it also has the disadvantage of being too diverse. Membership in APEC will often require a dilution of a specific ASEAN position to accommodate the larger and more heterogeneous membership of APEC. To what extent is the trade-off acceptable? The answer is unclear but ASEAN must be pragmatic in making the choice.

Conclusion

This chapter has attempted to examine the policy issues of regional trading arrangements in the light of the multilateral system. In simplistic terms, it attempts to address the controversy of regionalism

versus multilateralism. The question has been posed naively in terms
of a dichotomy, a mutually exclusive choice between growth through
a regional preferential arrangement (theoretically leading to an
economic or even a political union), and growth through the open
multilateral system.

Intellectually, this chapter argues without ambiguity that an
effective and open global system, operating on a non-discriminatory
basis, would be in the best interest of the ASEAN economies
individually and as a group. However, intra-regional integration in
ASEAN, if pursued with realism, can be positive in helping the
organization to cope faster and more effectively with the global
system, irrespective of how small the immediate impact of regional
integration may have on trade expansion.

In public policy terms, these choices are only meaningful as
initial abstractions. ASEAN is still ambiguous about the choice. Its
behaviour reveals that it does not regard the choice as a rigid
alternative but as a part of a continuum. Thus, while the debate on
regionalism versus multilateralism, or the debate on ASEAN versus
the WTO, are useful intellectualization of possible policy options,
which are potentially mutually exclusive, political realities require
ASEAN to combine the options, making them mutually compatible.
In this ambiguous situation, ASEAN is confronted with the need to
choose and/or combine between various options. We have argued
for a "constructive ambiguity".

Attempts to put a free trade area, AFTA, in place is a positive
development, not because the economic results are necessarily
significant, but because the alternative is for the ASEAN states to
declare that there is no room for further developments in regional
co-operation. Passivity is disastrous because it would close the door
to the kind of co-operation that is needed in practical terms. Taking
flexible initiatives would give the region a goal to strive for, and
therefore to take important, though not too dramatic, steps that are
needed to ensure that such goals can be implemented operationally.

Therefore, on matters of regional integration in ASEAN we
should be cautious about being euphoric, but we should also be
cautious about falling into the trap of complacency and mental
paralysis and not take initiative. Taking an approach of "constructive
ambiguity", we have argued for a "soft" integration in ASEAN. By
taking steps in "soft" integration, the ASEAN economies would be
moving towards the prevailing norms of best-technical practices in

the world, making them able to be more in tune with the highest level of global practices, however small these steps may be in increasing intra-ASEAN trade, and to liberalize the economy domestically to prepare better for the global system.

Many of these steps need to be taken. They fall under the "soft" categories of *trade facilitation* and *institutional developments.* There is much to be done in this field, if we take seriously the meaning of the term "facilitation" and if we do not dismiss this issue merely as trivial activities that do not require difficult decisions, and therefore not challenging. An increasingly workable ASEAN intra-regional interdependence through "soft" integration would over time (and it may take a shorter time than we think) serve as an "insurance policy" just in case the global system ceases to function the way it was intended. This insurance policy may become increasingly more valuable as the region expands the web of interdependence through consultations, through standardization of important economic practices, and through investment inter-links.

This chapter is an appeal, from someone who is more committed to the multilateral rather than the regional system, to be indulgent about the real prospects of ASEAN regional integration as the mechanism to make the ASEAN economies more prosperous. No matter how skeptical we are of the *economic* value arising from intra-regional trade in the short- and medium-term, the *political* pay-off is very high. Over time, as argued by Noordin Sopie, "Asian governments need only to watch while economic integration occurs naturally around them." In the meantime, ASEAN needs to focus on ensuring that the open global system remains open and to develop the capability of competing globally.[47]

NOTES

* The author was formerly Ambassador of Indonesia to the GATT during the Uruguay Round negotiations (1986–94). He is presently Vice-Chairman and Executive Director of the Center for Economic and Business Negotiations and Dispute Settlement, Jakarta.

1 At the time when the GATT Uruguay Round was initiated, the Institute of Southeast Asian Studies invited scholars to examine trade policy options for ASEAN in the light of the multilateral system. There was a shared view about the importance of international trade to the economies of each of the original ASEAN members. See Mohamed Ariff and Tan Loong-Hoe,

eds., *The Uruguay Round: ASEAN Trade Policy Options* (Singapore: Institute of Southeast Asian Studies, 1988).

2 The experience has been described in Jagdish Bhagwati, *Protectionism* (Cambridge, Mass., MIT Press, 1998), pp. 1–9.

3 The ASEAN economies enjoyed high growth because of the favourable external trading situation. It was the international system which made this possible, together with appropriate discipline in macroeconomic and exchange rate policies. This was recognized when ASEAN entered the Uruguay Round. See Narongchai Akrasanee, "ASEAN Trade Policy Options: An Overview", *The Uruguay Round: ASEAN Trade Policy Options* (Singapore: Institute of Southeast Asian Studies, 1988), pp. 200–2. It explains the active interest of the ASEAN countries in the negotiations.

4 For the period 1980–93, the ASEAN-5, except the Philippines, registered growth of production higher than 5 per cent, with Thailand averaging 8.2 per cent. For the same period, the growth of exports was significantly higher than production, with the exception of Indonesia where the growth of exports was only slightly higher than growth in production; the other ASEAN-5 countries had growth rates of exports twice the rate of growth of production. Moreover, in 1993 for the ASEAN-5, trade as a percentage of GDP had been high, with Indonesia at 42.6 per cent, while Malaysia was at 144 per cent, Singapore at 288 per cent, and Thailand at 66 per cent. See Suthiphand Chirathivat, "ASEAN Economic Integration with the World Through AFTA". *AFTA in a Changing International Economy*, edited by Joseph Tan (Singapore: Institute of Southeast Asian Studies, 1996), p. 22.

5 It is this threat arising from major trading powers becoming more introverted that has led to some serious concern. See Brian Hindley and Patrick Messerlin, "Guaranteed of Market Access and Regionalism", *Regional Integration and the Global Trading System*, edited by Kym Anderson and Richard Blackhurst (London: Harvester Wheatsheaf, 1993), p. 360.

6 I have borrowed the term from John Croome who attributes it to Alan Oxley, Australia's Ambassador to the GATT during the first half of the Uruguay Round negotiations, in describing the pragmatic process in the GATT when explicit rules are difficult to apply in any given moment, but when decisions are required. See John Croome, *Reshaping the World Trading System: A History of the Uruguay Round* (Geneva: World Trade Organization, 1995), p. 147.

7 This point has been stressed by Hoekman and Kostecki. See Bernard Hoekman and Michel Kostecki, *The Political Economy of the World Trading System: From GATT to WTO* (Oxford: Oxford University Press, 1996), p. 214.

8 Among the important works on economic integration which emerged at the time that Western European economic integration was being initiated are the work of Balassa and Scitoversusky. See Bela Balassa, *The Theory of Economic Integration* (Homewood, Ill.: Richard D. Irwin, 1961); and T.

Scitoversusky, *Economic Theory and Western European Integration* (London: George Allen and Unwin, 1958).

9 Bernard Hoekman and Michel Kostecki, *The Political Economy of the World Trading System*, pp. 214.

10 Ibid.

11 In the early days of post-war Europe, it had taken political courage, imagination and a sense of urgency to develop economic devices to encourage co-operation between previously traditional enemies. American encouragement and resources made the prospect more achievable. For a useful summary of the developments on the earlier years of the EEC, see Dennis Swann, *The Economics of the Common Market*, 2nd edition (Harmondsworth: Penguin Books, 1972). But it posed difficult conceptual issues in the GATT, as we shall see.

12 The emergence of the European Economic Community (EEC-Europe 6) had resulted in many disputes arising from its process of internal preferences and its renegotiation of tariff commitments with third countries. Kenneth W. Dam, *The GATT: Law and the International Economic Organization* (Chicago: University of Chicago Press, 1970), pp. 87–91.

13 Outsiders, indeed, have credited ASEAN as one of the most successful regional co-operation efforts. See Rita Beuter, "The Association of Southeast Asian Nations: Towards Closer Economic Co-operation", *Free Trade Agreements and Customs Union: Experiences, Challenges and Constraints*, edited by Madeleine O. Hosli and Arild Saether (Maastricht: Tacis/European Institute of Public Administration, 1997), p. 179.

14 If GATT had insisted on full compliance of its rules concerning the process of integration in the EEC at the time, GATT would have fallen apart. See Kenneth Dam, op cit. p. 291.

15 The unambiguously political goal of unification was further strengthened when the 1992 Single Market Project was being shaped. Symbolically, it was the Frenchman Jacques Delors, who, as President of the European Commission, energetically pushed for the project, ending the French obsession of *l'Europe des patries*. See Commission Européenne, *1992: le defi*, Report on a research project financed by the European Commission on the "cost of non-Europe" (Paris: Flammarion, 1989).

16 When the Single Market Project was well under way there was considerable worry whether Europe would continue to move towards a "fortress Europe". This received much attention in ASEAN and Asia in general. There is no clear answer to the question. See Nigel Holloway, "Economic Relations: Spat in the Supermarket", *Far Eastern Economic Review*, 8 October 1992, pp. 68–76.

17 The persistence of the debate between regionalism and multilateralism has led to a series of papers commissioned by the GATT Secretariat in preparation for the annual report of the GATT in 1992. The Secretariat was careful to note that the views expressed were personal views of the authors and that the Secretariat maintained a neutral view on the subject. The

papers were published in *Regional Integration and the Global Trading System*, edited by Kym Anderson and Richard Blackhurst (London: Harvester Wheatsheaf, 1993).

18   These provisions are found in Article 24 (para. 6). See *Text of the General Agreement on Tariffs and Trade* (Geneva: GATT, July 1986), p. 42.

19   Jacob Viner, *The Customs Union Issue* (New York: Carnegie Endowment for International Peace, 1950), pp. 41–56.

20   Article 24 also requires an interim agreement which was controversial and remains difficult to resolve satisfactorily unless its application is done flexibly. See Dam, op. cit., pp. 262–63.

21   Article 5 of the GATS specifies that economic integration must involve substantial sectoral coverage in terms of the number of sectors, the volume of trade, and the modes of supply. For developing countries, however, flexibility is provided. See "General Agreement on Trade in Services", *The Results of the Uruguay Round of Multilateral Negotiations: Legal Texts* (Geneva: WTO, 1995), p. 331.

22   *Analytical Index: Guide to GATT Law and Practice* (Geneva: GATT, 1994), p. 766–69.

23   During the Uruguay Round, developing countries, especially those that were trade dependent, at the end agreed to compromise with the developed countries in order to strengthen the multilateral system and in order not to be excluded from trade opportunities because of the emergence of trading blocs. See John Whalley, "Developing Countries and System Strengthening in the Uruguay Round", *The Uruguay Round and the Developing Countries*, edited by Will Martin and L. Alan Winters (Cambridge: Cambridge University Press, 1996), pp. 409–34.

24   See Hindley and Messerlin, op. cit.

25   Already in 1992, during the Uruguay Round negotiations, the World Bank warned of the implications of introverted free trade areas on developing countries outside the region. *World Bank Economic Prospects 1992* states that "... interest in regional free trade arrangements appear to have grown in recent years. The EC single market due in 1992 and the United States – Canada arrangements are two important examples. Already 45 percent of world trade is within such regional arrangements, and this could rise to 50 percent if current talks are concluded successfully ... But the risk that regional trade arrangements may turn hostile towards each other cannot be discounted. Not only would this be damaging to world trade, but countries outside the orbit of such blocs, especially small developing countries would be hard hit". See *Global Economic Prospects and the Developing Countries* (Washington, D.C., World Bank, 1992), p. 3.

26   Considering that for most ASEAN countries, relations with the EEC were less extensive than with either the United States or with Japan, both in investment and in trade, this initial step displayed other than trade or investment considerations. It was a search for a model of regional co-operation. Since intra-regional economic relations were more difficult to start than extra-regional relations, the first step ASEAN took was to

develop a common forum to deal with third parties. Thus, the step was taken to deal collectively on economic issues with third parties. For an account of those early efforts of ASEAN, see H. S. Kartadjoemena, "MEE dan ASEAN: Evolusi Suatu Hubungan Trans-Regional", *Prisma* (Jakarta, 1973); and H. S. Kartadjoemena, "Regional Co-operation in Southeast Asia: An Indonesian View", *Performance and Perspectives of the Indonesian Economy*, edited by Muh. Arsjad Anwar et al. (Tokyo: Institute of Developing Economies, 1976).

27 Efforts towards increasing intra-regional trade were made timidly with the introduction of high-sounding and technically sophisticated names but without much result. For a convenient and brief account of the evolution, see Rita Beuter, op. cit., pp. 180–81.

28 Jayant Menon points to the promising area of manufactured products which will provide the boost towards a more intensified intra-regional trade through intra-corporate trade. See Jayant Menon, *Adjusting towards AFTA: The Dynamics of Trade in ASEAN* (Singapore: Institute of Southeast Asian Studies, 1996), pp. 13–21.

29 In the 1980s, various proposals had emerged on creating an ASEAN free trade area. Hans Christoph Rieger proposed a two-tier system where Malaysia, Thailand, Indonesia, and the Philippines should establish a customs union, which collectively would establish a free trade area with Singapore. See Hans Christoph Rieger, *ASEAN Co-operation and Intra-ASEAN Trade*, Research and Discussion Paper No. 57 (Singapore: Institute of Southeast Asian Studies, 1985).

30 We need to recall that at that time, very few tariff lines in ASEAN were bound in the GATT. Countries were free to adjust upward most of the existing tariffs at that time. Therefore, the tariff level to third parties, many of which were not bound, could have been raised without having to renegotiate in the GATT. To take the example of Indonesia which, before the Uruguay Round, had bound tariffs of 8 per cent of all tariff lines, in the Uruguay Round Indonesia made a binding commitment for 95 per cent of all tariff lines (8,878 out of 9,382 lines), and 92 per cent of all imports. For a summary, see *The Uruguay Round and Its Benefits to Indonesia* (Jakarta: Ministry of Trade/USAID TIPS, October 1994), p. 4.

31 As mentioned, Rieger provides a variance to dealing with regional integration, which is somewhat complex to answer just such concerns: a *customs union* of Malaysia, Thailand, Indonesia, and the Philippines, which in turn would collectively negotiate a *free trade area* agreement with Singapore. Rieger, op. cit., and Menon, op. cit., p. 4.

32 The greater the preference margins in a free trade area or custom union, the greater the temptation for trade deflection and falsification on rules of origin documents. An example of a sector where trade is largely distorted is textiles where champions of textile trade distortions, such as the United States and the EU, insist in policing tightly the procedures to prevent "circumvention" of trade restrictions. For an account of the problem of administration when high differential treatment is applied, such as in the

case of textiles, see Marcelo Raffaelli and Tripti Jenkins, *The Drafting History of the Agreement of Textiles and Clothing* (Geneva: International Textiles and Clothing Bureau, 1995), pp. 101–8.

33 Since the early attempts, more explicit efforts for establishing an ASEAN free trade area have been pushed further. An analysis of AFTA done by scholars on ASEAN economic affairs is found in the collection, *AFTA in the Changing International Economy*, edited by Joseph Tan (Singapore: Institute of Southeast Asian Studies, 1996). See also Rita Beuter, op. cit., pp. 183–87.

34 The text is conveniently found in *AFTA in the Changing International Economy*, pp. 195–216.

35 Heinz W. Arndt, "AFTA and After", *AFTA in the Changing International Economy*, edited by Joseph Tan (Singapore: Institute of Southeast Asian Studies, 1996), p. 48.

36 See Jayant Menon, op. cit., pp. 78–80.

37 Ibid. The more imaginative steps in regional co-operation are in the areas of investment policy and investment co-operation requiring co-ordination and harmonization of policy in that field, and capitalizing on attractive investment location. See Suthiphand Chirathivat, op. cit., pp. 29–30.

38 As we move beyond trade issues to investment and corporate operations versus harmonization of regional policies on investment, competition policy becomes an important policy issue in regional co-operation. While ASEAN may wish to prevent an international and binding agreement on investment from being a part of the WTO system because it is not appropriate, in ASEAN the issue needs to be tackled in the context of a more open region. For an attempt to discuss investment and competition policy from the perspective of a developing country, see H. S. Kartadjoemena, *Aspek Internasional dari Masalah Competition Policy: Menghadapi Perundingan WTO Tahun 2000* (Jakarta: Yayasan Indonesia Forum, 1999).

39 Narongchai Akrasanee, "ASEAN Trade Policy Options: An Overview", *The Uruguay Round: ASEAN Trade Policy Options*, pp. 199–211.

40 There is an interesting institutional dimension in ASEAN that should be noted as we deal with economic policy in the region. Initially, as a political initiative, ASEAN was the creation of the foreign ministries. As trade issues became important, trade ministries also entered the picture. Interestingly, however, there is another dimension to institutional development. When macroeconomic issues needed co-ordination, the participation of the ministries of finance and the central banks was required. However, they are accustomed to another forum, which is more long-standing, the IMF-World Bank annual meetings. Thus, finance ministries and central banks do not have the same "sense of ownership" of ASEAN. Southeast Asian central banks have their own forum, the SEACEN, which is the association of Southeast Asian Central Banks. But the ministries of finance and the central banks need a distinct forum if macroeconomic management is to have a sense of co-ordination. A different set of institutional practices needs to be developed. This is not just an ASEAN issue. At the broader level,

co-ordination among the ministries of finance and the central banks of the
G-7 has also received wide attention. See C. Fred Bergstein and C. Randall
Henning, *Global Economic Leadership and the Group of Seven*
(Washington, D.C.: Institute for International Economics, June 1996).

41 At the broad policy level, economic integration requires macroeconomic
discipline of some kind. Institutionally, the mechanism has yet to be
considered. Serious political decisions must also be taken on how much
common discipline the ASEAN governments are willing to commit on
macroeconomic policy. For a discussion of these issues, see Hans Genberg
and Francisco Nadale de Simone, "Regional Integration Agreements and
Macro-economic Discipline", *Regional Integration and the Global Trading
System*, edited by Kym Anderson and Richard Blackhurst (London:
Harvester Wheatsheaf, 1993), pp. 167–95.

42 A constructive approach to *competition policy* without necessarily implying
the need for *competition law* has been developed in the APEC study group
by Kerrin Vautier and her associates, where the focus is on developing
competition-driven policies by governments, while not adamant on the
manner and mechanism in which such policies ought to be implemented
formally. See Kerrin Vautier, *PECC Competition Principles* (Singapore: PECC
Secretariat, 1999).

43 The notion of an "insurance policy" has been mooted in an article in *Far
Eastern Economic Review* in connection with Prime Minister Mahathir'
Mohamad's proposal to create an East Asia Economic Grouping (EAEG).
The article concluded in the same way that this chapter does, that an open
global system is superior to regionalism, and regionalism should be the
intermediate goal. Nigel Holloway, Anthony Rowley, Shada Islam and
Michael Vatikiotis, "East Asian Trade Grouping at Top of Region's Agenda:
An Insurance Policy", *Far Eastern Economic Review (FEER)*,
25 July 1991, pp. 52–53.

44 An editorial in the same issue of the *FEER* cited above is more forthcoming
about the need for East Asia to proceed with the EAEG. Given the
unrealistic objective of creating the EAEG and the potential trade hostility
that the EAEG would provoke, the approach in this chapter focuses on
ASEAN and APEC as the instrument of insurance policy. See the editorial
"Defense Tactics", *FEER*, 25 July 1991, pp. 52–53.

45 The objective of taking an insurance policy under ordinary circumstances
is to prepare for an occurrence of an undesirable event. Should that event
occur, the holder of the policy does not normally expect a full restitution
of conditions prior to such an event, but merely to have a cushion which
mitigates some of the worst effects of such an event. Peter Lloyd who argues
that ASEAN-AFTA and the New Zealand/Australia Closer Economic
Agreement (CER) should link in the event that the global system falters,
has suggested a variance to the notion of insurance for ASEAN. See Peter
J. Lloyd, "Should AFTA and CER Link?" *AFTA in the Changing
International Economy*, edited by Joseph Tan (Singapore: Institute of
Southeast Asian Studies, 1996), p. 191.

46   During the financial services negotiations in the Uruguay Round, the
      ASEAN countries, together with other countries which are members of
      SEACEN (Southeast Asian Central Banks), managed to maintain a well
      formulated and strong position, although ASEAN could not fully withstand
      the combined strength of the United States, the EU and other European
      countries. Nothing much has been written about the negotiating history
      seen by ASEAN participants. The author is currently working on notes
      about the negotiating history in financial services based on the experience
      of participants in the negotiations.
47   Quoted in Nigel Holloway et al., "East Asian Trade Grouping at Top of
      Region's Agenda", p. 53.

REFERENCES

Joseph Tan, ed. *AFTA in the Changing International Economy*. Singapore:
      Institute of Southeast Asian Studies, 1996.
Akrasanee, Narongchai. "ASEAN Trade Policy Options: An Overview". *The
      Uruguay Round: ASEAN Trade Policy Options*. Singapore: Institute of
      Southeast Asian Studies, 1988.
Analytical Index: Guide to GATT Law and Practice. Geneva: GATT, 1994.
Arndt, Heinz W. "AFTA and After". *AFTA in the Changing International
      Economy*, edited by Joseph Tan. Singapore: Institute of Southeast Asian
      Studies, 1996.
Bergstein, C. Fred, and C. Randall Henning. *Global Economic Leadership and
      the Group of Seven*. Washington, D.C.: Institute for International
      Economics, June 1996.
Bhagwati, Jagdish. *Protectionism*. Cambridge, Mass.: MIT Press, 1998.
Balassa, Bela. *The Theory of Economic Integration*. Homewood, Ill.: Richard
      D. Irwin, 1961.
Beuter, Rita. "The Association of Southeast Asian Nations Towards Closer
      Economic Cooperation". *Free Trade Agreements and Customs Union:
      Experiences, Challenges and Constraints*, edited by Madeleine O. Hosli
      and Arild Saether. Maastricht: Tacis/European Institute of Public
      Administration, 1997.
Chia Siow Yue and Joseph L. H. Tan, eds. *ASEAN in the WTO: Challenges and
      Responses*. Singapore: Institute of Southeast Asian Studies, 1996.
Chirathivat, Suthiphand. "ASEAN Economic Integration with the World
      Through AFTA". *AFTA in a Changing International Economy*, edited by
      Joseph Tan. Singapore: Institute of Southeast Asian Studies, 1996.
Commission Europeénne. *1992: le defi*. Paris: Flammarion, 1989.
Croome, John. *Reshaping the World Trading System: A History of the Uruguay
      Round*. Geneva, World Trade Organization, 1995.
Dam, Kenneth W. *The GATT: Law and the International Economic Organization*.
      Chicago: University of Chicago Press (Midway Reprint), 1970.

"Defense Tactics." *Far Eastern Economic Review*, 25 July 1991.

GATT. *Text of the General Agreement on Tariffs and Trade*. Geneva: July 1986.

Genberg, Hans, and Francisco Nadale de Simone. "Regional Integration Agreements and Macro-economic Discipline." *Regional Integration and the Global Trading System*, edited by Kym Anderson and Richard Blackhurst. London: Harvester Wheatsheaf, 1993.

Hindley, Brian, and Patrick Messerlin. "Guaranteed of Market Access and Regionalism". *Regional Integration and the Global Trading System*, edited by Kym Anderson and Richard Blackhurst. London: Harvester Wheatsheaf, 1993.

Hoekman, Bernard, and Michel Kostecki. *The Political Economy of the World Trading System: From GATT to WTO*. Oxford: Oxford University Press, 1996.

Holloway, Nigel. "Economic Relations: Spat in the Supermarket". *Far Eastern Economic Review*. 8 October 1992.

Holloway, Nigel, Anthony Rowley, Shada Islam and Michael Vatikiotis. "East Asian Trade Grouping at Top of Region's Agenda: An Insurance Policy." *Far Eastern Economic Review*, 25 July 1991, pp. 52–53.

Jackson, John, Willam J. Davey and Alan O. Sykes, Jr. *Legal Problems of Economic Relations: Cases, Materials and Texts*, 3rd edition. St. Paul, Minn.: West Publishing Co., 1995.

Kartadjoemena, H. S. *MEE dan ASEAN: Evolusi Suatu Hubungan Trans-Regional*. Jakarta: Prisma, 1973.

_____ . *Aspek Internasional dari Masalah Competition Policy: Menghadapi Perundingan WTO Tahun 2000*. Jakarta: Yayasan Indonesia Forum, 1999.

_____ . "Regional Cooperation in Southeast Asia: An Indonesian View." *Performance and Perspectives of the Indonesian Economy*, edited by Muh. Arsjad Anwar, et al. Tokyo: Institute of Developing Economies, 1976.

Lloyd, Peter J. "Should AFTA and CER Link?" *AFTA in the Changing International Economy*, edited by Joseph Tan, p. 191. Singapore: Institute of Southeast Asian Studies, 1996.

Menon, Jayant. *Adjusting towards AFTA: The Dynamics of Trade in ASEAN*. Singapore: Institute of Southeast Asian Studies, 1996.

Ministry of Trade/USAID TIPS. *The Uruguay Round and Its Benefits to Indonesia*. Jakarta, October, 1994.

Mohamed Ariff and Tan Loong-Hoe, eds. *The Uruguay Round: ASEAN Trade Policy Options*. Singapore: Institute of Southeast Asian Studies, 1988.

Raffaelli, Marcelo, and Tripti Jenkins. *The Drafting History of the Agreement of Textiles and Clothing*. Geneva: International Textiles and Clothing Bureau, 1995.

Kym Anderson and Richard Blackhurst, eds. *Regional Integration and the Global Trading System*. London: Harvester Wheatsheaf, 1993.

Rieger, Hans Christoph. *ASEAN Co-operation and Intra-ASEAN Trade*. Research and Discussion Paper No. 57. Singapore: Institute of Southeast Asian Studies, 1985.

Scitovsky, T. *Economic Theory and Western European Integration*. London: George Allen and Unwin, 1958.

Snape, Richard H. "History and Economics GATT's Article 24". *Regional Integration and the Global Trading System*, edited by Kym Anderson and Richard Blackhurst. London: Harvester Wheatsheaf, 1993.

Swann, Dennis. *The Economics of the Common Market*, 2nd edition. Harmondsworth: Penguin Books, 1972.

Urwin, Derek W. *Western Europe Since 1945: A Political History*, 4th edition. New York: Longman, 1993.

Vautier, Kerrin. *PECC Competition Principles*. Singapore: PECC Secretariat, 1999.

Viner, Jacob. *The Customs Union Issue*. New York: Carnegie Endowment for International Peace, 1950.

Whalley, John. "Developing Countries and System Strengthening in the Uruguay Round." *The Uruguay Round and the Developing Countries*, edited by Will Martin and L. Alan Winters. Cambridge: Cambridge University Press, 1996.

World Bank. *Global Economic Prospects and the Developing Countries*. Washington, D.C., 1992.

WTO. "General Agreement on Trade in Services." *The Results of the Uruguay Round of Multilateral Negotiations: Legal Texts*. Geneva, 1995.

10

ASEAN and Its Inter-Regional Economic Links

MAHANI ZAINAL ABIDIN

Introduction

ASEAN was founded in 1967 with political motives and was not intended to be a cohesive economic entity or bloc. The ASEAN economies are mostly open in nature and as a consequence, they depend very much on economic relations with other countries outside the region. This is generally thought to be one of the key factors in both ASEAN's formation and its success. The Bali Summit in 1976 formalized the nature and structure of ASEAN's external political and economic relations, and these relations must be consistent with the following objectives:

a) To accelerate their efforts in improving market access for their raw materials and finished products outside the ASEAN region by way of seeking the elimination of all trade barriers in these markets, in developing new usage for these products, and in adopting approaches and actions in dealing with regional groups and individual economic powers;

b) To co-operate in the field of technology and production and improve the quality of exports and products, and to develop "new products" with the specific view of diversification of export products;

c) To adopt joint approaches to international commodity problems
    by way of the existing instruments with a view to contributing
    to the establishment of a New International Economic Order;
d) To give priority to stabilization and increase of export earnings
    of those commodities produced and exported by ASEAN through
    commodity arrangements, including buffer stock schemes and
    other means.[1]

Three factors pushed ASEAN to seek extra-regional relations:
economic, political, and the need to strengthen the evolution of
ASEAN. The economic reasons were the most compelling. At the
early stage of their development processes, the ASEAN countries
depended on primary commodities, and they were thus very
vulnerable to international price fluctuations. If ASEAN were to
have closer relations with the developed countries, which were
the biggest buyers of these commodities, then such co-operation
would be a first step towards stabilizing prices. Most of the ASEAN
economies adopted export-oriented industrialization as their engine
of growth and for this they needed good export market networks.
ASEAN was also the recipient of a large flow of foreign direct
investment (FDI), in industries that assembled or processed
imported intermediate goods to be exported back to the developed
countries. Therefore, ASEAN needed close and cordial relations
with the countries which were the sources of these investments.
Equally important, as developing countries, the ASEAN members
had to seek external financial and technical assistance for their
development process.

    ASEAN external relations have two components: first,
economic relationships that include trade, investment, and trade
facilitation. The second is based on politics and regional security
needs. For the older ASEAN members (Indonesia, Malaysia, the
Philippines, Singapore and Thailand) the huge share of trade in
their economies indicates the importance of external economic
relations. Similarly, FDI dominates certain industries, which are
the key to ASEAN economic growth and, since 1990, ASEAN has
also received a large flow of short-term capital.

    Political and security relations were the foundation for
ASEAN's external relationship and the *raison d'être* for its
existence. One of the primary objectives of the formation of ASEAN
was to create a zone of peace and neutrality to contain the spread

of communism. The ASEAN Regional Forum (ARF) brought together all the key political and regional security players to support this objective. By achieving its political and security objectives, ASEAN was able to concentrate on economic growth, particularly from the early 1980s. ASEAN's political and regional security relations have taken a new dimension with the end of the Cold War and the emergence of new issues such as human rights. The addition of new members in ASEAN has raised concerns from ASEAN's partners. For example, the European Union (EU) and the United States objected to the membership of Myanmar. The claims over the Spratly Islands have also engaged both ASEAN members and their external partners in a potentially damaging dispute. More recently, the turmoil in East Timur has seriously tested Indonesia's relationship with Australia. Thus, the political and security dimension of ASEAN's external relationships may once again overshadow the economic issues, but this is beyond the scope of this chapter.

ASEAN's external economic relations are two-pronged: co-operation with dialogue partners; and co-operation with regional groupings.

Dialogue partnership is bilateral co-operation, with a more formalized mechanism carried out through annual meetings. This relationship began at the early phase of the ASEAN process, even as early as the mid-1970s. The Dialogue Partners include Australia, Canada, the EU, India, Japan and the United States. The relationship with regional groupings involve a larger group of countries but the issues covered are not as detailed as those with the Dialogue Partners. The regional groupings that are ASEAN's partners include the Asia-Pacific Economic Co-operation (APEC), North America Free Trade Agreement (NAFTA), Australia-New Zealand Closer Economic Relations and Trade Agreement (ANZCERTA), Mercado Comun del Cono Sur (MERCOSUR), and the South Asia Association for Regional Co-operation (SAARC). The possible emergence of new regional groupings is also important to ASEAN as they can impact on ASEAN's existing relationships or even affect the ASEAN economies directly.

This chapter analyses the progress of ASEAN's external relationships and examines the relevant issues affecting the future direction of these relationships. The next section discusses the outward structure of the ASEAN economies, which is the primary reason for its need to develop strong external links. Following this is a review of ASEAN's relationship with its Dialogue Partners, and an assessment of its co-operation with other regional groupings. The final section raises the pertinent issues that can determine the future direction of ASEAN's external relationships. These include the types of co-operation and their priorities, the areas of co-operation, and how ASEAN's external relationships fit in with the larger objective of a free multilateral trading system promoted by the World Trade Organization (WTO).

ASEAN External Relationships

A salient feature of the ASEAN economies is their openness, and ASEAN's external relationships are very much determined by its trade and investment links. Trade (exports and imports) constitutes a large part of these economies. For example, the share of exports and imports in Malaysia's gross domestic product (GDP) is 80 per cent and 70 per cent respectively. Likewise, the share of exports in Thailand's economy is also at about the same level, while for Indonesia and the Philippines, the percentages are smaller. Singapore's total trade is about two to three times that of its GDP. As the newer members of ASEAN are still in transition to a market economy, it is not unusual that trade contributes only a small part to their economies. Trade also influences the relationship between ASEAN and its Dialogue Partners and other regional groupings. Table 10.1 shows that APEC is the most important trading partner (exports and imports). The North America Free Trade Agreement (NAFTA) comes second, followed by the European Community (EU) and the ANZCERTA. Trade links with MERCOSUR and the European Free Trade Area (EFTA) are relatively small. The table also gives the bilateral trade pattern. In terms of exports, the United States is the largest market for ASEAN exports, followed by Japan and the EU. However, the ranking of sources for imports differs from exports — Japan is the largest source of ASEAN imports while the United States comes second and the EU a close third.

For foreign direct investments (FDI), Japan is by far the largest investor in ASEAN (see Table 10.2), with the EU taking second position, and the United States a distant third. In Indonesia, Singapore, and Thailand, Japanese share in total FDI declined from 1980 to 1993 but its share increased in Malaysia and the Philippines during the same period. On the other hand, the EU's share only increased in two countries, Indonesia and the Philippines, while in

TABLE 10.1
Direction of ASEAN's Exports and Imports
(In US$ millions)

Exports

	1992	1993	1994	1995	1996	1997
World	185,864	211,808	259,309	317,375	339,665	351,570
Intra-ASEAN	37,034	44,524	60,410	72,659	70,646	86,252
Dialogue Partners						
CER	—	4,262	5,209	5,941	6,918	7,192
Japan	30,483	33,144	37,245	45,782	51,191	42,009
Korea	—	6,126	7,005	8,575	9,447	10,668
India	—	1,484	1,970	2,821	3,723	4,473
Russia	—	423	931	915	3,169	876
PR China	3,784	5,089	6,838	8,568	9,756	10,772
US	36,582	42,258	51,560	59,852	64,355	70,030
Canada	—	1,956	2,155	2,244	1,988	1,882
EU	28,335	30,285	35,573	43,436	47,850	46,087
Rest of the World						
Taiwan	—	6,144	7,394	8,761	11,317	14,167
EFTA	—	—	—	712	1,201	—
MERCOSUR	—	—	—	1,319	1,627	1,681
SADC	—	—	—	928	1,776	—
NAFTA	38,748	44,856	54,757	62,996	67,959	73,229
APEC	128,428	148,742	185,876	225,122	238,839	263,835

Imports

	1992	1993	1994	1995	1996	1997
World	200,092	229,570	278,568	344,626	369,746	373,465
Intra-ASEAN	33,646	40,268	48,826	61,128	66,692	67,603
Dialogue Partners						
CER	—	5,940	7,245	8,039	9,839	9,261
Japan	46,999	56,020	69,289	85,485	82,857	71,264
Korea	—	7,125	9,036	11,591	13,294	14,857
India	—	1,392	1,547	1,881	2,844	4,396
Russia	—	215	535	1,084	2,041	1,116
PR China	5,393	5,619	7,332	10,992	11,702	15,249
US	29,934	34,374	40,023	50,178	53,943	61,695
Canada	—	1,540	1,717	2,291	2,446	2,568
EU	28,780	32,119	38,619	50,144	55,618	51,010
Rest of the World						
Taiwan	—	8,141	9,530	11,241	12,797	18,030
EFTA	—	—	—	3,649	5,422	—
MERCOSUR	—	—	—	1,790	2,533	1,950
SADC	—	—	—	651	1,447	—
NAFTA	31,762	36,103	41,310	53,172	57,142	65,082
APEC	135,955	159,435	194,841	246,766	260,201	284,301

SOURCE: IMF, *Direction of Trade Statistics,* various years; and ASEAN Secretariat.

TABLE 10.2
Distribution of Inward FDI Stock and Average Annual FDI Inflows of
Selected ASEAN Economies from Main Source Countries, 1980–93
(In US$ millions, and percentages)

	Stock						Inflows (annual average)			
	1980		1985		1993		1985–1987		1990–1993	
	Value	Share of	Value	Share of	Value	Share of	Value	Share of	Value	Share of
INDONESIA	10,274	100	15,353	100	67,275	100	1,047	100	8,999	100
European Union	851	8	2,672	17	9,967	15	269	26	1,205	13
Japan	3,462	34	5,009	33	13,937	21	329	31	1,379	15
United States	437	4	974	6	3,701	5	123	12	450	5
NIEs	1,196	11.6	NA	NA	17,234	25.5	NA	NA	NA	NA
Subtotal	5,946	57.6	8,655	56	44,839	66.5	721	69	3,034	33
MALAYSIA	6,462[b]	100[b]	8,510	100	34,091	100	818[c]	100[c]	5,508	100
European Union	1,720[b]	27[b]	2,264	27	5,842	17	84[c]	10[c]	837	15
Japan	1,135[b]	18[b]	1,602	19	7,435	22	284[c]	35[c]	1,142	21
United States	413[b]	6[b]	604	7	3,586	11	65[c]	8[c]	709	13
NIEs	2,353	36.4	NA	NA	11,506	33.7	NA	NA	NA	NA
Subtotal	5,621	87.4	4,470	53	28,369	83.7	433	53	2,688	49
PHILIPPINES	1,225	100	2,589	100	4,389	100	121	100	329	100
European Union	1,149	9	349	14	748	17	15	12	71	22
Japan	206	17	352	14	890	20	12	10	111	34
United States	669	55	1,961	57	1,937	44	79	65	55	17
NIEs	67	5.5	NA	NA	442	10.1	NA	NA	NA	NA
Subtotal	1,056	86.5	2,672	85	4,017	91.1	106	87	237	73
SINGAPORE	6,211	100	12,115	100	38,584[d]	100[d]	11,908	100	..[e]	..[e]
European Union	2,024	33	2,914	24	9,265[d]	24[d]	3,556	30	..[e]	..[e]
Japan	679	11	1,549	13	2,568[d]	7[d]	1,763	15	..[e]	..[e]
United States	1,219	20	2,931	24	6,813[d]	18[d]	3,213	27	..[e]	..[e]
NIEs	845	13.6	NA	NA	2,743	7.1	NA	NA	NA	NA
Subtotal	4,767	77.6	7,394	61	21,389	56.1	8,532	72	NA	NA
THAILAND	981	100	2,221	100	13,918	100	259	100	2,050	100
European Union	156	16	350	16	1,484	11	24	9	210	10
Japan	285	29	622	28	4,579	33	100	39	602	29
United States	322	33	721	32	2,412	17	69	27	311	15
NIEs	181	18.5	NA	NA	4,370	31.4	NA	NA	NA	NA
Subtotal	944	96.5	1,693	76	12,845	92.4	193	75	1,123	54

[a] Data for Indonesia, Malaysia and Thailand are estimated on the basis of cumulated inflows and are on approval basis.
[b] 1981
[c] 1987 only
[d] 1991
[e] Geographical breakdown of FDI inflows is available only up to 1989.

SOURCE: S. Y. Tham, "Competition and Co-operation for Foreign Direct Investment: An ASEAN Perspective", *Asia-Pacific Development Journal* 5, no. 1 (June 1998).

the other three it dropped quite substantially. The increased importance of Japanese investment from the second half of the 1980s was the result of the relocation of Japanese firms from the home country to ASEAN because of the appreciation of the yen. In the 1990s, investments from the newly industrialized East Asian economies (Taiwan, South Korea, and Hong Kong) became very significant.

The closer trade and investment relationship between ASEAN and its external partners (bilateral partners or regional groupings) is the result of the liberalization measures introduced by the ASEAN countries, the reduction of tariff barriers promoted by the multilateral trading system, and the relocation of investments by international firms. The introduction of the ASEAN Free Trade Area has turned the region into a potentially large common market. The ASEAN members have extended their trade liberalization commitments in AFTA to other trading partners and this has had an overall effect of lowering tariff rates. The ASEAN members also took significant steps beyond tariff reduction in their WTO agreement, such as commitments in trade-related intellectual property rights and anti-dumping measures. In the area of investment, besides offering incentives by individual countries, ASEAN has also embarked on a programme to develop an ASEAN Investment Area (AIA). Under this programme, the ASEAN countries would streamline their investment regimes and improve investment facilities. The AIA, together with a large integrated market (the total population in ASEAN is about 500 million), provides a strong incentive for foreign firms to invest in ASEAN.

ASEAN Dialogue Partners

ASEAN's commitment to develop its external relations was stated at the first meeting of the ASEAN heads of government in 1976, through a "Dialogue Partnership". Participation in a common stand on the external front has validated intra-ASEAN integration, both political and otherwise. Intra-ASEAN economic integration was slow to start and faced many difficulties; the member countries compete economically and a move towards a "common market", as it was perceived, might have delayed the development of some member countries. A united front, however, helps to address some shared external problems, particularly concerning economic development.

Having reached a consensus, ASEAN leaders built stronger links with the Dialogue Partners through the mechanism of periodical dialogues on selected issues. The ASEAN countries later extended this into a series of sectoral partnerships, which hold discussions on specific areas of common interest.

In 1976 the first group of countries with which ASEAN's external relations began were its major trading partners — Australia, Japan, New Zealand and the United Nations Development Programme (UNDP). Dialogue partnership was later extended to the United States in 1977, the European Union in 1980, Canada in 1981, and the Republic of Korea in 1991. India had been a Sectoral Dialogue Partner of ASEAN since 1993 and became a Dialogue Partner in 1995. China and Russia, which began consultative relations with ASEAN in 1991, were accorded Dialogue status in 1996. Pakistan also established Sectoral Dialogue relations with ASEAN in 1997.

ASEAN discusses with its Dialogue Partners not only economic topics but also politics and international relations. ASEAN has taken full advantage of its external relationships to obtain crucial support for its economic growth through direct investment and trade. Apart from these, ASEAN's economic co-operation with its Dialogue Partners includes industrial development, transfer of technology, energy, communications, transport, and tourism. The emphasis of this development co-operation has changed from specific project financing to partnership and shared projects in selected areas. Co-operation was also extended to include non-economic matters, such as politics, science and technology, human resource development, environment, and social, cultural and international relations as these are also critical to the existence and survival of ASEAN.

The Dialogue Partnership consists of three main types: first, relations with the EU which is, in the truest sense, inter-regional co-operation; secondly, relations with individual countries; and thirdly, relations with an international development institution (UNDP).

ASEAN–Australia

ASEAN–Australia co-operation started in 1974, with the formation of the ASEAN–Australia Economic Co-operation Programme

(AAECP). The Programme, involving mainly trade and investment, forms the major ASEAN–Australia dialogue. Projects covered under this programme include environmental management, transportation, biotechnology, telecommunications and information technologies, and agro-based industries. Cultural co-operation, which is under a separate working group, covers the exchange of information officers as well as human resource development projects in the performing arts, film archiving, heritage preservation, theatre management, and distance education.

In the economic area, the ASEAN–Australia dialogue covers trade and investment relations, sub-regional growth areas, the ASEAN Free Trade Area, the Australia–New Zealand Closer Economic Relations and Trade Agreement, and other international arrangements, such as APEC and the General Agreement on Tariffs and Trade (GATT). Of special interest is the implementation of AFTA and its effect on trade between ASEAN and Australia.

The strength of ASEAN–Australia co-operation is evidenced by the fact that the AAECP is now entering its fourth phase and it will be extended to the new ASEAN members. It has been suggested that the co-operation programme be renamed ASEAN–Australia Development Co-operation Programme to better reflect the development focus of the bilateral relationship. A key area of co-operation is the enhancement of human resource development and technology transfer, which can facilitate further the ASEAN–Australia relationship. A new area of co-operation arising from the East Asian crisis is the commitment by Australia to support the recovery of the ASEAN economies, and the exchange of views on measures to deal with the crisis as well as to mitigate the social impact of the crisis.

Apart from economic issues, the dialogue meetings also discuss regional security matters; for example, the Southeast Asia nuclear weapons free zone and political developments in Myanmar and Cambodia. There has also been discussion of topics of potential difficulty, such as the Australian immigration and overseas students' policies. Of course, the elimination or reduction of trade barriers by both ASEAN and Australia have always been the underlying concern as this is a *sine qua non* of the expansion of trade between ASEAN and Australia.

ASEAN–Canada

Although the dialogue relationship was already in place in 1977, the ASEAN–Canada Co-operation Agreement was signed in September in 1981 and covers industrial, commercial, and development co-operation. Canada's major contribution came through the ASEAN–Canada regional training programme, which provided training for ASEAN government officials. In February 1999, in a review of the bilateral relationship, Canada agreed to help mitigate the social impact of the financial crisis, strengthen regional financial systems, combat transnational crime, and tackle transboundary haze.

In the area of international trade ASEAN and Canada have shared concerns with respect to the implementation of the GATT, and have ongoing discussions particularly about financial services, telecommunications, and government procurement. The more tangible form of co-operation is in the field of science and technology; for example, ASEAN has proposed and Canada has responded positively to two projects on the environment, namely, natural resource and environmental accounting, and application of economic instruments for pollution control.

ASEAN–China

The ASEAN–China relationship has reached a high level of institutionalization with the establishment of various consultation mechanisms. China has invited ASEAN to participate in the trade and investment opportunities arising from the Chinese push for higher economic development. New initiatives include the exchange of personnel, seminars for young ASEAN diplomats on understanding modern China, increasing knowledge on ASEAN–China economic and trade co-operation, increasing co-operation among ASEAN and Chinese scientists, and promotion of bilateral investment flows.

ASEAN–EU

The EU is ASEAN's oldest Dialogue Partner, which began informally in 1972 and was formalized in 1980 through the ASEAN–EU Co-operation Agreement. Following this agreement, a Joint Co-operation Committee (JCC) was set up to review and guide the direction and implementation of ASEAN–EU co-operation. The main areas of co-operation are the promotion of trade and investment flows, industrial complementarities, standards and conformance, intellectual propriety rights, science and technology, environment, human resource development, and institutional linkages. Additional areas of co-operation include greater involvement of EU financial institutions in ASEAN projects and access to European technology and know-how. There is potential for a much higher trade flow than at present. The EU operates its own Generalized System of Preferences (GSP), but ASEAN has not made the fullest use of this. FDI from the EU is also less than optimal. One possible explanation is that EU cross-border investment decisions first consider other parts of Europe, while corporate Japanese and U.S. investors have ASEAN as one of their preferred destinations.

In order to strengthen the present links, the ASEAN–EU agreement may be renegotiated to broaden and deepen the scope of co-operation. One possible addition is to encourage private sector participation in joint-venture projects. Furthermore, a co-ordinating group may be established to monitor the progress in ASEAN–EU development co-operation.

ASEAN–India

When India was accorded Dialogue Partner status in 1995, the two sides had agreed to expand their areas of co-operation to include human resource development and people-to-people contacts. Another area of co-operation that is active is science and technology, particularly in computer expertise. A study on AFTA–India linkages for the enhancement of trade and investment will be conducted. ASEAN and India have also agreed to start their political dialogue at the Senior Officials level.

ASEAN–Japan

The first ASEAN–Japan forum was held in Tokyo in 1977 and heralded the Japanese commitment of financial assistance to ASEAN countries, amounting to about US$1 billion. The most prominent areas of co-operation are human resource development, agricultural science, engineering science, medical science, and basic research and frontier technology.

Because Japan is one of the major trading partners of ASEAN, trade, commercial, and economic issues naturally dominate their relationship. The trade balance has always favoured Japan and ASEAN believes that its trade deficit could be narrowed through the import by Japan of more ASEAN industrial and manufacturing products. In addition, the strength of the yen has caused the trade imbalance to worsen to such an extent that it may restrict the economic growth of the ASEAN countries. In 1993, ASEAN–Japan co-operation was deepened to include the development of small and medium-scale industries, standards and quality control, intellectual property, and industrial technology research.

A new body, the AEM-MITI Economic and Industrial Co-operation Committee was established in 1997 to promote further industrial co-operation in ASEAN, improve ASEAN competitiveness, and provide development assistance to new members of ASEAN. Among its objectives, the new committee is to run programmes to assist ASEAN economic recovery, facilitate greater market access for ASEAN exports in the Japanese market, and introduce Japanese investors to opportunities created by AFTA, ASEAN Industrial Co-operation (AICO), and AIA.

Japanese financial aid through the US$30 billion Miyazawa Fund is essential in providing funds for the ASEAN recovery programme. Japanese financial assistance began even earlier with the proposed Asian Monetary Fund in 1997, but this initiative did not materialize because of strong objections by the United States.

ASEAN–New Zealand

Dialogue with New Zealand began in 1975, focusing on the long-term objective of achieving sustainable development in ASEAN. New Zealand has offered co-operation on the economic and technical fronts and has committed 12 per cent of its overseas development aid to ASEAN. A significant portion of the co-operation efforts will be in agriculture — for example, surveys on end uses of timber, animal husbandry, dairy training centres, and afforestation projects.

In 1990/91, to further increase co-operation, ASEAN and New Zealand introduced the Inter-Institutional Linkages Program (IILP), and Trade and Investment Promotion Program (TIPP). The objective of IILP is to establish self-sustaining links between ASEAN and

New Zealand institutions in the academic, professional, scientific, and commercial spheres. The TIPP, on the other hand, was formed to overcome constraints hindering the promotion of trade and investment by the business communities of both sides. An important feature of the TIPP is that it is allowed to fund private sector projects.

In 1998, New Zealand proposed that in view of the East Asian crisis, bilateral co-operation should focus on trade facilitation, public sector reform, science and technology, and English language.

ASEAN–Republic of Korea

Co-operation between ASEAN and Korea covers trade, investment, tourism, education, environment, science and technology, human resource development, and development co-operation. A fund has been established and 41 projects have been funded under this programme. ASEAN and Korea have also agreed to jointly work to bring their economies out of the crisis by promoting and facilitating trade (including countertrade on essential items), and encouraging the flow of investment and boosting tourism.

ASEAN–Russia

The Russian Federation became ASEAN's Dialogue Partner in 1996. The bilateral co-operation is centred on science and technology but economic difficulties experienced by both partners have slowed down the planned activities.

ASEAN–United States

The United States is a major trading partner for all the ASEAN countries and the ASEAN–U.S. dialogue co-operation started in 1975. U.S. ties with ASEAN cover not only economic issues but also political, security, social and cultural matters. However, trade issues, as in most other relationships, take centre stage and close attention has been given to shared concerns, such as unilateral U.S. trade protectionist measures (Section 301), voluntary restraint agreements, and non-tariff barriers, and the U.S. domestic lobby against certain ASEAN agricultural exports.

The United States has given financial assistance to ASEAN, particularly in the area of technical co-operation, expansion of intra-ASEAN and ASEAN–U.S. trade and investment, and upgrading of management and technical skills. Recently, the favoured vehicles for development co-operation have been the Private Investment and Trade Opportunities (PITO) Project, and the Environment Improvement Project (EIP), which began in 1989 and 1991 respectively. The aim of PITO is to establish a structure and mechanism to promote and expand private sector involvement in trade and investment between ASEAN and the United States. The objective of the EIP is to create a decision-making environment in which business will take the necessary steps on its own initiative to prevent or reduce pollution, through the adoption of cleaner production technology and procedures.

The ASEAN–U.S. dialogue has also taken up political and security issues of mutual concern. These include those involving Cambodia, the Middle East, Bosnia-Herzegovina, the South China Sea, and Indochina's refugees.

ASEAN–UNDP

The United Nations Development Programme (UNDP) has operated many programmes in ASEAN during the past decades and it is considered a very important promoter of industrial development, hence its inclusion as one of the Dialogue Partners. The projects sponsored and funded by the UNDP are primarily technical and are designed to help capacity-building and institutional development.

ASEAN–Pakistan

The Sectoral Dialogue with Pakistan covers trade, investment, industry, science and technology, tourism, drugs and narcotics, and human resource development. In February 1999, more specific fields of co-operation were identified to match the priorities of ASEAN with the expertise of Pakistan. These fields of co-operation include food-processing technology, environment protection, water resource management, and non-conventional energy research.

In summary, ASEAN dialogue and sectoral partnerships address developmental co-operation. It started with the Dialogue Partners from the developed countries assisting ASEAN in economic growth and strengthening the ASEAN integration process. Promotion of trade and investment is the hallmark of this relationship. Subsequently, when the partnership was extended to other countries, the scope of co-operation was widened to cover more specific areas, particularly in science and technology, human resources, cultural and social development, and the environment. Interestingly, the East Asian crisis has opened a very challenging dimension to bilateral co-operation, namely, the formulation of joint support programmes to revive the ASEAN economies, including financial support and schemes to mitigate the social impact of the crisis.

Relationship with Regional Groupings

Apart from its existing dialogue relations, ASEAN also agreed, during the Fourth Summit in 1992, to intensify co-operative relationships with interested non-Dialogue countries and international organizations. The Fifth ASEAN Summit in 1995 re-emphasized the importance of expanding ASEAN's external relationships. This move recognized an increasingly interdependent world, in which ASEAN has to optimize its growth and development prospects by maximizing gains from global integration. In this regard, ASEAN has to reassess its established ties with regional groupings such as APEC, the EU, NAFTA, and ANZCERTA. Moreover, ASEAN has expanded co-operation with new partners, such as the MERCOSUR, and the SAARC. ASEAN will also have to develop relationships with emerging regional groupings, such as the Japan–South Korea Free Trade Area and the Transatlantic Economic Partnership.

The main objective of regional groupings is to promote integration by giving preferential treatment to its members that discriminates imports but encourages internal trade. ASEAN is a regional grouping with similar characteristics but its preferential treatment is extended to all its trading partners. Unlike its bilateral links, ASEAN's relations with other regional groupings are limited to trade and investment liberalization because wider co-operation would take a long time to reach agreement. For example, the large and diverse membership of the EU limits the relationship with ASEAN to trade and investment areas that can benefit both sides. On the other hand, a bilateral ASEAN dialogue partnership extends the area of co-operation to specific fields, such as project funding, human resource development, industrial complementarity, and the environment. With this limitation, the primary aim of ASEAN's relationships with other regional groupings is to best employ their respective strengths and enhance each other's comparative advantage.

ASEAN's links with other regional groupings is determined by the nature of their relationships and by the level of integration within the regional grouping. Unlike its relations with other regional groups, ASEAN is a member of APEC and therefore its goals should be in tangent with APEC's. On the other hand, ASEAN is free to determine the direction and depth of relations with other groupings because it is not restricted to a set of predetermined goals. Another challenge in ASEAN's external relationships is the fact that relations with a particular country can have three forms: for example, Australia has a bilateral relationship with ASEAN (Dialogue Partner), it is a fellow member of APEC, and has a regional relationship through its membership in ANZCERTA. Thus, the three relationships must be aligned to avoid any inconsistencies or ambiguities.

The following analysis of ASEAN's relationships with other regional groupings is confined to the economic sphere. In this context, the ASEAN Free Trade Area initiative is chosen as the basis of analysis, because the current focus of that relationship is on trade and investment.

ASEAN–APEC

APEC was established in 1989 for the purpose of trade and investment facilitation and liberalization through co-operation and consultation. Its membership has been extended to twenty-one: namely, Australia, Brunei, Canada, Chile, China, Hong Kong, Indonesia, Japan, Korea, Malaysia, Mexico, New Zealand, Papua New Guinea, Peru, Philippines, Russia, Singapore, Chinese Taipei, Thailand, USA, and Vietnam. The objectives of APEC are:

• free and open trade and investment in the Asia-Pacific region no later than 2010/2020; and
• expansion and acceleration of trade and investment facilitation programmes, to attain sustainable growth for the APEC region.

These definitive goals were translated into each country's own Individual Action Plan (IAP), known as the Manila Action Plan for APEC (MAPA). MAPA represented a compilation of the IAPs, as well as collective action plans for trade and investment liberalization and facilitation, and joint activities on economic and technical co-operation. The IAPs offer:

- significant unilateral tariff reductions;
- a standstill on new measures of protection;
- commitments to reduce non-tariff measures and liberalize services trade; and
- implementation of trade and investment facilitation measures.

Investment liberalization in APEC is addressed through the agreement on non-binding investment principles. At the individual level, the policy direction taken by most APEC economies over the past two decades has generally been towards easing of restrictions on, and/or lowering or removal of barriers to attract inward foreign direct investment. However, accessibility for foreign investors may still be difficult because liberalization of formal rules has not necessarily led to an increase in the transparency of investment regimes, and informal investment barriers are now relatively more important than formal barriers. In terms of trade liberalization, rapid progress in APEC has been made since the late 1980s. APEC members implemented unilateral reforms and deregulation programmes that resulted in a significant reduction of their overall tariff rates in the 1990s. As a result of these various measures, the unweighted average tariff rate in the APEC region fell from 15.4 per cent in 1988 to 9.1 per cent in 1996. Unilateral reforms done primarily under the Uruguay Round Agreement have brought about a significant decline in the incidence of non-tariff measures (NTMs) on imports by the APEC economies since the late 1980s. For APEC as a whole, the incidence of NTMs has been cut nearly in half, declining from 9 per cent of import coverage in 1988 to 5 per cent in 1996.

To accelerate the liberalization process, APEC has embarked on the Early Voluntary Sectoral Liberalization (EVSL) package. The EVSL effort for information technology products was successful when the tariff rate was reduced to almost zero. Under the pressing economic circumstances faced by many APEC members during the regional crisis, the EVSL failed to make further progress at the Kuala Lumpur Summit in 1998. Progress in APEC's economic and technical co-operation has been slow.

Although ASEAN's objectives complement APEC's goals, the different rates of progress in their respective integration processes may weaken their relationship. APEC consists of diverse economies at different stages of development, with different economic structures and located in a wide geographical area. As a result, the process of integration is much slower as member economies have different priorities. In contrast, the ASEAN economies have strong intra-regional links, similar structures, and the same stage of development. Furthermore, the ASEAN Free Trade Area initiative will integrate these economies faster, where internally traded goods will face at most 5 per cent import duty by the year 2003. In addition, the AFTA process will make significant advances in improving trade facilitation, such as harmonization of standards and customs procedures.

The success of APEC's liberalization programme is very dependent on the unilateral efforts of each member economy. Since APEC's approach is based on the concept of open regionalism, it cannot provide an exclusive preferential treatment that can serve as an incentive for liberalization. On the other hand, AFTA, with its preferential treatment, offers an advantage to its members operating in an integrated regional market. The failure of the EVSL indicates APEC's difficulty in pushing for further liberalization, whereas the advantages of a free trade area will encourage ASEAN to commit further liberalization.

The usefulness of APEC to ASEAN was questioned during the East Asian crisis. APEC, with the world's two largest economies as its members, could not provide any support to mitigate the crisis. The United States prematurely shot down the Japanese proposal on the Asian Monetary Fund while the Chinese voiced a tacit disapproval. The argument given was that APEC was not established to deal with a financial crisis as its focus is on trade and investment. Nonetheless, in the future APEC cannot avoid this issue because of the importance of international capital flows and the fast liberalization of the financial sector. The new demands on APEC include the establishment of an early warning system, strengthening institutional capacity, and developing a macroeconomic and financial sector co-operation mechanism.

Notwithstanding the concerns on the future direction of APEC's relationship with ASEAN, the latter can still benefit the former, especially in the area of trade facilitation and economic and technical co-operation (ECOTECH). Trade facilitation, in effect, can complement and enhance development efforts made by ASEAN, and substantial gains can be made through ECOTECH, particularly in developmental co-operation in infrastructure and energy supply.

ASEAN–NAFTA

NAFTA, which formed a preferential trading group among the United States, Canada, and Mexico, has evolved into a formidable economic area. The combination of a developing country (Mexico), with two developed countries (the United States and Canada), created a strong and complementary regional group. The developing country provides low-cost labour, while the developed partners supply capital, technology, and skills. With the formation of NAFTA, it is feared that products from Mexico, which enjoy preferential treatment, will displace competing exports from ASEAN. In particular, labour-intensive products, such as clothing and garments, will be disadvantaged. This concern deepens when there are indications that NAFTA will be expanded to other countries in Latin America, under the proposal for a Free Trade Area of the Americas.

Nevertheless, investment and trade figures do not indicate any serious trade diversion or investment relocation from ASEAN as a result of the formation of NAFTA. Table 10.1 shows that exports to NAFTA almost doubled from 1992 to 1997; ASEAN exports to NAFTA increased from US$38 billion in 1992 to US$73 billion in 1997. Even though this increase may be largely due to higher exports of electrical and electronic products, labour-intensive exports, in particular clothing and garment, did not decline. Mohamed Ariff, Mahani and Tan (1996) show that from 1990 to 1995, the Malaysian export quota allocations for garment and clothing to the United States were fully utilized. Furthermore, Kim and Weston (1993) found that "... while the East Asian exposure to the North American market and the structural overlap with the Mexican exports have been growing, neither suggests that any East Asian country will be seriously threatened by NAFTA". The U.S. market is critical for the recovery of the ASEAN economies that have been hit by the East Asian crisis as it absorbs exports from these economies, and thus allow them to export their way to recovery. For investment, the pattern of FDI flows from the United States into ASEAN represents the NAFTA investment flow because the share of the other two members (Canada and Mexico) is small compared to that of the United States. The pattern of FDI flows into ASEAN from 1990 to 1993 was mixed. In terms of value, the U.S. investment increased substantially: for example, in Malaysia, U.S. investment in 1980 was US$413 million and it rose to US$3,586 million in 1993. However, as a share of total investment, except for Malaysia, the U.S. presence in the other ASEAN countries showed a decline.

The relationship between AFTA and NAFTA is mutually beneficial, although there was fear of a trade diversion when NAFTA was first formed. The fast-growing NAFTA economies, in particular the United States, will consume more imports from ASEAN. Besides trade liberalization, ASEAN has introduced other measures to open up their economies and to integrate further with the global economy, including the creation of the ASEAN Investment Area, which will attract more NAFTA investment into the region. In particular, ASEAN efforts to lure high-value-added and technology-intensive investment, especially in the information technology industry, by offering investment incentives and streamlining trade facilities will provide an opportunity for investment in a high growth industry. Plummer and Imada-Iboshi (1994) suggest the possibility of linking NAFTA with AFTA because both have similar tariff liberalization goals and both are considering an expansion of membership. This move can accelerate market access in both regional markets to circumvent the APEC process, in which both are members.

ASEAN–EU

Unlike other Dialogue Partners, the EU is the only one that represents a regional grouping. Even though some ASEAN members had been linked historically through colonial ties, the relationship between ASEAN and the EU has not been as strong as the other Dialogue Partners, such as Japan and the United States. Although ASEAN's trade with the EU accounts for a significant share of its global trade (about 13–14 per cent), the converse is not true for the EU — its trade with ASEAN constitutes only a small part of its total trade. Similarly, while EU investments are significant for ASEAN, they form a much smaller share in the EU's total investments. In the 1990s, EU investments in ASEAN were smaller than those of Japan and the newly industrialized East Asian countries. Dialogue partnership between the EU and ASEAN was less active when compared with other partners and this may be due to the high demands of the EU's internal integration. Another reason may be that the structure of the EU requires many stages of bureaucratic process in its negotiations with ASEAN because as a regional group it represents many interests. The Asia-Europe Meeting (ASEM) set up in 1996 gave a new impetus to the bilateral relationship.

ASEAN initially feared the EU's integration because it was seen as creating a "fortress" that favoured the developing economies within the group, other Eastern European countries, and developing countries from Africa and the Caribbean, which were formerly European colonies. At the same time, ASEAN plays an important role as a part of the EU production process because it supplies raw materials and produces intermediate goods for Europe. Cuyvers (1995) has estimated that ASEAN exports to the EU are affected to a limited extent by the accession of Austria, Finland, and Sweden. However, the Association's agreement with Eastern European countries (Hungry, Poland, Czechoslovakia, Romania, and Bulgaria) will cause substantial trade diversion.

The ASEAN–EU relationship has matured from the earlier donor–recipient relationship in development co-operation to one based on a partnership of equals. The future direction of the ASEAN–EU relationship is naturally to promote further liberalization and to facilitate investment flows. The EU should liberalize further its trade regime to allow greater competition from efficiently produced imports, which will encourage the reallocation of resources to reach its optimum utilization. Perhaps the EU should promote the concept of "open regionalism" to support the larger WTO objective of a free global trading system. The enlargement of both the EU and ASEAN will provide new challenges to these regional groups because both have to assimilate the new members and to encourage them to free their trade and investment regimes. The co-operation between ASEAN and the EU should also move towards APEC's approach, going beyond trade and investment liberalization to include trade facilitation and economic and technical co-operation.

In view of the regional economic crisis and the important role of an exchange rate regime, ASEAN can learn valuable lessons from the monetary integration process of the EU. No doubt, there is an urgent need to address the issue of a stable exchange rate, as it is crucial for economic sustainability. The Euro has provided that stability and macroeconomic discipline for the EU economies and this hopefully will minimize future financial crises.

ASEAN–ANZCERTA

The proposal for linking ASEAN with ANZCERTA was first raised in 1993. It received positive responses from Australia and New

Zealand, while ASEAN's reaction was more restrained. It is argued that a formal regional link between ASEAN and ANZCERTA would bring about higher growth because their economic structures complement each other and the combined market offers enormous potential. Another advantage of a formal link is that together the two regional groupings could have a stronger bargaining power in international trade negotiations. In addition, both are outward-looking economies, where the external sector contributes substantially to their economic growth. Liberalization in ANZCERTA is deeper and more comprehensive and all border restrictions on intra-ANZCERTA trade have been removed. ANZCERTA integration has advanced to services trade, where national treatment is accorded to service providers from both countries. In contrast, ASEAN trade liberalization is mainly in manufactured goods, while sectors such as agriculture and services are still subjected to selected protection.

As Dialogue Partners, both Australia and New Zealand have extensive close links with ASEAN, including development co-operation. A formal link with ASEAN may take some time to be realized but future co-operation can be directed towards trade facilitation and economic and technical links, like those proposed under APEC. ASEAN's priority is to deepen its integration, ensure that its industries are competitive, and address the issue of a developmental gap among its members. In all these areas, it can learn from the experience of ANZCERTA on the gains of closer regional integration. For example, the introduction of a competition policy to promote domestic competition by New Zealand can provide valuable lessons to ASEAN.

Other Regional Groupings

Besides the major regional groupings (APEC, EU, and NAFTA), ASEAN is also expanding its relationship with other trade areas, such as MERCOSUR and the South Asian Association for Regional Co-operation. Argentina, Brazil, Paraguay, and Uruguay established MERCOSUR in 1991. Their aim was to create a common market by 1994 through a common tariff scheme that would reduce tariff rates to between 0 and 20 per cent, with an overall average tariff of 11 per cent. Thus, MERCOSUR has shared goals with AFTA and these two groupings are forming links to increase co-operation.

MERCOSUR can offer a window for ASEAN producers to enter a large and integrated South American market, and conversely the same applies for MERCOSUR producers. The economies of the two regional groupings have the potential to achieve a high growth rate, and this can be attained when their markets are enlarged. In fact, an economic link through investment joint ventures can provide a foothold for ASEAN to enter other South American markets and, likewise, MERCOSUR producers can take advantage of the growth potential in Asia by establishing a base in ASEAN.

The SAARC's (comprising Bangladesh, Bhutan, India, Maldives, Nepal, Pakistan and Sri Lanka) progress towards economic and regional co-operation has been very limited although it was formed about nineteen years ago. This regional grouping has vast growth potential and because some member economies have a high degree of protection, liberalization that comes with regional integration will be a strong catalyst for growth. ASEAN should strengthen its links with the SAARC and in this way encourage the group to liberalize their economies. ASEAN can provide a good example of how developing economies can integrate well into the global economy.

ASEAN should also assess the potential impact of new regional initiatives and maximize co-operation with these groups. One such grouping is the proposed Transatlantic Economic Partnership between the United States and the European Union. This proposal, if realized, will have a major impact on the global economy because it links two large economic entities, thus creating a high-income market. The partnership will also resolve many trade disagreements between the United States and the EU, and this will strengthen the WTO process. However, the most important question is whether the partnership will open and extend the benefits to non-members, a concept very similar to open regionalism practised by APEC. The current proposal is for the partnership to promote bilateral liberalization to further the objectives of the WTO. The partnership will also have on its agenda trade and investment facilitation. Undoubtedly, ASEAN can derive benefits if the partnership is also open to others outside the two regions.

The proposal on the Japan–South Korea Free Trade Area is still at the conceptual stage. However, the formation of such an arrangement will affect ASEAN significantly because it may divert trade and investment from ASEAN to the new free trade area. ASEAN is a competitor to South Korea in certain industries as it supplies Japan with intermediate goods, and free access to the

Japanese market will give Korean firms an advantage over ASEAN suppliers. Similarly, Japanese firms may prefer South Korea as an investment location because of geographical proximity and low tariffs.

Another development that should impact ASEAN is the progress of regional integration in Latin America through the Andean Community and the Free Trade Area of the Americas. The Latin American market offers a huge potential for trade and investment co-operation with ASEAN. Liberalization and improved trade and investment facilitation resulting from the economic integration process will facilitate the regional linkage between ASEAN and its counterparts in Latin America.

Issues in ASEAN's External Relationships

The 1976 Declaration of Concord and the Treaty of Amity and Co-operation laid down the principles of ASEAN's external relations:[2]

- co-operation with ASEAN as a group should not be at the expense of existing bilateral arrangements;
- co-operation should serve to complement ASEAN's capabilities and not to supplant them;
- co-operation should be for projects conceived by ASEAN which are of regional character and for the benefit of all ASEAN countries; and
- co-operation should be unconditional.

ASEAN has observed these principles in its external relationships, both at the bilateral and regional levels. These relationships have brought large gains through trade expansion and increased investment, which have produced high economic growth. Its bilateral relationships have worked well but increasingly regional links are becoming more dominant. The future of ASEAN's external economic relationships is now in question because of developments inside and outside the region. Internal developments include the expansion of ASEAN membership and the progress of regional economic integration. On the other hand, WTO liberalization and advancement in other regional groupings are also critical in shaping ASEAN's external relationships. Another aspect to this relationship is the level and scope of future co-operation. After taking full advantage of its trade and investment links, ASEAN's future external relationships are likely to be more complex because they now have to cover a wider set of interests, such as capital flows and macroeconomic policy. It may be more difficult for ASEAN members to reach a consensus on the issues and the level of integration with its external partners. Going forward, there are a number of issues that will determine ASEAN's relationship with other regional groupings, and ASEAN must ensure that they can contribute positively to its integration and prosperity:

- The pace of progress within each grouping will change the priority of the relationship between ASEAN and its regional partners. A contrasting pattern is observed when ASEAN's relationship is compared with APEC and the EU. In the first case, ASEAN is a more cohesive unit compared to APEC, whose membership is very diverse. ASEAN has a schedule of commitments to achieve free trade, through AFTA. Although APEC's integration covers a wider area, such as economic and technical co-operation, its timetable for free trade is based on a more flexible schedule. As a result, ASEAN is likely to integrate and achieve the goal of free trade faster than APEC. In such a case, ASEAN may move to another stage of integration, especially in monetary and financial union as a solution to the crisis experienced by the region in 1997 and 1998. If ASEAN takes this route, it is possible for it to focus less on APEC and to initiate a closer relationship with other regional groups with a similar level of integration.

  If ASEAN's relationship with APEC is hampered by the relatively slow progress in the latter, the reverse would be true in the case of ASEAN and the EU. As a fully integrated region, the EU may find it difficult to deal with ASEAN, which does not have a supranational institutional structure to handle bigger issues, such as the environment, research and development (R&D), and technological development. It is easy to deal with the EU because it has achieved an economic and monetary union and has common standards practised by its members. Most importantly, it has a supranational political institution that expedites the decision-making process. In contrast, ASEAN lacks most of these features and its trade and investment policy integration is still nascent. Thus, the EU may place less emphasis on its relationship with ASEAN and focus on other more integrated regional groupings, or the EU may prefer a stronger bilateral relationship with individual ASEAN members.

- The enlargement of ASEAN membership creates new challenges for ASEAN integration and its external relationships. The newer members are at a lower stage of development and their priority is to develop a market economy and to generate employment. The older members of ASEAN, on the other hand, had experienced a long period of growth and are ready to be fully integrated with the global economy. For example, AFTA will be implemented in two stages: a faster timetable for the six original members, while a longer adjustment period is given to the four new members. This poses the problem of a differentiated level of liberalization, which can create constraints in dealing with external partners. The free trade area approach for economic integration, as proposed by AFTA, poses another constraint in ASEAN's external relationship. Under this approach, ASEAN members only have to maintain a common internal tariff regime but each is free to set its own external tariff rates. As such, it discourages external partners from treating ASEAN as an economic block because they have to deal separately with each member on trade matters. Furthermore, in advancing economic co-operation with other regional blocks, these partners would demand reciprocal treatment, including deeper liberalization. However, ASEAN may not be able to comply because it may have to limit liberalization to safeguard the interests of the new members.

- The progress of liberalization under the auspices of the WTO will influence the nature and level of relationship between ASEAN and its regional partners. The WTO agreements cover wider areas than the regional relationships: trade liberalization is regarded as a basic commitment, and the WTO obligations are extended to agriculture, services, and intellectual property rights, and may expand to non-core economic issues such as the environment and labour standards. In addition, WTO principles, such as most-favoured-nation (MFN) treatment, reduce the benefits of bilateral relationships because these principles prohibit special treatment to selected partners. Moreover, there are moves for the WTO to encroach on domestic policy, thus decreasing further the ability of a country or a regional grouping to give exclusive benefits to its external partners. Therefore, as the influence and jurisdiction of the WTO increase, the incentive to expand and the effectiveness of ASEAN's external relationships will decrease.

However, the possibility of the WTO overshadowing inter-regional relationships was lessened with the failure of the WTO Millennium Round in Seattle in 1999. Talks on services liberalization, in particular, financial services, were to be the main agenda of the Round but they were stalled for a variety of reasons, among them objections by developing countries and vocal resistance by non-governmental organizations. Many developing countries, including ASEAN, are unwilling to open their services sector because they do not have a comparative advantage. ASEAN should mobilize its inter-regional relationship to encourage other developing countries to form a common stand on this issue. Similarly, ASEAN should work with its partners, such as the EU and its ASEAN+3 partnership to determine the WTO agenda. There is, however, a need for a new area of co-operation, especially in the services sector.

- ASEAN should identify and prioritize new areas of co-operation to be pursued with its external partners. Do ASEAN interests lie mainly with trade-related areas, such as trade facilitation and harmonization, or cross-border issues such as infrastructure and the environment? Trade and investment liberalization and facilitation are insufficient to bring about the maximum benefits of regional integration. To derive the maximum gains, the scope of co-operation must be extended to cover economic and technical co-operation, including capacity building, and human resource development. There are questions about the form of relationships that ASEAN should follow — the APEC or the EU model. The APEC model allows for more flexible co-operation but progress may be slow. Open regionalism also reduces discriminatory treatment in inter-regional relationships and avoids contradicting the principles of the WTO. Thus far, ASEAN external relations do not show such inclination. Yet, the slow progress of open regionalism makes the inter-regional relationship *a la* EU a more attractive alternative. The presence of a regional structure will facilitate and expedite decisions on matters concerning external relationships and, as such, the scope of co-operation can be deepened and widened significantly. Still, the issue facing ASEAN is how its external relationship can support or strengthen the WTO process.

- Is there a need for ASEAN to review the role of its Dialogue Partners in the context of inter-regional relations? Some Dialogue Partners (such as the United States) are also members of another regional grouping (NAFTA). The dialogue partnerships seem to have a comprehensive and close relationship with ASEAN but they do not negotiate directly on trade liberalization on a bilateral basis because of their regional commitment. These Dialogue Partners' commitments to their respective regional groupings take precedence over their bilateral relationship with ASEAN. Does this mean that the Dialogue Partners will concentrate on secondary trade issues, such as trade facilitation and standard harmonization, and will not engage in direct bilateral trade liberalization? It is timely to review the dialogue partnership in the context of the larger picture of ASEAN inter-regional relationships.

- With the possible emergence of mega-regional groupings, such as those between the EU and the United States and the Free Trade Area of the Americas, ASEAN should re-evaluate its position to ensure that such developments will not be a disadvantage to its members. In fact, ASEAN should also find ways to link with these regional groups to maximize its economic growth and developmental objectives.

- The crisis has given a new perspective to ASEAN's external relationships, particularly on whether there can be inter-regional co-operation to minimize a country's or group of countries' vulnerability to such a crisis. The crisis tested ASEAN's relationship with its external partners. Generally, the relationship was a disappointment: there was no assistance to stabilize ASEAN currencies, and assistance only came through the International Monetary Fund with its set of conditions. Japan mooted the idea of an Asian Monetary Fund to provide an emergency fund to help the affected ASEAN countries but the United States objected to it. Similarly, APEC was incapable of organizing any assistance because its focus was on trade co-operation and not financial matters. The EU and Japan did, however, establish some funding arrangements to help ASEAN exporters and small- and medium-scale manufacturers. In sum, there was no clear indication of benefits from external relationships in times of severe crisis.

• As ASEAN integration progresses, its success will change the agenda of its relationship with other regional groupings. In other words, as it moves towards maturity, ASEAN's external relationship will be different from that in the early stages of its development. Similarly, other regional groupings are also making good progress in terms of economic integration. The question is how should ASEAN tailor its needs at the various stages of economic transition to match its external relationships.

The various issues discussed above will, no doubt, determine the future direction of ASEAN's inter-regional relationship. The formulation of a strategic direction for this relationship is paramount in order to increase ASEAN's global role and influence. ASEAN is too small to remain inward-looking and only by expanding its external relationship can ASEAN be a key player in the international arena. A strong external partnership will give ASEAN the opportunity to garner political support and form a collective stand on common concerns at the international level. The likely direction of ASEAN's external relationship is to strengthen the ASEAN+3 co-operation. This move coincides with the earlier proposal by Malaysia to create an East Asian Economic Caucus (EAEC), which receded after receiving strong objections from the United States. The contagion effects of the East Asian crisis clearly show that the market recognizes the ASEAN+3 economies as an economic group. Closer co-operation among the ASEAN+3 will allow better co-ordination of economic policies and surveillance on short-term capital flows, with the ultimate aim of preventing the reoccurrence or lessening the impact of future crises. The confirmation of ASEAN's strategic direction is also necessary to synchronize individual member's initiative in seeking stronger bilateral relationships with selected partners beyond what is achieved by the regional group.

In conclusion, it is generally agreed that the concept and conduct of ASEAN's external relations have been eminently successful. The initial development co-operation mainly focused on technical and scientific support, but this was found to be inadequate for the promotion of trade and investment, which are considered essential for economic growth and development. Thus, co-operation was extended to include, and even emphasize those areas. The most significant achievement of ASEAN's external relationships is the role they played in making the ASEAN economies internationally competitive. It is also agreed that economic links will be more effective if there is active participation from the private sector. For this reason, the private sector is now included in ASEAN's external relationships.

NOTES

1   Quoted in D. S. Simandjuntak, "Problems and Perspectives of ASEAN–EEC Economic Co-operation", *Indonesia Quarterly* 11, no. 4 (1983): 87.
2   Ibid.; Hamzah (1989), p. 9.

REFERENCES

ASEAN Secretariat Website at *http://www.aseanaec.org*
Asia-Pacific Economic Co-operation (APEC). *The Impact of Subregionalism on APEC*. Singapore: APEC Secretariat, 1997.
Avila, J. L. "ASEAN's Relationship with other Regional Economic Groupings". Paper presented at the International Conference on "ASEAN at the Crossroads: Opportunities and Challenges", Malaysian Institute of Economic Research, Kuala Lumpur, 25–26 November 1997.
Chia, S. Y., and J. Tan, eds. *ASEAN and EU: Forging New Linkages and Strategic Alliances*. Singapore: Institute of Southeast Asian Studies, 1997.
Cuyvers, L. "The Trade Diversion Effects on ASEAN of the European Union Enlargement with EFTA Countries and the Association Agreements with Eastern Europe". CAS Discussion Paper No. 4. December 1995.
Hamzah, B. A. *ASEAN: Relations with Dialogue Partners*. Kuala Lumpur: Pelanduk Publications, 1989.
Imada-Iboshi, Pearl, and Michael G. Plummer. *Direct Foreign Investment and Development in ASEAN*. Honolulu: East-West Center, 1994.
IMF. *Direction of Trade Statistics*. Various years.
Kim, H. S. and A. Wetson. "A North American Free Trade Agreement and East Asian Developing Countries". *ASEAN Economic Bulletin 9, no. 3* (March 1993).
Mahani, Z. A. "Institutional Mechanism for ASEAN–India Co-operation: Trends And Prospects". *Journal of Asian Economics* 7, no. 4 (1996).

————. "APEC's Relationship With Sub-Regional Trading Arrangements". Paper presented at the PAFTAD 25th annual conference on "APEC: Its Challenges and Tasks for the Future", Osaka, June 1999.

Mohamed Ariff, Z. A. Mahani, and E. C. Tan. "Study of the Emerging Global Trading Environment and Developing Asia: The Malaysian Perspective". Study submitted to the Asian Development Bank, Manila, 1996.

Simandjuntak, D. S. " Problems and Perspectives of ASEAN-EEC Economic Co-operation". *Indonesia Quarterly* 11, no. 4 (1983).

Tan, J., ed. *AFTA in the Changing International Economy.* Singapore: Institute of Southeast Asian Studies, 1996.

Tham, S. Y. "Competition and Co-operation for Foreign Direct Investment: An ASEAN Perspective". *Asia-Pacific Development Journal* 5, no. 1 (June 1998).

APPENDIX I

ASEAN's Relevance:
Has It Become Questionable?

C. P. F. LUHULIMA

Has ASEAN's relevance become questionable? Perhaps this question can be answered promptly by saying that ASEAN is still very relevant in the field of politics and conventional security, to moderate political and security disagreements among members. It seems, however, to be less relevant in the field of economics.

ASEAN's Major Objectives

ASEAN's major goals as set out in the ASEAN Declaration in Bangkok on 8 August 1967 were, first, to reconcile intra-regional strife which characterized Southeast Asia at the time (in the form of border and territorial disputes, ethnic conflicts and animosities, religious prejudices, and the fear by smaller states of the bigger states). The second was to manage those conflicts and tensions and create a Southeast Asian regional order on the basis of the social and economic systems of each member country and the territorial status quo, and thus to "promote regional peace and stability". Both goals were to be achieved by way of a third goal, which was to speed up "the economic growth, social progress and cultural development in the region". ASEAN's founding fathers were confident that economic and societal development, on the one hand, and peace and stability on the other, were tightly linked. They were further determined, and the fourth goal was "to ensure their stability and security from external interference in any form or manifestation" to "preserve their national identities in accordance with the ideals and aspirations of their peoples".

ASEAN was thus the result of its members' recognition of their inability to solve their disputes and conflicts bilaterally. On the other hand, it was also meant to serve as a political-cum-security framework.

These four major goals of regional endeavours in Southeast Asia were subsequently cast into four instruments for political and security building: the ASEAN Declaration; the Declaration on the Zone of Peace, Freedom and Neutrality (ZOPFAN), which was primarily meant to secure the recognition and respect for Southeast Asia as such a zone; the Bali Concord; and ZOPFAN's legal instruments, the Treaty of Amity and Co-operation (TAC) in Southeast Asia and the Treaty on Southeast as a Nuclear Weapon-Free Zone, which was meant to promote perpetual peace, everlasting amity and co-operation among the Southeast Asian nations. These instruments formalized ASEAN's role as an important contributor for peace and stability.

Since the Association's establishment, the ASEAN member countries have proved that they are capable of co-existing in peace and harmony. Although regional disputes and differences have not been resolved, the ASEAN countries have learned to diffuse or abate their conflicts and not to exploit it for their own interests at the cost of the Association. Hence, ASEAN's existence is a security guarantee for peaceful and harmonious bilateral relations, and as a corollary for long-term economic development.

It has become increasingly difficult to visualize a conflict between two or more ASEAN member states. Sub-regional relations have developed an ASEAN spirit, which strongly supports ASEAN regionalism. Despite the legal character of the Treaty of Amity and Co-operation in Southeast Asia, ASEAN's preference is for informal approaches to solving conflicts, placing emphasis on relationships rather than on formal structures, and emphasizing consensus building. There is a general distrust for a structured and legalistic manner of approach to conflicts without sufficient consideration of the situation and the emotional state of the conflicting parties.

But will this hold in the twenty-first century, which will be complicated by the deluge of globalization and fierce competition and, as a corollary, the multilateralization of security approaches and multidimensionalization of threats to security?

Multilateral Security Approaches

Multilateral organizations in Asia were born during a period of great geopolitical change. The disintegration of the Soviet Union and the end of the Cold War, in combination with the U.S. departure from its bases in the Philippines, provoked considerable uneasiness among political and security specialists in Asia on the future of regional security in the post-Cold War environment. The result was a proliferation in the early 1990s of official and unofficial multilateral security dialogues intended to address the imperatives of a new multipolar world. Academics and scholars were the driving force behind many of the first dialogues, including the Council on Security Co-operation in the Asia-Pacific (CSCAP), established in Kuala Lumpur in June 1993, and the Northeast Asian Co-operation Dialogue (NEACD), established in California later that year.

The most important of the organizations to emerge from this ferment was the ASEAN Regional Forum (ARF). In 1993, the Clinton Administration reversed its previous policy of hostility to multilateralism and joined ASEAN as a founding member of the ARF, the first region-wide consultative body in Asia focusing on security issues.

The great variety of actors and the number of strains and conflicts in the region created the ASEAN Regional Forum to provide the region with an institution to absorb multilateral dialogues on security and to develop further the concepts of confidence-building, and preventive diplomacy, to find ways to resolve regional tensions and conflict, and to develop instruments for conflict resolution in the region based on the model of the TAC. The need to maintain stable relations among the major powers, which is a crucial and integral element underpinning regional stability, should be continuously emphasized and operationalized.

The ASEAN Regional Forum in its first session in Bangkok (25 July 1994) agreed to accept the objectives and principles of the TAC as "a code of conduct governing relations" between states and a unique diplomatic instrument for regional confidence-building, preventive diplomacy, and political and security co-operation"

(Par. 6). At the sixth ARF in Singapore (25 July 19999), members recognized the TAC as "a key regional instrument for strengthening security in the region". This will involuntarily promote the development of a "region-wide code of conduct" (Par. 10). Following this train of thought, the acknowledgement of non-Southeast Asian countries of the Treaty on Southeast Asia as a Nuclear Weapon-Free Zone is expected to contribute to the comprehensive denuclearization of the region.

Multidimensional Security Approaches

The post-Cold War developments in the Asia-Pacific region have also produced new disturbances and threats, beyond the conventional field of foreign policy and security. It has expanded the threat dimensions to sustainable development and democracy. It is this complexity that creates the need to multidimensionalize the concept of security, comprising those aspects of security against narcotic traffic, international crime, formerly dubbed low-intensity threats, and increasingly against environmental degradation, biodiversity loss, emerging diseases, over-population, and political unrest as a consequence of these new kinds of threats.

Biodiversity loss is the fastest moving of all environmental problems and it is irreversible. It also hampers future prospects of achieving stability. So is environmental degradation, which is a threat driven by the production and consumption of goods and services in a manner that is not environmentally benign, such as the haze problem following forest fires in Kalimantan and Sumatra since 1997 (which for some time questioned the seriousness of the Indonesian Government to solve what is increasingly seen as a sustained crisis). This will need the institutionalization of disaster management. Emerging diseases are also a threat to security. Infectious diseases affecting humans, plants, and animals, which are spreading rapidly as a result of trade and travel, and — amplified by malnutrition — threaten the public, and productivity on a broad and intensive scale. Still another problem is over-population as a consequence of population growth. It is putting excessive demands on human and physical capacity to meet the needs for food, housing, health, employment, and education. Finally, political unrest also has its consequences. Warfare, ethnic and social clashes set back efforts to meet critical human and environmental needs. They tend to be regional problems with global impact as a consequence of forced migrations and other disruptive effects.

The unpreparedness of Indonesia and other ASEAN countries to recognize and deal with the new dimensions of security straightforwardly is complicated by the emergence and widely applied concept of human security. The term means safety for people from challenges, threats, and disturbances, both violent and non-violent. The principal and conventional objective of national security is the protection of national territorial integrity and political sovereignty from external aggression. It is now considered to be insufficient in guaranteeing people's security. The concept takes people as its point of reference rather than focusing exclusively on the security of territory or sovereignty. Human security (which also emphasizes that women are equal partners of men in all walks of life and throughout their life-cycle) entails taking preventive measures to reduce vulnerability and minimize risk, and if prevention fails, remedial action is necessary. A human security perspective thus asserts that the security of the state is not an end in itself.

The concern for human security, or the safety of people, extends beyond national borders. It is seemingly a logical extension of current approaches to international peace and security. The United Nations Charter embodies the view that security cannot be achieved by a single state in isolation. The term "international peace and security" implies that the security of one state depends on the security of other states as well. A human security perspective seemingly builds on this logic by noting that the security of people in one part of the world depends on the security of people elsewhere. It seems to imply that the security of states, and the maintenance of international peace and security, is ultimately constructed on the foundation of people who are secure. Human security will thus have to be incorporated in the dimensions of national and regional security in the Southeast Asian region.

Economic Approaches to Security

Asia's economic relevance came starkly into question during the dramatic financial crisis in 1997–98. It failed to find answers to the breakdown in their financial and economic systems (to their weak financial systems, to their excessive unhedged borrowing by the private sector and to the lack of transparency in government and corporate sectors). Each member resorted to individual approaches to safeguard its own interests. Each member tried to overcome the crisis individually, each in co-operation with global financial institutions, the International Monetary Fund (IMF) and the World Bank, and each followed its own prescriptions for economic recovery. Leaders often contradicted each other on the basic policies they had earlier agreed upon. It was even feared that relations with neighbours might be sacrificed in the process of finding solutions to domestic instabilities. These developments have turned the attention of member states inwards and, as such, made intra-ASEAN relations less cohesive, and indeed pointed to the resurfacing of longstanding tensions among member states.

Although ASEAN leaders met in December 1997 in the light of the crisis, and although they acknowledged that the depreciation of their currencies had resulted in serious regression in the economic well-being of their countries, their business, and their peoples, they failed to outline or pursue a united approach towards the IMF and the World Bank in dealing with the crisis. They only stressed "that ASEAN countries must remain united and show resolve in responding to the challenge posed by the currency situation".

These developments have led to the view that the Association lacks the resilient mechanisms to handle the dramatic impact of the crisis and justified the question of ASEAN's further relevance for the countries in Southeast Asia. It came short of the establishment of an ASEAN Surveillance Mechanism, which may constructively propose to a member country to modify or change its financial-economic policies which may have adverse effects on its neighbours or the region as a whole.

The Hanoi Action Plan was an attempt to again commit themselves to "greater integration" of their economies "as a primary expression of our co-operation and solidarity". The major thrust of the Hanoi Action Plan is to enhance greater economic integration and the speedy creation of an ASEAN economic region. ASEAN leaders will "spare no efforts to quickly restore financial and microeconomic stability, bring about early economic recovery and maintain sustained growth". ASEAN will continue with its open market policies, and its commitment to trade and investment liberalization and facilitation, as it recognizes that long-term investments are the key to strengthening and stabilizing the region's currencies and economies. ASEAN has also boldly committed itself to accelerate AFTA, the ASEAN Industrial Co-operation (AICO) Scheme, and the ASEAN Investment Area (AIA) through consistent investment laws and policies. This is aimed at regaining business confidence, enhancing economic recovery, and promoting growth. An important decision is the wider use of ASEAN currencies in intra-ASEAN trade settlements, which was agreed in 1997. These commitments will be supported by further development of regional infrastructures, such as networks of electricity grids, gas and water pipelines, and transport and telecommunications links, which will enhance ASEAN's competitiveness.

The great scope and ambition of the programmes raise the question whether ASEAN will be capable of massively mobilizing the political will and resources in time and execute them with great determination. Unilateral approaches to face and handle the crisis still predominate among the member countries.

The latest developments have shown that the AFTA programme is more political economy than economy *per se*. It is an attempt to provide an adhesive for intra-ASEAN co-operation rather than a genuine mechanism for trade liberalization and facilitation. Even APEC has not been able to provide the necessary conditions for trade and investment liberalization and facilitation. It seems to have lost its momentum. APEC's summits have evolved into a talking shop for issues unrelated to trade, particularly to trade of the developing countries. They have developed into discussions on topics of liberalization and facilitation that are more of interest to the developed APEC members. Moreover, in the past three years APEC forums were dominated by non-trade issues: the financial crisis in 1997, the Anwar Ibrahim case in 1998, and the East Timor case in 1999.

The World Trade Organization seems to be a better avenue to liberalize and facilitate trade and investment policies of its members. If AFTA is to serve as an instrument for trade liberalization, it would have to be open to a wider commitment, which means that it has to be integrated into the WTO framework.

Whither ASEAN?

ASEAN has developed a well-tested mechanism for co-operation and co-ordination in facing conventional threats under favourable economic conditions, but it was paralysed by the regional crisis and has since not been able to devise and develop a mechanism in times of crisis, to face conventional and non-conventional security threats. ASEAN will not be capable of solving its conventional and non-conventional threats if it is unable to design and develop a new institutional infrastructure to face conventional and non-conventional security threats alike, in line with the concepts of national and regional resilience, of comprehensive or total security, or redefine or redesign existing institutions, such as the ASEAN Regional Forum, for the purpose.

The severe financial and economic crisis which had profound effects on the security outlooks and designs of the ASEAN countries seems to have shattered ASEAN dreams and simultaneously exposed the fragility of its security outlook and doctrine, and of ASEAN as a regional institution. It has failed to provide immediate answers to the economic collapse and thus individual approaches to safeguard the interest of each constituent member have prevailed. The leaders have frequently contradicted each other on the basic policies they had earlier made. It is feared that relations with neighbours may continue to suffer in the process of finding solutions to domestic instabilities. Long-standing tensions among members may resurface in new attire. It is from the political and security perspective that ASEAN still has a very important role to play, to safeguard the region from internal and external threats to its development, to its modernization programmes and processes as a consequence of unfettered globalization and fierce competition. It still has a very important role to play to guarantee the security of sea-lanes of communication for the trade and commerce of any member country. However, the expansion of the security spectrum has simultaneously made it possible for external forces and states and international institutions to intervene in the internal affairs of the Southeast Asian countries, particularly in the name of human security, sustainable development, and democracy.

These issues will have to be examined to find approaches to resolve them, by incorporating measures into the Treaty of Amity and Co-operation in Southeast Asia to make it compatible with the new security issues with its challenges to the independence, sovereignty, and territorial integrity of the Southeast Asian nations, and the challenge of non-interference in the internal affairs of one another. This is our task for the twenty-first century. If such an attempt were to fail, then new, more comprehensive instruments will have to be designed to meet the demands of the time.

It is important to factor non-conventional threats and threat perceptions into the existing security instruments, or design new instruments to include the new sources of threats. The security concepts and outlook and the recent developments clearly indicate that it will be very difficult indeed to sustain an artificial dividing line between the various dimensions of security and the levels on which they operate. It will also become increasingly difficult to refuse outright the proposal for "constructive intervention" (Anwar Ibrahim) or "flexible engagement" (Surin Pitsuwan, *Thailand's Non-Paper on Flexible Engagement Approach*, 27 July 1998) as the dividing line between domestic affairs and external or transnational issues becomes less clear. "Many domestic affairs have obvious external or transnational dimensions, adversely affecting neighbours, the region and the region's relations with others". Next to the haze problem, the East Timor and Bank Bali scandals are cases in point.

In the near term, it would be necessary not only to sustain ASEAN's relevance for member countries but also to make it more relevant, in order to achieve ASEAN's Vision 2020, which is in the process of review.

APPENDIX II

Is ASEAN Still Relevant?
Some Thoughts from a European Perspective

ROLF J. LANGHAMMER

Changing Institutional Underpinnings in Globalizing
Goods and Capital Markets by the Turn of the Century:
What Is Exogenous for ASEAN at the External Frontier?

While the number of World Trade Organization (WTO) contracting parties is rising, the number of relevant actors in the world trading order is shrinking. Big players like the United States and the European Union (EU) increasingly act as catalysts for neighbouring countries which harmonize their national trade policies with those of the players. Most countries pursue harmonization via free trade areas (Mexico, Israel, Norway, Switzerland), very few (Turkey) have already gone further by forming a customs union with these players. Other smaller players intend to first implement a customs union among themselves before linking their union to the big players' trade policy via a regional free trade agreement (such as relations between the Mercado Comun del Cono Sur [MERCOSUR] and the EU). Each of the three paths will lead to economies of scale in trade policies. At the very end, few trading blocs (defined as customs unions) will decide on the outcome of multilateral negotiations, which in fact are already oligopolistic negotiations.

The "open regionalism" style of APEC has not (yet) delivered convincing results in stimulating global liberalization from bottom-up. It needs success stories soon, otherwise it will lose to the traditional preferential EU style of regionalism pursued by the majority of emerging economies in Latin America and Europe, as well as by the ASEAN Free Trade Area (AFTA).

Parallel to the declining number of trade policy actors, the number of relevant currencies traded in the financial markets will also decline. This is not only due to the European Monetary Union but also to the lessons from the Asian economic crisis. These lessons suggest that exchange rate regimes which do not seem sustainable will be tested. Such tests speak against in-between-exchange rate regimes, such as different exchange rate crawls. Thus, the two polar cases (either fixing exchange rates completely [currency boards] or full floating) are credible alternatives. Many small economies with both strong trade and capital links to a major player will take the first (admittedly dangerous) option into more serious consideration than in the past.

In many cases, regional trading blocs and regional currency blocs will have overlapping membership, thus reinforcing each other (Mexico with respect to the United States, and Eastern Europe with respect to the EU). The larger the overlap, the stronger is the position of the anchor currency (in the capital account) and the anchor country (in the current account of the smaller economies), respectively.

Where does ASEAN find its niche if the two scenarios materialize? Its position is difficult for two reasons. First, unlike Europe and Latin America, currency blocs and trading blocs do not overlap in ASEAN (and Asia), and secondly, there is no dominant economy in ASEAN or in neighbouring Asia playing the role of the anchor country or anchor currency.

The State of ASEAN Economies in 1999:
What is Exogenous for ASEAN at the Internal Frontier?

Seen from Europe, divergences with ASEAN seem to have grown from different angles. To start with the least controversial one, membership has been extended to the low-income Indochinese economies which are rudimentary with respect to market economic principles and which have been given longer adjustment periods to meet AFTA commitments than the other AFTA members. The EU pattern of concentric circles around a core group comes to mind, but unfortunately divergences have also grown among the ASEAN founding member states. Given the political foundations of ASEAN, political divergences seem to be more relevant than economic disparities in terms of (temporarily) widening growth gaps. Political divergences, for instance, comprise dissenting views on more or less use of controls in transborder trade and capital transactions or on pros and cons of getting involved in partner countries' internal issues. Such dissenting views can strongly impede common targets, such as the implementation of AFTA, or of an ASEAN free investment zone, or extending free trade agreements to neighbouring non-ASEAN members.

The Asian economic crisis has supported views that ASEAN as an actor in international politics owed its reputation primarily to past non-economic achievements than to present economic achievements. Its reputation would be at risk if internal political controversies are aggravated further and if each member state sees domestic and regional stabilization as trade-offs. The implementation of AFTA would be endangered too. This could become a vicious circle since postponing the AFTA liberalization timetable would further fuel sceptical views on the "economic teeth" of ASEAN.

With political uncertainties in the largest ASEAN member state as a heavy burden, ASEAN (again seen from Europe!) can regain its reputation rapidly if it actively contributes (directly or indirectly) to solving (or easing) its partner countries' internal problems first. There is no substitution process between "external collective bargaining power" and "internal trouble solving". Speaking with one voice to dialogue partners is non-credible if internal trouble-solving fails.

Markets need a convincing signal that the implementation of AFTA and other "binding" commitments to ASEAN-wide liberalization (including investment) are beyond any doubt, whatever happens internally. Europeans would fix such commitments in a treaty. How does the ASEAN way of "tying hands" solve this?

ASEAN Integration and Co-operation Widening and Deepening: Two Substitutable Options?

The Asian economic crisis of 1997–98, which clearly demonstrated current account transactions being wiped out in importance by capital account transactions, seems to have induced ASEAN to consider areas of co-operation besides trade. An ASEAN investment area is one such area, which is not necessarily new, given previous endeavours — for example, the Individual Action Plans (AIP), the ASEAN Industrial Complementation schemes (AICs), and the ASEAN Industrial Joint Ventures (AIJVs). Areas with cross-border spillovers, such as the environment, can be added to this list.

Apart from an issue-related widening of ASEAN integration and co-operation, a country-related widening of integration is under way, covering the Indochinese economies first, but ultimately the Australia–New Zealand area too.

The experience of Europe, the only integration area with a simultaneous process of widening and deepening, suggests that deepening and widening are sequences but not substitutable options. Before widening the country coverage as well as the issues, an integration area needs a solid core area with a good record of liberalization achievements. This is what is called the *acquis communautaire* in the EU. For ASEAN, the core group comprises the founding member states, and the issue is the free trade area. Hence, completing the AFTA programme is of utmost importance for the core group to maintain credibility. To be consistent with the WTO, AFTA should lower and/or bind external tariffs to internal tariff dismantling. The next step of free investment could be done by establishing general principles of investment in the national investment codes of the member countries. Free investment (that is, the freedom of establishment and free mobility of investment-related labour), however, seems to be a more distant target. Under the current conditions, this target seems overly ambitious, particularly seen against the background of member countries with different policies regarding the control of cross-border capital transactions.

Is ASEAN Relevant?

By world standards, and measured in terms of gross domestic product (GDP) (not population), AFTA is a mini-integration scheme still in the making. So is ASEAN as a co-operation scheme. Outside Asia, the trend points towards mega-schemes even if it will take time to implement them. If the term "mega" cannot be equated with "efficient", the specific advantage of large schemes should not be under-estimated. Larger schemes benefit from the existence of stable core countries, either in institutional or in economic terms. Such countries, being often the largest beneficiaries of the schemes, are the relevant engines for both deepening integration and co-operation, and compensating periphery members for short-term adjustment costs. What is important is that they are accepted by other members to act as engines and mediators. Such core countries which are able and accepted as engines to deepen integration and to shoulder burdens for other members are today difficult to identify within ASEAN. If "relevant" is equated with "promising", there is doubt whether ASEAN is relevant.

Today, purely trade-oriented free trade areas are considered standard and do not draw much attention from potential investors. Schemes which are more ambitious and may leave an impact on financial markets are at least customs unions, including free mobility of capital. For economies oriented to the world market and exporting a large part of their international supply to non-member countries (as in the ASEAN case), internal liberalization is less important than external liberalization. However, even if it is true that internal liberalization can improve the collective bargaining power in external trade negotiations, the ASEAN member countries stand to lose if they use too much resources on liberalization within a mini-scheme. There are opportunity costs if skilled international negotiators are in short supply and if an increasing number of trade issues like e-commerce spreads beyond regional boundaries.

ASEAN is a white sheet of paper in financial market integration. There is no ASEAN-wide bond market, no common position in handling international capital transactions, no common peg or common exchange rate basket, no common standards for the accounting sector, no common position towards the Basle standards for capital adequacy, no common prudential standards, not to speak of a common currency. In financial market integration, including banking supervision and prudential standards, ASEAN as an entity does not exist. Thus, the ASEAN-10 is more heterogeneous than ever. Should markets see overlaps between the direction of trade and capital flows as a promising indicator (and therefore relevant to deep integration), then again ASEAN is not relevant.

Given all these (admittedly) intuitive remarks, I conclude that ASEAN's pre-crisis reputation was considerably larger than its reputation today and that its relevance (in terms of potential gains for the economies) has declined. This is not only due to the financial crisis, which was outside the realm of ASEAN, but also due to its incapability to handle typical internal co-operation issues efficiently (such as the haze issue).

In spite of the sceptical view raised above, I conclude with an optimistic forward-looking note, which, however, is bound to conditions. To reappear as an internationally recognized actor, ASEAN must implement AFTA on time in order to demonstrate credibility and bad-weather quality, not because AFTA is critical to economic recovery. Simultaneously, external liberalization should be announced and bound with the WTO to meet Article 24 of the GATT (General Agreement on Tariffs and Trade) requirements. ASEAN should not go the easy way through notification under the "free-rider" Enabling Clause of 1979 (special and differential treatment). Secondly, negotiating and implementing ASEAN-wide minimum standards for prudential regulations and banking supervision in the financial sector of the founding member states would be helpful to signal the entry of ASEAN into the capital account sphere. Thirdly, anchoring the most-favoured-nation (MFN) scheme and national treatment as ASEAN-specific elements in all national investment regulations would qualify ASEAN as a player in the forthcoming negotiations on trade and investment in the WTO. Finally, to overcome the disadvantage of being small, ASEAN should initiate an ASEAN–OCEANIA economic partnership focusing on trade and investment facilitation, as well as issues with cross-border spillovers, such as environmental protection, cross-border crime control, meteorological research, natural disaster prevention, and emergency relief.

However, it goes without saying that the success of the latter proposal in particular, and of the entire ASEAN rehabilitation programme in general, is inseparably linked to political stabilization and economic recovery in Indonesia.

INDEX

environment, 201
exports
  intra-regional, 66
free trade area, 72
GDP
  per capita, 69
institutional developments, 225, 226
integration, 53, 208, 211, 221, 222, 263, 286
  monetary, 263
investment, foreign direct, 102
  in ASEAN, 246
preferential treatment, 215
regionalism, 206, 284
reserves, foreign, 138
exchange rate, 16, 18, 19
  flexible, 15
  pegged, 18
Executives' Meeting of East Asia-Pacific (EMEAP) Central Banks, 135–37, 139

financial architecture, international reform, 14
financial crises
  panic, 16, 17, 18
    economic policies during, 18–20
  rescue packages, 26
  three-stage process, 15
  understanding, 14–18
financial panic
  trigger, 17
food security, 155–56
foreign exchange reserves
  depletion, 15
Free Trade Area of the Americas (FTAA), 72, 261, 266

General Agreement on Tariffs and Trade (GATT), 204, 208, 210, 211, 213, 215, 235, 288
  agreement, 212, 213, 214, 236
  on investment, 119
  jurisprudence, 214
  Secretariat, 235

Uruguay Round, 51, 67, 71, 210, 236
General Agreement on Trade in Services (GATS), 54, 55, 212, 213, 214, 236

Hong Kong, 136
  economic fundamentals, 130

India
  -ASEAN relations, 253
Indonesia, 46, 288
  in AFTA
    CEPT, 64, 65
  agriculture, 151, 157, 165
    crops, 152
    rice, 167
  banks
    non-performing loans, 38
  bond market capitalization, 127
  competitiveness, 23, 43, 44
  CPI, 150
  economic fundamentals, 130
  economic growth
    predictions, 25, 38
  economy
    characteristics, 20
    performance, 11
  education
    science graduates, 44
  energy
    availability, 159
    requirement, 159
    supply per capita, 158
  exchange rates, 21, 42
  exports
    growth, 34, 38
    hi-tech, 44
  financial crisis, 22
    panic, 19
  financial panic
    and GDP change, 24
  financial sector
    indicators, 127
  fires, 184–93, 200, 277
    cost, 190